Participatory Development in Appalachia

Participatory Development in Appalachia

CULTURAL IDENTITY, COMMUNITY, AND SUSTAINABILITY

EDITED BY SUSAN E. KEEFE

The University of Tennessee Press / Knoxville

Library of Congress Cataloging-in-Publication Data

Participatory development in Appalachia: cultural identity, community,
and sustainability / edited by Susan E. Keefe. — 1st ed.
        p. cm.
Includes bibliographical references and index.

ISBN-13: 978-1-57233-657-5
ISBN-10: 1-57233-657-9

1. Community development—Appalachian Region. I. Keefe, Susan E. (Susan Emley)

HN49.C6P3684 2009
307.140974—dc22   2008043580

Contents

Preface

This book is intended to serve Appalachian communities by recommending ways to better represent the goals and values of mountain people in public decision making. Participatory development refers to a process that is more inclusive and democratic, more bottom-up than top-down. It relies on citizen involvement and local knowledge. It involves research that aims to discover participants' view of things, either through research executed by the participants or through the use of ethnographic methods. It involves strengthening both the social and economic infrastructure, and it puts greater power and control into the hands of local people, increasing the likelihood of sustainability. It puts the public into public decision making.

The authors of these chapters include anthropologists, sociologists, and other professionals who have been engaged, sometimes for decades, in Appalachian communities. I have asked them to incorporate ideas and concepts developed in my introduction, including participatory development, participatory research, community-based development, community assets, capacity building, cultural competency, community identity, and social capital. These theoretical concepts provide a common thematic framework for the book. I have also written a summary paragraph introducing each chapter by highlighting its contribution to the book's main ideas.

I would like to acknowledge the support of the Department of Anthropology and the College of Arts and Sciences at Appalachian State University as I have edited this volume. Tim Ezzell kindly shared with me references on participation in planning and related fields. I would also like to thank Jeff Boyer, Diane Mines, Pat Beaver, and Greg Reck for their stimulating discussion regarding social capital and participatory development. Finally, I want to express appreciation to Elvin Hatch for many thoughtful discussions of mountain life and his patient encouragement during the development of this book.

Grateful acknowledgment is extended to *Appalachian Journal,* published by the Center for Appalachian Studies at Appalachian State University for permission to reprint sections of an earlier version of the chapter by Helen M. Lewis "Rebuilding Communities: 12-Step Recovery Program," vol. 34, nos. 3–4 (Spring/Summer 2007): 316–25.

Introduction

What Participatory Development Means for Appalachian Communities

Susan E. Keefe

Critiques of the modern development paradigm in the last three decades pose unique possibilities for action in Appalachian communities. Generally conceived of as impoverished, backward, and victimized, the people of the southern mountains have always been ripe for development projects conceptualized and controlled from outside the region. Just as development around the world has been driven by the ideology of modernism, where the West is the Best and the Rest is Poor, so we find Appalachian communities have been overwhelmed by a master narrative and economic development projects in which they play the poor country cousin awaiting cultural enlightenment and expert assistance. This book proposes an alternative paradigm for conceptualizing and engaging in development projects in Appalachian communities. Based on a critical analysis of the modern development process and the emerging participatory approaches to action, our model assumes that local culture has value, that local communities have assets, and that local people have the capacity to envision and lead their own social change. This requires reframing the development process with a new narrative in which Appalachian communities are cast as the plucky and hardworking self-starters. But let's not get ahead of the story. To begin with, we must examine the philosophical roots of the reigning modern development paradigm that create an inherent disadvantage for mountain people working on their own social change.

The Modern Development Paradigm

During the eighteenth century, Enlightenment philosophers and social intellectuals began to rework ideas about humans, society, and nature in a way that fundamentally challenged the dominant Christian worldview. Freeing themselves from traditional forms of knowledge based on religious authority, such as the Bible, they envisioned a society awakening from ignorance and superstition to a new age of reason in which people might, in the words of Immanuel Kant, "dare to know." According to Enlightenment philosophers, modern knowledge was based on human experience, scientific evidence, and rational thought, and humans everywhere might have this fundamental capacity for understanding the world around them. Science, in particular, was thought to be the "key to expanding all human knowledge" and a principle to be applied in all domains of life (Hamilton 1992). There was confidence that the scientific method would create secure truths arrived at through observation and experiment, and that this secular knowledge based on universal principles and laws might be accumulated, organized, and used for the benefit of mankind.

In contrast to the absolute monarchies legitimized by the medieval church, authority in modern society was believed to be based on the individual who became the starting point for all knowledge and action, empowering the government through a rational social contract and assuming authority through secular institutions and structures. The individual became the fundamental social unit, and society therefore must be the product of the thought and action of individuals. Optimistically, Enlightenment philosophers believed in the progressive improvement of the human condition through the application of science and reason, producing increasing well-being and happiness. And so it was that people came to believe they were "able, entitled, and even compelled" to exert control over the processes of the natural and social world in the name of progress (Schech and Haggis 2000:4).

Modernity is generally seen in contrast to traditional social order and beliefs. For eighteenth-century European intellectuals, this was epitomized by the Christian churches that controlled the basis for all knowledge and power.

As modernity was spread, initially through colonization, it became the basis for global comparisons of regions around the world. Societies and cultures encountered in distant lands became identified by their degree of traditionalism. A general unilinear process of social development was imagined in which it was believed that all humanity had the capacity for progressing from ignorance and backwardness to enlightenment and progressiveness. Since it was assumed that Europe rightly stood at the apex in this historical trajectory, the highest point of civilization, progress was ultimately the process of shedding traditional culture and becoming more and more like Europeans. The colonial enterprise in the nineteenth century in Asia, Africa, and Latin America provided opportunities to exercise the civilizing mission of European administrations (Schech and Haggis 2000).

The perception of a Western modern ideal continued into the twentieth century when the United States assumed global prominence. It was following World War II that "development" clearly emerged as a cultural and economic project led by the West. Arturo Escobar (1995) begins his book, *Encountering Development: The Making and Unmaking of the Third World,* with a quotation from Harry S. Truman's inaugural address as president of the United States in 1949. Truman defined half of the world's population as poor, hungry, diseased, and underdeveloped and argued that the West had the scientific and technical knowledge necessary to alleviate their suffering. Escobar elaborates on the process by which the "Third World" was created through discourses and practices that totally restructured "underdeveloped" societies through industrialization and urbanization, the growth of production and consumption, and imposed modern educational systems and cultural values. Development became fused with modernization and it was expected that not only economies but also ways of "thinking, acting, and living" would be transformed. As Schech and Haggis observe, it is almost impossible to differentiate modernity from the development process as engaged in by Western theorists and practitioners, and that "the shorthand of this connection is development = modernization = westernization" (2000:30). Escobar concludes that at the century's end, however, rather than producing the dream societies envisioned by Truman and others, the modern development project in Latin America and elsewhere in the Southern Hemisphere produced "massive underdevelopment and impoverishment, untold exploitation and oppression" (Escobar 1995:4). Dependency theorists argue that this is the product of an interlinked capitalist world system in which the Third World's "underdeveloped" social, economic, and political conditions are the flipside of the same historical exploitative process by which the First World became "developed" (Cockcroft, Gunder Frank, and Johnson 1972).

Escobar (1995) would add, drawing on Foucault, that development discourse was part of the destructive process that resulted in a Third World that came to perceive itself as poor and backward, demanding external intervention. In this sense, the perceived "truth" is constructed within relations of power where certain modes of being and thinking become permissible while others become impossible. Thus, "knowledge" about the nature of poverty, who is poor, and how poverty and underdevelopment can best be alleviated is inextricably tied up with power and the discourse between all social actors, rich and poor, North and South.

The process of development in Appalachia has followed a path similar to that of the Third World. Settled by small-scale subsistence farmers, the region experienced an invasion of "mature capitalist institutions" during the late nineteenth century (Billings, Blee, and Swanson 1986). Industrialization of the region began in earnest in the 1880s as federally subsidized railroads were constructed for the extraction of natural resources including timber and minerals, especially coal. Outside capitalists and speculators began purchasing land and mineral rights, and the federal government also began to condemn and buy land for the developing National Park system. Resource extraction helped to fuel urbanization and industrialization on the East Coast, especially the Northeastern United States. Meanwhile, the inevitable rising taxes in the mountains and the need for money in an increasingly market-driven rather than subsistence-based economy forced farmers to sell out or take on wage labor jobs to supplement household incomes. The nature of the industries that took root in the region did not require a sophisticated labor force, and management actually benefited from the perpetuation of a monoeconomy forcing workers to accept undesirable and dangerous jobs for low pay. As a consequence, "modernization and industrialization in Appalachia did not result in a rising standard of living but instead produced one of the highest rates of poverty in the country" (Keefe 1998:139).

This early industrial period, during which ownership of basic resources largely passed from local to absentee ownership and the region became an "internal colony" largely controlled and exploited by outside interests, was also a period of reimagining the area as a "strange land and peculiar people." A nineteenth-century literary period now known as the "local-color movement" produced travel sketches and short stories laced with mountain dialect describing the geographic wonders, biological curiosities, and cultural peculiarities of the southern mountains for readers in eastern cities (Shapiro 1978). Stereotypic themes that persist today of mountaineers as violent feudists, criminal moonshiners, and ignorant hillbillies fed the growing perception of Appalachian cultural deviance that served to justify the process of dispossession of their land and resources during the early era of capitalism. Missionary, settlement school, and benevolent workers were drawn to the region in the effort to "uplift" the population, which had profound consequences for identity and the sense of cultural differentness among mountaineers (Whisnant 1983). During the twentieth century, mass media fed this image through such diverse outlets as the Grand Ole Opry radio show, *Ma and Pa Kettle* films, "Li'l Abner" and "Snuffy Smith" comic strips, and *The Beverly Hillbillies* television show. Through the creation and manipulation of these images of "Otherness" by those from outside the region, Appalachian people came to be seen by the nation and often to see themselves as a social problem in need of being solved (Batteau 1990).

In the 1960s Appalachia became firmly identified with the issue of poverty in the American consciousness when social activists—such as Michael Harrington, author of *The Other America* (1962)—expressed outrage that one in four Americans lived in an underclass of grinding poverty hidden out of sight of middle-class America. The worst pockets of economic hardship were identified in the urban ghettoes of America's largest cities and the rural poor in the mountains of Appalachia and in the South. John F. Kennedy took up this issue in his widely televised 1960 Democratic presidential primary campaign in West Virginia. In 1964, President Lyndon Johnson launched the War on Poverty from the home of an impoverished family in eastern Kentucky. Documentaries such as *Christmas in Appalachia* (1965), narrated by Charles Kurault, created visual images that equated the Appalachian landscape with extreme poverty. The discourse continues today in the recent documentary focusing on an impoverished East Kentucky extended family entitled *American Hollow,* directed by Rory Kennedy(1999), the daughter of Robert Kennedy. Moreover, in a recent article, Susan Sarnoff (2003) confirms that Central Appalachia is "still the other America."

The modern development process in the southern mountains has been conceptualized from the beginning as both an economic development project and a campaign to change the traditional "backward" culture of southern mountaineers. The process gained momentum during the New Deal in the 1930s when the Tennessee Valley Authority was federally authorized to provide "unified, public, multipurpose development" through the construction of dams for power production, better navigation, and flood control (Whisnant 1980). In the 1950s, TVA converted to coal-fired steam generation and more recently has developed nuclear power production to produce cheap energy to support economic development. Along with a focus on the development of electrical power, federal legislation produced funding in the region for the Area Redevelopment

Administration in 1961 focusing on job development. Later, the region was included in a nationwide effort to fight poverty with the Economic Opportunity Act in 1964, which was charged with pulling the poor out of their "culture of poverty" and into the mainstream. While these efforts were relatively short-lived, the Appalachian Regional Commission (ARC) established with federal legislation in 1965 has provided a regional development approach for several decades. The ARC has focused on creating an infrastructure for conventional economic development, especially highways, industrial parks, vocational education, and health care to hypothetically attract industry (Gaventa and Lewis 1991). Well over three-quarters of all ARC money goes to build highways and more than 2,600 miles have been constructed at a cost of almost $10 billion.

There is no question that some results of these development programs have been impressive. Yet, the emphasis on physical infrastructure has not managed to significantly change the relative degree of poverty in the region, as many areas in Appalachia remain some of the poorest in the United States (Plaut 1999). Nor has this approach necessarily provided capacity-building resources for communities. David Whisnant's assessment in 1980 remains relevant: "Pressing problems of strip-mining, black lung and other occupational diseases, secondary and higher education, housing, and community-based primary health care have been dealt with belatedly . . . if at all" (Whisnant 1980:xxi). Instead, the region has seen the emergence of mountaintop removal as the new efficient but environmentally destructive form of strip-mining. Rural mountain communities continue to deal with inadequate water supply, sewage disposal facilities, and health care facilities. Factory-flight and the new tourism economy, with its low-paying service industry jobs, now define regional economic under-development. Despite infrastructure development and regional, state, and federal monies devoted to expanding human resources, Appalachian communities still struggle with problems largely defined and "solutions" provided by non-Appalachian individuals and agencies.

Current economic indicators reveal, in fact, a growing gap between rich and poor rather than an amelioration of inequality in the region (Billings and Blee 2000; Gaventa, Smith, and Willingham 1990a). Those critics who have studied economic development from a global perspective see this growing inequality as a consequence of an economic restructuring that has formed an essential component of late capitalism since the 1960s (Korten 2001; Phillips 1998; Seligson and Passe-Smith 1993). This process, and its political counterpart "neoliberalism," involves the unification of world markets, the globalization of capitalism, and a growing reliance on the profit-oriented market for organizing social and economic activities. The shift in significance from the nation-state to the global world system increases the role of multinational and transnational corporations that can more easily penetrate far-flung areas due to their economic rather than politically based order (Giddons 1990). Driven by the need for profits and economic growth, corporate globalization has pressured nation-states for deregulation of economic activity, the privatization of public services and assets, and the elimination of tariff barriers (Friedmann 1992). As a result of subsequent changes in public policy encouraging a "free market economy," the role of the private sector has become more significant, leaving to nongovernmental organizations (NGOs) and voluntary organizations (many specifically concerned with poverty and social injustice) much of the responsibility for social welfare and redistribution activities formerly assumed by governments. At the same time, citizens' democratic participation in matters that affect their lives is threatened as the control of resources moves into more centralized corporations operating with less and less government oversight (Korten 2001). Professionals involved in the development process have become increasingly concerned, therefore, with the intersection of these closely related issues of economic development, social justice, and political democracy. John Gaventa and Helen Lewis (Gaventa 1991; Gaventa and Lewis 1991; Gaventa, Smith, and Willingham 1990a; Hinsdale, Lewis, and Waller 1995), Stephen Fisher (1993), and Richard Couto (1999), among others, have developed these themes in the Appalachian context.

Critics of the modern development process have become convinced that it is incapable of producing economic and social development. Postmodern critique of metanarratives such as the Enlightenment idea of progress and the belief that rational, universal principles might provide answers for peripheral regions has produced "the quest for another development" (Veltmeyer 2001:2). The new paradigm, often called participatory development, recognizes "the radical heterogeneity of experience, the existence of multiple paths toward development, the local community as the basis of the process involved, and people themselves as the only effective agency for change" (3). Unlike the modern development process, participatory development begins with locally led development by and for Appalachian people and communities, and the narrative becomes one of local empowerment and cultural persistence.

The Participatory Development Paradigm

The participatory development paradigm has emerged in direct response to the modern development paradigm, or what is sometimes called "corporate development," given its values, aims, and assumptions (see Table 1). The foundation of corporate development is the belief in a universalistic scientific knowledge. The rational scientific paradigm assumes facts exist independently in nature, can be empirically measured and analyzed using dispassionate and "value-free" methods and theories, and can produce a single best solution to any human problem. The application of this form of positivistic science and technology has led historically to the standardization of products, a goal of rational efficiency, the emergence of specialized knowledge and a professional intelligentsia, and the growth of bureaucratic hierarchical organizations. Corporate development is also founded on the notion that human beings might rationally harness natural and social resources in increased production and so improve peoples' quality of life. The corporate development paradigm thus promotes a focus on material infrastructure and technological development based on eighteenth-century classical and, more recently, neoclassical economic theory. Resources are viewed theoretically as unlimited, and increased consumption is highly valued. Capitalist development strategies hinge on investment in big business and industrialization, where growth is expected to trickle down to benefit all levels of society and success is measured as growth in gross domestic product, or the value of all goods and services produced in any year. This kind of economic success is often equated with moral superiority and worthiness.

Alternative models developing in the 1980s critiqued the fundamental assumptions of corporate development and their implications (Cernea 1985; Chambers 1983; Gran 1983). Analysts pointed out that the "one solution fits all" approach denies the potential viability of different, often contrasting, cultural concepts and values, and it tends to exclude voices beyond the mainstream. Putting development in the hands of professional power holders, it is argued, is paternalistic and encourages dependency. Beneficiaries assume the role of passive recipients of knowledge they may neither understand nor control. Spiraling growth and an exploitative utilitarian view of nature is accused of producing ecological destruction and a waste of finite natural resources. Furthermore, the focus on material things as opposed to people results in little social change and reinforces the status quo. Progress, in this case, assists a small powerful elite rather than the populous at large, undermining the potential for a democratic social order. Finally, the rational scientific approach excludes important and perhaps immeasurable factors that can affect the development process, such as cultural heritage, traditions and historical memory, religious and spiritual convictions, social capital, and sociocultural identities other than worker versus management. What is needed, critics argue, is a development process done *by* the people, not one done *to* them.

During the 1990s, a new model of development was articulated. Often called "participatory development," this model counters much of the corporate development model point by point. Rather than pursuing a universalistic form of modernization and development, the participatory model aims to understand

Table 1. Differences between Corporate and Participatory Development

Corporate Development	Participatory Development
1. Values science and "value-free" methods and theories to produce the single best solution for human problems	1. Values local culture and social organization and sees development taking multiple paths
2. Reliance on professionals with specialized expertise	2. Collaboration between professionals and community members, strengthening stakeholders and empowering them to contest power holders' control of meaning
3. Belief in progress and use of natural and social resources to increase economic and production	3. Values economic production *and* production of social capital and strengthening spiritual other ways of knowing
4. Resources viewed as theoretically unlimited; values individualism and consumption	4. Protection of local environment and natural resources necessary for cultural survival; cooperation in satisfaction of basic needs
5. Focus on infrastructure and technological development	5. People-focused development fostering research skills and local leadership; inclusion of women, ethnic minorities, the poor
6. Success measured by economic factors	6. Success measured by sustainability after the experts leave

and adapt to local culture and social organization. Moreover, rather than assuming that culture is a fixed category of shared knowledge, culture is understood as a dialectical process based on discourse between various elements of the society (Geertz 1973). Power becomes an important element in this discourse and stakeholders may be manipulated and controlled by thoughts and behaviors deeply etched more through symbolic means than simple direct oppression by power holders (Foucault 1977). This can result in stakeholders' acquiescence to authority and power relations even though it is obviously detrimental to their own self-interest (Gaventa 1980). Low self-worth and apathy are the inevitable outcomes that serve to reinforce the low status of the powerless. The purpose of intervention through participatory development is to strengthen stakeholders in contesting power holders' authoritative control of cultural meaning. In this sense, power is conceived not solely as a limited good in the hands of an elite but also as a capacity for action that can be strengthened among the less powerful as they develop greater self-confidence, self-reliance, and self-worth; higher levels of trust within the community; and a sense of "creation and control" (White 1994). It is noteworthy, in this regard, that much of the literature on participatory development has emerged in the public arena from grassroots training manuals for community action rather than in the academic community.

The work of Brazilian activist and educator Paulo Freire (1970) provides a critical unification of theory and praxis for the participatory development paradigm. Assuming the existence of agency or individual initiative in actively transforming society, Freire proposed a dialogical method of "conscientization," or cultivating a critical consciousness among the poor illiterates with whom he worked. Through a process in which students and teachers cooperatively engage in learning, students acquire a sense of dignity and a sense of their ability to transform the world around them, ultimately struggling to change the structure of society. Teachers become co-investigators learning about the students' cultural world, and together students and teachers work toward a cultural synthesis as a basis for action.

A key component of participatory development is participatory research. This method of research involves community members in theorizing, organizing, and implementing research on issues of interest to the community. It challenges basic tenets of traditional positivism, such as objectivity of the researcher, the discovery of universal truths, and science as the domain of experts (Mora and Diaz 2004). It also speaks to postmodern critiques of modernist forms of social science that have come to be seen as ways of maintaining traditional forms of power and privilege (Banks and Mangan 1999). In participatory research, community members are understood to be active, knowledgeable agents who can understand issues, develop research questions, and collaborate in data collection and analysis. In this process, the social science researcher is not the external expert but the facilitator working with a community. John Gaventa (1993) argues that in the political economy of a "knowledge society" in the postindustrial world, participatory research provides a means by which people can produce their own "knowledge for action" and, in the process, become educated, develop consciousness, and mobilize for change. Moreover, Banks and Mangan (1999) see participatory research as a means of producing a community narrative (as opposed to a scientific metanarrative) that strengthens identity and provides a basis for continued cooperation. Nonpositivist methods such as theatrical performance, artwork, and story-telling can contribute to the creation of this community narrative (Cornwall and Jewkes 1995).

Several shifts in values are evident in the participatory development model as contrasted with the corporate development model. The participatory model is founded on the value of diversity and respect for local cultures and people. Rather than seeking homogenization, participatory development honors cultural differences and encourages their reenactment and preservation. Moreover, alternative or indigenous knowledge is recognized as having value in its own right, the idea being that the "people's science" rivals Western scientific positivism as a way of understanding the world (Fals-Borda 1991). It is also holistic and humanistic in that it acknowledges that a peoples' knowledge base relies on their cultural histories, traditions and cultural heritage, philosophies, spirituality, value systems, and worldview (Titi and Singh 1995). The participatory development model seeks sustainability not only through reliance on local people and their cultural knowledge but also through the protection of the local environment and natural resources that are vital to cultural survival (Hoff 1998; Sargent et al. 1991; Thiele 1999).

The participatory model also values the inclusion of diverse voices, including women and ethnic minorities. The goal is to ensure that all stakeholders are incorporated into a democratic process. Furthermore, the participatory model values local social organization and the indigenous way in which people are tied to one another. In kin-based societies, participatory development acknowledges the priority of kinship and the extended family and seeks to build on these kinds of linkages.

Lastly, participatory development values parity between participants and researchers/professionals. The outside professional facilitator is recognized as being a necessary catalyst, but there is a shift in the locus of power during the development process. In the words of Robert Chambers (1997), the professional must "hand over the stick" and urge participants to take the lead in developing research goals, to become involved in data collection and analysis, to make decisions regarding action, and to take responsibility for carrying out development projects.

The goal of participatory development is to empower participants through the process of development. This is first and foremost a people-centered transformation as opposed to change that is primarily material and technological. Participatory development encourages self-confidence, self-reliance, and self-development. It assumes that power is not finite, residing only in the hands of power holders, but can also be created through participation in dialogue (Freire 1998; Gramsci 1971). Democracy is more likely to result from this focus on community-based economies and increased sociopolitical participation, it is argued, than by raising the gross domestic product to try to compete in the global economy (Friedmann 1992; Gaventa and Lewis 1991).

Aspects of participatory development have actually been incorporated into public policymaking for decades. Since the 1960s, federal legislation in the United States has moved to incorporate public participation in policymaking—for example, in urban poverty programs and the Office of Economic Opportunity. The National Environmental Policy Act passed in 1969 institutionalized public participation at the federal, state, and local levels. Combined with privatization, this movement has led to an increased emphasis on collaboration in policy management in the United States where many government agencies have experimented with community-based collaborations, community advisory boards, citizen review panels, and online discussion forums. Public participation has also spread to other countries through work by the United Nations and the World Bank. At the same time, there has been criticism of the way participation has been incorporated into governance (Cooke and Kothari 2001). In a widely cited article on levels of citizen participation in public policymaking, Sherry Arnstein (1969) notes that the most common (but passive) role for the public is to review and comment on agency decisions at public hearings while shared decision-making authority over policy and planning is likely to be found mostly in nongovernmental organizations. As Depoe et al. (2004) point out, participation by the public is often allowed only as an adversary as part of a "decide-announce-defend" agency process.

Nevertheless, there is emerging evidence of public participation and collaboration in shared decision making by stakeholders including grassroots citizen organizations, nongovernment organizations, and state and federal government. An interesting example from environmental management is the Applegate Partnership in southwestern Oregon, where forest and mill workers confronted protesting environmentalists over the Bureau of Land Management and Forest Service plan to harvest timber in areas where the northern spotted owl and other old growth–dependent species were endangered. A board was established representing a cross-section of interests and values in the Applegate Valley, including federal land managers, environmentalists, timber company employees, a community organizer, and a soil and water conservation district manager. The partnership worked through open, inclusive, and transparent decision-making processes toward comprehensive land management and ultimately addressed a wide variety of issues in planning and development (Koontz et al. 2004).

Examples promoting public participation could be cited in many other fields. In the field of public health, partnerships involving community organizations, agencies, coalitions, and government institutions form the basis for the World Health Organization's approach to global primary health care in *Health 21: Health for All in the 21st Century* (WHO Europe 1999). Citizen participation is being promoted in such diverse fields as community psychology, nursing, social and economic justice, community development, environmental planning, and sustainable architecture (Depoe et al. 2004; Edwards and Gaventa 2001; Francis et al. 1987; Green and Haines 2002; Jason et al. 2004;

Koch and Kralik 2006; Robb 1999; Sassi 2006). Perhaps one of the best-known examples of collaborative planning is used in design and planning fields: the "charrette," or intense planning period, which includes all stakeholders in developing and refining plans with opportunities for feedback at each stage of the process (Lennertz and Lutzenhiser 2006).

Participatory development has had its advocates in Appalachia, although researchers may not have used the term. Probably best known has been the work of the Highlander Research and Education Center and its founder, Myles Horton (Horton 1989; Horton and Freire 1990; Lewis 2001). An important early example of participatory research in the region was the study of landownership by a coalition of citizens and technical researchers (Appalachian Land Owner-ship Task Force 1983; Horton 1993). John Gaventa (Gaventa 1991; Gaventa, Smith, and Willingham 1990b) has examined underlying connections in theory and praxis between Appalachian social, political, and economic struggles and those of the Third World in the global system. Stephen Fisher's (1993) edited volume explored the significance of Appalachian regional culture as a force of resistance and social change. Richard Couto (1999; Couto et al. 1995) has used Appalachian case studies to illustrate how community-based organizations with their emphasis on social capital (social networks and resources for cooperative action) help to promote democratic process. Thomas Plaut and the health and human service providers of Madison County, North Carolina, joined with local citizens in a model of rural coalition building to improve residents' health and quality of life (Landis et al. 1996). In Ivanhoe, Virginia, Helen Lewis and her associates enacted participatory development principles in their work with the Ivanhoe Civic League (Hinsdale, Lewis, and Waller 1995). Similarly, Rhoda Halperin (1998, 2006) has provided a detailed account of her professional/ community partnership intended to revive and reclaim an urban Appalachian community and a neighborhood school in Cincinnati, Ohio. Finally, Mary LaLone's (1997, 1998) edited work on the oral history of coal miners in the New River Valley, Virginia, has relied on her own extended collaboration with students and community partners.

Community-Based Development

Participatory development is, above all, local development. It involves working with individuals in the context of their communities. This shifts the development focus from industry or technological expertise to local people and community resources. It shifts development from a top-down to a bottom-up approach, which is inherently more democratic. It produces research and the systematic development of knowledge that is useful to people in their everyday lives. Anchored in a particular community, development is grounded in the social and cultural attributes of the local people. Those professionals who facilitate development must be reflexive practitioners, aware that their cultural frameworks for understanding may differ from those in the community they serve. Community-based development requires a commitment to learning local knowledge and relying on community assets in addition to making connections to external resources. It requires adopting a critical approach to ideas and narratives privileging progress as defined by those in power and authority. Participatory development is ultimately a transformative process for individuals and communities because it contributes to the creation of self-reliant and sustainable communities (Kumar 2002). In this sense, growth becomes defined as the cumulative competence gained by community members through action taken on behalf of the community's welfare.

DEFINING COMMUNITY

The concept of community is complicated when applied to the southern mountains. Appalachian communities have often been invisible to those from outside the region. In fact, the "absence of community" is identified by Henry Shapiro (1978) as one of the principle characteristics by which Appalachian otherness was defined at the turn of the twentieth century. The outbreak of feuds and conflict with the law over moonshining contributed to this picture of disorganization and antisocial tendencies. This helped to fuel the attraction of a wave of benevolent workers to the region who envisioned the need to provide community through bringing mountain people together and reestablishing a common culture by encouraging the study of folk music, handicrafts, and folklore at settlement schools. In the mid-twentieth century, the perception of a lack of community in Appalachia was associated with the concept of a "culture of poverty," which is characterized by psychological reactions of apathy and alienation, a lack of trust in institutions, and the breakdown of social relations beyond the family (Gazaway 1969). Whether explained by social isolation at the turn of the twentieth century or impoverishment at midcentury, the general assessment has been that Appalachian people are socially deficient.

These interpretations have been critiqued by scholars from a number of perspectives. Shapiro (1978) argues that the accurate description of mountain people's way of life was never the objective of turn-of-the-century writers and travelers; rather, the creation of Appalachian otherness emerged as these authors wrestled with assumptions about the nature of America and American civilization. Appalachian scholarship has also suggested that the outbreak of feuds and conflicts with the law over moonshining are better interpreted as a reaction of mountain people to the strains of modernization, industrialization, and expanding federal power (Miller 1991; Waller 1988). Many also contend that the development of apathy, distrust, and a sense of fatalism in the mountains is understandable when considered in the context of social and economic development controlled by external capitalists (Gaventa 1980; Lewis et al. 1978). Moreover, Whisnant (1983) has demonstrated that the folk culture imported and taught by settlement schools and benevolent workers in the region was more that of an imagined mountain culture and actually bore little resemblance to the native culture they were hoping to "revive." In fact, little objective description of mountain culture was begun until the last half of the twentieth century.

One of the reasons the absence-of-community mountain stereotype became (and remains) anchored in the American imagination is that it makes sense given a certain mainstream cultural definition of community that envisions densely clustered housing and neighborhoods, the presence of formal institutions and markets, formal leadership and political organization, and so forth. Early-twentieth-century travelers from the Northeast, for example, found little in the mountains that might resemble the familiar town-square variety of New England towns and villages.

Mountain communities are better understood, as Patricia Beaver (1986) points out, as a set of overlapping informal and flexible social networks serving a range of purposes. Appalachian communities are certainly defined by geography. In other words, a community is a locale, a place. And place is shaped by the mountain topography in which the people between ridges generally share an identity and feel set apart to some extent from those on the other side of the ridge. But more than this, it is defined by social relations and local association in families, churches, neighborhoods, and "interaction flows along the roads" that twist through the valleys winding from one intersection to the next (54).

The mountain version of community is also a moral system. It rests on the idiom of kinship as a value about how people *should* behave toward one another (Beaver 1986). The commonly heard "We're all kin here" indicates that mountain people perceive themselves to be like one another, of the same flesh and blood (Bryant 1981). Nonkin are often incorporated into kinship networks as equals through the extension of kinship terms and obligations (Beaver 1986; Halperin 1990). These themes of familism and egalitarianism are echoed in mountain churches where people address one another as "Brother" and "Sister" who assemble as a "family of Christ" (Keefe 1998). The small mountain churches that dot the countryside are typically made up of members bound by ties of kinship, and the annual church homecomings celebrate the reunion of actual kin groups as well as church members. Self-sufficiency is expected in mountain families and communities, and individuals are expected to work hard and to be able to take care of themselves. At the same time, neighbors expect to help neighbors and to go out of their way to help members of their church and community in times of crisis. As with any small society, there is the value of peaceful cooperation and the desire to avoid conflict in personal relations. Successful community leaders are able to avoid arguments and bring about consensus without offending others. The moral system that sustains mountain communities forms an interconnected ideology, and the values of egalitarianism, independence, familism, neighborliness, conflict avoidance, and a religious worldview reinforce each other in complicated ways (Beaver 1986; Keefe 1998). Rather than being wholly distinctive, rural communities in Appalachia resemble rural communities across America in their set of values and *gemeinschaft* patterns of social interaction (Flora et al. 1992; Salamon 2003).

Appalachian communities are largely invisible to the untrained eye and "lie below the surface during most of the year," becoming manifest in times of crisis, such as a disastrous flood, or when an opportunity for community development arises and the social community provides the resources and energy to "pull the neighborhood along" (Beaver 1986:55). This interpretation finds that, contrary to the stereotype, Appalachian communities often have been able to provide the very basis of survival for mountain people during the social and economic upheaval of industrialization, modernization, and globalization of the twentieth century. There is evidence that Appalachian neighborhoods in cities beyond the mountains work in the same ways (Halperin 1998).

COMMUNITY ASSETS AND CAPACITY BUILDING

John O'Looney (1996) remarks that the human service field has been "revolutionized" in recent years by an approach of "community capacity building" in which citizens and providers work collaboratively to identify and strengthen community assets and resources rather than focus on weaknesses and needs. John L. McKnight and John Kretzmann have made key contributions to this "asset-based community development" approach (Kretzmann and McKnight 1993; McKnight and Kretzmann 1996). McKnight and Kretzmann argue that by beginning with an inventory of abilities and skills, members of a community become empowered by seeing themselves as contributing citizens and producers. Assets include often-overlooked categories of people with gifts and time on their hands, including youth, seniors, and the disabled who might be pulled into community-building work through public and private institutions such as churches, libraries, and schools. The authors describe a five-step blueprint for community mobilization that begins by mapping the capacities and assets of individuals, citizen's associations (both formal and informal), and local institutions; later steps are taken to build relationships among local assets, mobilize assets for economic development and information sharing, collaborate on a community vision and plan, and, finally, leverage resources from outside the community (Kretzmann and McNight 1993). Asset-based community development contradicts the traditional social service model that identifies needs and deficiencies of individuals and communities and provides them with services, turning people into welfare recipients and weakening natural community supports. McKnight (1997) argues that policymakers must begin to divert resources from social service systems to provide more community-based economic opportunity. Private foundations are already funding these kinds of approaches, especially in the field of public health (Bruce and McKane 2000; Minkler 1997).

Many social critics argue that it is only through small-scale grassroots action that more equitable and democratic development will take place (Gran 1983, Shuman 1998; Veltmeyer 2001). A fundamental difference characterizing this kind of development has to do with the conceptualization of economics. Rather than being concerned with growth in production and consumption, participatory development is concerned with "community economics," which is defined by community self-reliance. This approach would emphasize nurturing locally owned businesses that use local resources sustainably, employ local workers at decent wages, and primarily serve local consumers (Shuman 1998). Community economics relies on a number of values, including personal responsibility, respect for others, harmony with nature, social caring, empowerment of all, and minimized dependence on others. This is a humanistic economics that is organized around meeting peoples' moral, social, and material needs and not desires for profits and consumption (Gran 1983). Clearly, this kind of community economics is founded on the ideal of a community with shared institutions, common beliefs, and social bonds of mutual obligation.

Communities with these shared traits have what has been called a "moral economy" (Scott 1976). In these kinds of economies, people are bound together by social obligation and reciprocal exchange. Kin-based societies are common examples in which individuals give material goods and services freely to others in their kin group, knowing that they will receive in kind. These types of exchanges are not conceptualized as primarily of instrumental value, but rather as part of the social obligations owed to relatives. In other words, the primary reason people say they participate in these exchanges is because they want to help a kin member, without an explicit economical calculation of payback. To do otherwise would turn the social obligation into something more like a bribe. Nevertheless, the net result is that these moral economies can operate efficiently in providing for the needs of community members. The kinds of communities that are organized around moral economy are based on intimate social bonds with others, trusting relationships, and a high degree of social cooperation. This "social capital" is important for community development and will be addressed in a later section.

Communities with these kinds of strong social ties are threatened by modernity and the forces that result in disentangling social connection and meaning. Philip Selznick argues that the technologically advanced, industrial, commercial, and urban society, emerging since the eighteenth century in the Western world, fragments social experience: "The most important element is the steady weakening of traditional social bonds and the concomitant creation of new unities based on more rational, more impersonal, more fragmented forms of thought and action" (Selznick 1992:4). He calls for the development of more coherent meaning in contemporary life through a recommitment to a "moral commonwealth" by engaging the elements of community, including shared identity, institutions, and culture. Many of those in the community development field argue that this focus on strengthening the social and cultural infrastructure is more important than chasing industry or improving physical infrastructure (Gaventa and Lewis 1991; O'Looney 1996).

Rural Appalachian communities tend to be anchored on kinship and rely on a moral economy at the local level. Related families often live near one another and cooperate in organized activities such as gardening and canning food, farming, house-building, and car maintenance (Beaver 1986). Neighbors exchange goods and services and employ multiple livelihood strategies that enable the family to be less dependent than if they had a single, possibly unreliable, source of income (Halperin 1990). In other words, in many mountain communities, there already exists the kind of social infrastructure the previously cited authors hope to reestablish in American society. It is imperative that community development in the mountains strengthens and preserves these precious assets and that it builds on local social organization for economic development purposes.

CULTURAL COMPETENCY AND COMMUNITY DEVELOPMENT

The recognition of community assets requires cultural competency. So often, practitioners unversed in Appalachian culture know only the stereotypes and see only cultural deficiencies because they begin with mainstream America as the norm. The concept of cultural competency implies that community residents have cultural knowledge; this knowledge contributes to their livelihood and survival; and cultural knowledge is a resource that can be harnessed for action on behalf of the community. Clearly, the idea of cultural competency is based on the concept of culture as developed by anthropologists in the twentieth century (Keefe 2005b). Culture consists of the meanings shared by members of a society and the practices by which shared meanings are produced. In this sense, the term culture refers to both a way of life and the process by which a way of life is reproduced in a social group. The latter is complicated in hierarchical societies, where it is conceived as a dialectical process incorporating diverse actors with varying power and ability to manipulate and construct meaning (Bourdieu 1977). Cultural competency requires an understanding of a group's way of life as well as how group members might be mobilized in the struggle to interpret the social meaning of their life. In the case of mountain people, then, it is necessary to understand both indigenous cultural practices and the nature of political economy in the larger society in which mountain culture is perceived as being without value.

The term "cultural competency" comes from practitioner fields in medicine, mental health, and social services. The model was first elaborated in 1989 in the field of children's mental health by Cross et al. in *Towards a Culturally Competent System of Care,* in which they outlined a negative-to-positive continuum of care going from cultural destructiveness to cultural proficiency as practiced by individuals and institutions.

Several domains of competence are addressed by the cultural competency model (Hong, Garcia, and Soriano 2000; Mason, Benjamin, and Lewis 1996). The level of awareness involves the process of developing an awareness of one's own cultural heritage and cultural stereotypes about others and an ability to recognize and learn to respect cultural differences in other groups. This includes the development of a heightened self-awareness and the recognition that every individual, including oneself, has a cultural identity, a heritage, a set of values by which they navigate life (Lynch and Hanson 1998). This self-awareness necessarily involves reflexivity or becoming conscious of being self-conscious and considering how others might perceive us and vice versa. Thinking about the self as both subject and object causes individuals to think differently about the self and, subsequently, to alter the self. In this way, reflexivity creates a never-ending process of self-tuning in response to changing social and cultural contexts (Davies 1999). Those involved in community development are encouraged through reflexivity to put themselves in the shoes of community members, to question professional expertise as well as their own cultural baggage, and to remain open to new ideas, new ways of knowing, and new methods of action.

Reflexivity among practitioners in the Appalachian context is addressed in a recent edited volume, *Appalachian Cultural Competency,* by Keefe (2005a).

Other domains of competence include a knowledge level, a skills level, and an institutional level. In the knowledge level, practitioners actively seek to acquire specific knowledge about their own culture as well as the cultures of others through self-study, professional training, and the pursuit of cross-cultural experiences. Several excellent general resources with extensive bibliographies are available to practitioners on Appalachian culture and society (e.g., Ergood and Kuhre 1991; Higgs, Manning, and Miller 1995; Obermiller and Maloney 2002). Many practitioners in community development, education, and the health and human services fields currently attend the annual meetings of the Appalachian Studies Association for continuing education in Appalachian studies. More symposia developed specifically for practitioners would be helpful at these meetings. At the skills level, practitioners are expected to learn culturally appropriate skills for assessment, intervention, and evaluation. Only now are we beginning to see the conceptual development of these kinds of skills in the delivery of services in the Appalachian cultural context (Keefe 2005a). The institutional level addresses changes in institutional policies and structures in order to ensure that cultural competence is activated at the societal level. This conscious effort in the policy arena has yet to really begin on behalf of southern mountain people and communities.

Community Identity and Mobilization

Community-based development requires the ability to recognize and strengthen community identity. Appalachian communities, organized as they are on the basis of kinship and long-term social ties, generally have well-defined and tangible identities. Residents' sentiments of community attachment can be important assets for community-based development. Strong community identity can provide people with the will and the motivation to engage in work that contributes to the common good. If, as social critics argue, communities are being weakened by the very nature of the modern world, exactly what kinds of sentiments and practices should be cultivated in order to strengthen community identity? To begin the discussion, we must return to an analysis of the concept of community as a distinctive kind of social organization.

The whole notion of "community," as Jewkes and Murcott (1996) point out, can be traced to eighteenth-century Enlightenment thought. With growing urbanization, industrialization, and laissez faire capitalism in Europe, philosophers felt the relationship between individuals and society was being altered and the result was a loss of community. Ferdinand Toennies (1957) later conceptualized the distinction between community (gemeinschaft) and the larger society (gesellschaft) in a way that captured this idea about two basic types of human association for modern sociology. In gemeinschaft communities, individuals identify more with the larger association than with their own self-interest, and they experience fulfillment through efforts made on behalf of the community. Strong personal relationships and family ties provide the basis for social structure, and bureaucratic institutions are minimal. As a result of the strong collective loyalty, there is little need to enforce social control. Typically, communities are founded on a shared place and shared beliefs as well as kinship and common race and ethnicity. In the larger society of gesellschaft, the larger association never takes on more importance than individual self interest and the individual sees society as the instrumental means to further individualistic goals. Social cohesion in such societies derives from an emphasis on secondary relations in business and commerce and a more elaborate division of labor. In gesellschaft, shared values and mores are less important; there is less loyalty to the social good; and society is more susceptible to conflict. Contemporary social critics continue to be concerned about this shift to gesellschaft-like association and its impact on social relations, trust, and, ultimately, democracy and civil society in America. At the same time, community development activists have redoubled their efforts to better understand the cooperative enterprise at the local level.

Community studies by anthropologists and sociologists were a common undertaking during the early twentieth century. Even so, there was little agreement on the definition of community except that it deals with people (Jewkes and Murcott 1996). By the 1970s, community studies had been largely abandoned because of the growing recognition that it is impossible to study communities in isolation from external forces and connections. There was also increasing interest in the kinds of diversity that complicate social interaction (e.g., gender, race, ethnicity, class, age, religion, etc.), and the realization that no community can be described as a homogeneous unit with a single set of coherent interests and pursuits. Since the 1970s, more attention has focused on what action needs to be taken to strengthen communities rather than the pursuit of more detached study of them. Much of this concern comes from practitioners in the fields of social work, community development, public health, and mental health, where the decline of community is perceived as the root cause of many social problems.

The question of identity has emerged recently as the helpful focus of research on strengthening community. How do successful communities reinforce the identification of residents with the common good? How do individuals formulate personal identities that involve affiliation with the community and agency to act on its behalf? How is community identity maintained and adopted by the next generation as well as by newcomers to the community? Answers to these questions will contribute to practitioners' efforts to intervene and assist those communities that are ailing.

Sonya Salamon's research in small towns and rural communities in the Midwest for the past twenty years provides keen insights in this regard. Her book *Newcomers to Old Towns* (2003) describes the kinds of changes undergone in the Illinois countryside with creeping suburbanization as individuals move to small towns that become bedroom communities in which they live but do not shop, work, or affiliate in meaningful ways. In contrast to the gemeinschaft character of old-timers who live in these towns, the newcomers are less neighborly, more consumption oriented, and prefer looser social ties. The newcomers chafe at the coercive social control imposed in stable communities, preferring "loose connections and porous institutions that maximize autonomy and freedom" (Salamon 2003:16). They exhibit a kind of "moral minimalism" and feel children should be a family (rather than a community) responsibility. There is little tolerance for adolescent shenanigans, and youth in newcomer families form less attachment to place and are less likely to return there as an adult. New residents often segregate into new subdivisions where more housing is available, and these neighborhoods tend to be shaped by newcomers' emphasis on the home as the locus of consumption, the backyard as a private refuge, and the objectification of an artificial natural landscape. Newcomers arrive with a romantic notion about small-town life but tend to treat small towns like interchangeable suburbs. Avoiding face-to-face connections with old-timers facilitates their mobility. As a result of this in-migration of new residents with different social and cultural baggage, communities are transformed in their interconnectedness, and their social resources and civic engagement often decline.

Salamon details at great length the kinds of practices that contribute to customs of cooperation, trust, consensus-building, alertness, selflessness, and volunteerism that characterize community at its best. She identifies community as a sense of social relationships attached to place. The small towns with which she is familiar have a common ethnic heritage, a set of cultural practices of kin relations and land inheritance supporting attachment to place, and a particular history in the place and with certain people. The old-timers are lifelong residents who were born in town and have grown up within a dense social circle dominated by kinship, friendship, and neighborhood ties. Residential stability leads to multiple generations living nearby, and children are as much the responsibility of others, especially kin, as of parents. Adolescents are not only tolerated, they become stars as the schools pull in people across the generations. Youths quickly form a strong attachment to their hometown through athletic team rivalries with nearby towns. People who are old-timers know each others' family history and reputation. Because they engage in a lifetime of small-scale as well as large-scale reciprocal exchange, they build the kind of trust and responsiveness needed for civic work. Salamon emphasizes the time and repeated experiences necessary to create a sense of community: "Community does not exist abstractly or in a void, to be activated in an emergency for efficient mobilization. Old-timers know that community culture is deep and thick, although the daily interactions themselves may seem superficial and repetitive. But if community has been built, it is there to be mobilized when cooperation is needed" (2003:24). Newcomers often refuse to make the kind of social investment required to reproduce community culture. In only one out of the four types of towns Salamon describes are old-timers successful in pressuring newcomers to adopt norms of reciprocity and civil society, and these tend to be the smallest and most isolated hamlets.

Community identity then is anchored in these social networks of friends, neighbors, and kin who can be relied upon to reciprocate support, producing social trust and caring for the community as a whole. Identity incorporates the concept of community culture, which constrains and shapes what people think and do and what they feel and believe (Salamon 2003). Cultural attributes come from various sources including the community's settlement pattern, its history, its geography, people's ethnicity, and the demography of the place. A community story line is constructed that connects individual lives with the social processes of community so that individuals sense they are part of a caring community of givers and receivers with a capacity for positive change (Rappaport 1994). Community culture is produced and reproduced through daily interaction chatting with neighbors, eating at the local café, and meeting at the post office. Other practices contribute to community culture, including school activities, caring for dependent citizens, fund-raising for community causes, and organizing community festivals and celebrations. Regular interaction over a long period of time is required of individuals in order to prove their loyalty and to become integrated into the community.

Anyone who has lived in the small towns and rural communities in Appalachia will find these descriptions of "old-timer" community life familiar. Southern Appalachian communities are commonly rich in community culture and identity. Even communities in coal mining counties can be strongholds of kin-based networks and individuals with a sense of loyalty to people and place, often evidenced by the frequent return of out-migrants (Schwarzweller, Brown, and Mangalam 1971). At the same time, Appalachian communities, especially those in the southern part of the region, are also threatened by the in-migration of newcomers with different values, a different relationship to the natural environment, and less attachment to people and place (Anglin 1983; Keefe 1994; Keefe, Reck, and Reck 1991). Second homes and new "gated communities" are becoming far more common in the southern mountains. Seasonal residents may not be local voters, but they can easily overwhelm small mountain communities and change the character of community life. Certainly the agenda for community action may be rewritten as a result. An important focus for community development in Appalachia should be to identify, strengthen, and preserve the social resources that already exist in mountain towns and rural communities. Mountain communities are "communities of practice" reproducing places with which residents identify and feel compelled to support through action (Holland et al. 1998). In this sense, far from the stereotypical poor and deficient Other, mountain communities can be seen as precious resources that offer a foundation for future development.

Gary O'Dell (2005) provides an example of this kind of mountain community of practice in his examination of water development in McDowell County, West Virginia. Water supply systems in McDowell County are the legacies of coal companies who built them to serve workers in company towns. In the late 1980s water quality steadily deteriorated along the Big Creek area of the county after the local coal company filed for Chapter 11 bankruptcy and would no longer provide funding for the water company. According to O'Dell, many communities of coal miners were affected, with the water turning jet black from manganese in one community and rust colored from iron in another. One community resident, Frankie Rutherford, recalled: "I could run two inches of water in the bathtub to bathe my two-year-old, and when I put my hand in the water, it would disappear, you couldn't see it anymore." Despite complaints, the water company did nothing, and residents were forced to haul water for daily household needs. According to O'Dell (2005:61):

> For Rutherford, the pivotal moment arrived when, frustrated, she decided to hire a contractor to drill a water well on her property. The driller drove his rig to her home one evening and parked it in the yard, intending to begin work the next day. That night Rutherford, a single mother, thought seriously about the water problem. Having a well drilled might solve the problem for her own family, but would not help the many other children in the community who did not have access to safe drinking water. When the driller arrived on the next morning, Frankie Rutherford told him to go home. "I did not want to have a solution for myself alone until one could be found for all the children," she recalls.

Instead, Frankie Rutherford became an activist organizing meetings where community residents took legal and political action to secure clean water for McDowell County. Ultimately, she was appointed director of a new public service district established by county commissioners that took over responsibility for developing and maintaining water, sewer, and gas systems in the area. The successful mobilization of public support in this case relied upon the dense social communities of local miners and their families and the leadership of individuals like Rutherford who put the community's interest above self-interest.

SOCIAL CAPITAL AND COMMUNITY-BASED DEVELOPMENT

Involving local people in research, decisions, and priority setting is a prerequisite for long-term sustainability and effectiveness of community development initiatives. People's participation in this work is ultimately a matter of power and control (Hampshire et al. 2005). Power can be conceptualized in different ways. A Marxian view of power sees it in the hands of the dominant group, where it is used to oppress and control groups with less access to basic economic resources. From this point of view, power is coercive and top-down, and one gains power at another's expense. Power is conceptualized as control of the means of production, especially the businesses and factories, equipment, inventories, and employees' labor, which make up economic capital. Power can be enacted in several ways: as outright force or by excluding groups from the political process or by influencing the consciousness of the powerless who adopt the ideology of the powerful.

This chapter has focused on another way of conceptualizing power. Rather than a locatable entity that people can possess, power is a generative force that emerges in social relations (Foucault 1980). Power is diffuse and changing, and the empowerment of one does not necessarily mean the disempowerment of others. Power from this point of view can be based on many different forms of capital. Dominant groups have the authority to define authentic forms of capital and the power to perpetuate a status quo, but less powerful individuals and groups are considered to have agency and the ability to reflect and strategize, to create knowledge, and to resist domination through their own action.

In this second conceptualization of power, resources are understood to include forms of capital beyond Karl Marx's nineteenth-century formulation that referred solely to economic capital. These other forms of capital are far ranging and include human capital (individual skills and education), political capital (influence and power gained through the electoral process), cultural capital (knowledge about elite cultural taste), social capital (influence through social connections), symbolic capital (prestige and family name), psychological capital (personality traits improving leadership and entrepreneurial chances), and spiritual capital (influence through access to supernatural power).[1] In addition, it is generally assumed that each of these forms of capital can be converted into other forms. For example, Bourdieu (1984, 1987) has argued that cultural capital or knowledge accumulated while growing up in an upper-class family, including such things as taste in art, table manners, and knowing how to dress for success, contributes to access to economic capital and the reproduction of class stratification.

Capital clearly takes on a more generic definition in these new formulations. For example, Flora et al. (2003:8) offer a definition based on "resources or assets that are invested to create new resources thereby becoming capital." Ivan Light suggests a definition that implies its employment by social agents: capital is "a store of value that facilitates action" (2004:19). In this sense, what is of value may include productive resources, educational training, political influence, aesthetic taste, and/or social ties.

As Flora et al. (2003) point out, every community has capital or resources for investment within it. One thing that makes social capital unique among these various forms of capital, Ivan Light argues, is that social capital is the only one available to "the poor, illiterate, landless and downtrodden" (2004:23). The concept of social capital has been criticized especially by Marxist scholars for this notion that the poor might have capital, since by their definition they have none (Durrenberger 2002). In the new theoretical repositioning of the poor and the powerless, on the other hand, social capital assumes center stage as an essential resource for their survival, giving them agency. For example, Carol Stack's book, *All Our Kin* (1974), is often cited in the social capital literature as an example of how the everyday survival of the poor in urban black neighborhoods frequently depends upon close interaction between family and friends.

The literature on social capital in the last decade has become a minor academic industry. One of the reasons for this explosion, I would argue, is that the very term "capital" creates a meaningful metaphor for Westerners, who tend to see worth in economic terms, as profits or the bottom line. The term "capital" implies value that Westerners understand, for we often speak of "being rich in family and friends." We know that there are "payoffs" to social relationships (Field 2003). Anthropologists, having specialized in the study of small-scale societies, fundamentally understand that economic life is often "embedded" in social life, while economists have had greater difficulty in grasping the significance of social ties in economic life and are often frustrated in their attempt to apply measurement to social relationships. Nevertheless, it is apparent that the concept of social capital has enjoyed popularity in many disciplines including sociology, anthropology, political science, economics, history, health and social work, social policy, and urban policy. Political scientists are interested in how social capital might contribute to the development of democracy and civic engagement. Economists would like to quantify and incorporate "soft" social traits into their economic models. Social workers are interested in how social ties contribute to individuals' and communities' well-being. Health and mental health researchers are interested in how social relationships might help individuals prevent disease, recover from illness, and maintain good mental health. Policy makers are especially interested in the concept because they want to find new and cost-effective ways of achieving economic development, health promotion, and the reduction of poverty and crime (Field 2003).

As it stands, current economic models cannot adequately explain growth and development in many parts of the world (Grootaert 1997). There are countries, cities, and regions that have similar endowments of natural resources and physical and human capital but have different levels of economic performance. The "East Asian Miracle" is often cited as an example, where the countries of Hong Kong, Singapore, Thailand, Indonesia, Malaysia, Korea, Japan, and Taiwan have had higher than expected growth rates over the past three decades. It is assumed that social capital must explain much of the rest of the variance in the economic model.

Elements of Social Capital

Social capital can be defined as the "networks and norms that enable participants to act together effectively to pursue shared objectives" (Gittell and Vidal 1998:15). There are three elements of social capital identified in the literature: social networks and associations, norms of reciprocity, and trust.

Social Networks

Social networks are conceptualized as points and linkages providing connections between individuals and others, sometimes many points removed. An individual might be linked to others through many different kinds of social relationships, such as family, friends, neighbors, coworkers, club or association members, and so on. Kinship ties are generally considered stronger than other kinds of social ties. Relationships might be simplex (involving a single kind of tie) or multiplex (involving multiple kinds of ties); for example, in a multiplex relationship, a relative might also be a neighbor and coworker. Multiplex ties are considered stronger in social network analysis.

The implication is that gemeinschaft communities have stronger social networks due to the importance of local kinship ties and the multistranded nature of many social relationships. James Coleman (1988) examined the impact these kinds of ties have on educational achievement in his research on dropout rates in private-religious versus private-nonreligious versus public high schools. Dropout rates were much lower in Catholic high schools, where overlapping relations between clergy, neighbors, and kin in stable communities reinforced teachers' and parents' efforts to dissuade youngsters from truancy or skipping their homework. In this way, social capital was transformed into educational achievement and human capital.

Robert Putnam (2000) has distinguished between two kinds of social capital, bonding versus bridging, that differ in whether the social tie is internal or external to the community. Bonding social capital refers to the multiplex intra-group ties between family members, friends, neighbors, etc. in gemeinschaft communities. Bridging social capital, on the other hand, refers to external linkages to unrelated people, perhaps of higher social status, and associations having other kinds of resources. Bridging social capital, it is often argued, is more important for democracy and for economic development, linking the poor, for example, with people and organizations with more resources, including nongovernmental organizations and funding agencies. Other scholars point out that bonding and bridging social capital are both necessary for community development, and communities deficient in one or the other will be unsuccessful in accomplishing goals (Flora et al. 2003; Gittell and Vidal 1998).

Social networks can be viewed from the perspective of the individual on which a personal network is anchored. But more important in structural terms, social networks themselves are situated in a structural sense between the levels of individual and group. That is, social networks are aggregates of individuals, although the individuals may never gather together in an organized group. Networks can be activated and can set into motion far-ranging actions, as ideas and calls for mobilization move along linkages. This can be significant in rural communities where people may not often gather together in large groups but are tied together as part of complex networks through which information and goods and services move with frequency. Patricia Beaver (1986) has described how these networks in Appalachian communities can operate in crisis, such as a flood, drawing in disparate people who will put aside their differences to work as a neighborhood helping each other in times of need.

Researchers often put emphasis on networking through formal associations as an important means by which individuals can access large numbers of other people and thereby increase resources to be used for development purposes. Robert Putnam's first book, *Making Democracy Work* (1993), entailed a contrast in voluntary association membership and civic development in two regions in Italy. The northern Italian region, where voluntary associations flourished, experienced greater civic development in the last part of the twentieth century compared to the southern region, where voluntary associations were weak. Richard Couto's book, *Making Democracy Work Better* (1999), focuses on these kinds of voluntary organizations in Appalachia and advocates community-based organizations as a primary means of mitigating social, economic, and political inequality in the region. On the other hand, voluntary association membership is fairly uncommon in the southern mountains. The only voluntary associations that occur consistently in mountain communities are churches, volunteer fire departments, school parent-teacher organizations, and electrical and telephone cooperatives. Otherwise, mountain people are more likely to be involved in the kinds of informal associations described by Beaver (1986).

Key to maintaining informal networks is the time spent with others in easy, comfortable social interaction. Robert Putnam (2000) calls this "schmoozing." In the mountains, it is referred to as "fellowshipping." Mountain churches use the term "fellowship" to describe the occasions after services when members socialize over coffee and snacks (often in the "fellowship hall"). Church members also speak of having fellowship with God, especially through daily prayer. But fellowship goes on in many secular situations as well. Generally, in any small mountain town there are one or more places where people regularly gather for a sit-down chat, such as restaurants, coffee shops, fast food places, and convenience stores. Sometimes, other kinds of establishments such as a gas station or a women's clothing store serve the same purpose. Most often, gatherings are exclusive to one gender or the other. More spontaneous social interactions occur at the post office or the local grocery store, where people on errands run into others they know and often have not seen for some time, prompting a conversation. Fellowship greases the wheels of social networks in mountain communities, and people take the time to engage in it.

Reciprocity

Generalized reciprocity is the exchange of goods and services without requiring an immediate return of value. It is a "gift economy" that socially indebts people to one another. At the same time, it is the social relationship that has primacy in the moral economy based on reciprocity. In any case, reciprocity sets up obligation to others and thus creates the basis for community bonding.

While other anthropologists offer detailed descriptions of the way in which reciprocity binds together small-scale societies, Mayfair Yang (1994) provides an example of reciprocity in the urban industrial society of China. The Chinese use *guanxi* as a way to acquire resources. It is an "art" because the style and appropriateness of the exchange is critical to its effectiveness. It is a gift (and not a bribe), because the focus is on the relationship and obligation is the outcome but never the primary purpose. In China, guanxi provides a means for appropriate exchanges between people of different status, vertically connecting individuals in the social hierarchy. She gives the example of a lower status man who, through complicated maneuvers among his various connections around town, provides a rare herb as a gift to a doctor who has an interest in it. She and others suggest that guanxi and similar cultural forms in other societies provide an effective way to access resources in societies lacking midlevel institutions such as political parties, trade unions, and organized interest groups (Ledeneva 1998; Smart 1993). Smart (1993), for example, finds that by taking advantage of guanxi, investors in Hong Kong are able to set up businesses in China in only three months as opposed to the years it can take Western companies.

Ethnographies of Appalachian rural communities are filled with examples of reciprocal exchange between neighbors, friends, and kin. Rhoda Halperin (1990) provides a rich description of the reliance on livelihood strategies in which people in rural Kentucky employ reciprocal cooperative labor (especially in growing labor-intensive burley tobacco), as well as swapping services (e.g., nursing care, car maintenance) and barter to regularly obtain economic goods and services outside the cash economy. Halperin argues that multiple livelihood strategies based on social networks and reciprocity enable Appalachian people to resist dependence on capitalism and are the basis for their success in continuing a rural way of life, even in those "shallow rural" areas increasingly drawn into the market economy.

TRUST

Trust is implied in generalized reciprocity because gifts are given with the expectation of a return gift sometime later. It more likely characterizes social relationships between equals, but clearly guanxi functions between people of different status in Chinese society (Yang 1994). An example of the generalized trust possible with social capital is in the wholesale diamond market in New York City, which is dominated by Jews who live in Brooklyn, go to the same synagogues, and are related by intermarriage (Coleman 1988). In these communities, diamond dealers informally exchange bags of stones worth millions to examine before a sale, knowing that to steal a stone would jeopardize one's reputation and family, community, and religious ties. Trustworthiness facilitates productivity so that groups with it can accomplish much more than groups without it. Throughout the world, rotating credit unions, where all members contribute money each month but only a few withdraw funds at a time, are based on the trust established in face-to-face groups of closely related individuals (Velez-Ibanez 1983). In American ethnic groups with strong extended family ties, successful civic and business cooperation is often based on the trust provided by established kin networks (Light 1972).

In the developing world, a good example of this aspect of social capital is the Grameen Bank, founded in 1976 by Nobel Prize–winner Professor Muhammad Yunus (2003). Yunus launched an action research project to examine the possibility of designing a credit delivery system targeting the rural poor in Bangladesh. He was concerned that the poor were unable to qualify for bank loans and had to resort to exploitive moneylenders. One woman who made bamboo stools and chairs had to sell them to a moneylender who provided her credit to buy more raw materials. She paid interest at the rate of 10 percent a day (or 3,000 percent a year). By loaning her twenty-seven dollars, Yunus enabled her to establish her own self-employment in a few months and increase her income sevenfold as well as repay the loan.

In the Grameen Bank scheme, groups of five prospective borrowers are formed (these are usually groups of women who are family and friends). Only two are eligible for a loan, and only if these borrowers begin to repay the principal plus interest over a period of six weeks do the other members of the group become eligible for a loan. The collective responsibility of the group serves as collateral on the loan. The loans are used in micro-enterprises such as purchasing rickshaws, milk cows, goats, sewing machines, etc. As of July 2004, the Grameen Bank has over 3.7 million borrowers, 96 percent of whom are women. This concept has been endorsed by the World Bank and others and has spread to over 250 institutions in nearly one hundred countries around the world.

Development projects like the Grameen Bank are successful in rural communities because they build on the preexisting informal networks of relatives, friends, and neighbors that are necessary for sustaining daily life. Jennie Smith (2001) has written eloquently about these kinds of informal rural civic groups in Haiti and their potential for providing organizational structure for grassroots development among the very poor. She points out that these groups are often invisible to development workers because they are not "voluntary organizations" with a charter, closed membership, and formal hierarchical structure. Yet, life among rural peasants is filled with examples of organized cooperation, interdependence, and sharing; Smith describes in detail five different types of cooperative labor and reciprocal sharing, from simple labor rotation within extended families to large collectives of fifty to a hundred members with formal organizational structure who can work in mutual labor exchange or for hire.

The literature in Appalachian studies is filled with examples of these kinds of cooperative labor arrangements during the historical period of subsistence farming: corn shuckings, quilt making, sharing farm equipment and labor between neighbors, house-raising, and barn-raising. Neighbors in rural mountain areas still rely on one another for assistance, knowing they can always count on help in times of need. Elderly neighbors are often the recipients of help that comes unasked for: the road to the house gets plowed after a snowstorm, wood gets chopped for the stove, and food gets delivered in times of sickness. Historically, mountain people had a "pounding" for people in need, each community member giving a pound of flour or other necessity, resulting in enough food for the needy. Today, communal response is often evident at local stores where a collection jar is set out for a sick community member without insurance or a family who lost their home to a fire. Mountain churches are the mainstay of these kinds of mutual-aid traditions, employing prayer chains that provide spiritual assistance as well as material help to those in need. Longtime residents of mountain communities typically have the habit of offering help and trust in others when it is needed.

Putting Social Capital to Work

Much of the literature on social capital is consumed with figuring out how to create the bonding type of social capital in urban ghettoes and inner-city neighborhoods (Rubin and Rubin 2001). Scholars agree it is hard to create social capital where it does not exist (Gittell and Vidal 1998). The Appalachian region, on the other hand, is blessed with abundant bonding social capital; indeed it is the means by which rural mountain communities have survived over time. The relative merit of bonding social capital has been questioned by some writers who cite the "dark side" of exclusive networks and the potential reinforcement of antisocial behavior (Field 2003; Portes 1998). The mafia and street gangs, for example, are characterized by high bonding social capital. On the other hand, there are also a number of examples of negative stereotyping of traditional communities in the literature, such as Szreter's remark that it is evident social capital is absent in "the feuding and distrust of tight-knit 'hillbilly' Appalachian hamlets" (Szreter 2000:59). Traditional communities have also been criticized in the literature as racist, classist, and patriarchal (Hooghe and Stolle 2003; McLean et al. 2002). But many would argue that this makes them no different from the larger society. It would seem that development work in any community would necessarily involve moving residents toward less exclusion and more equality in participation. Another criticism of the interconnectedness of rural communities is that these dense ties limit people's options and reduce innovation and efficiency, as compared to "weak" ties that characterize voluntary associations and urban life in general (Granovetter 1973). Few would disagree that the thick social glue in gemeinschaft communities is a double-edged sword that contributes to the ability for collaborative action while it restricts individual behavior. Yet, without bonding social capital—that is, the "networks and norms that enable collective action" (Grootaert 1997)—communities are weakened in their response to powerful external forces. I would argue that one of the most important assets to consider in participatory development projects in Appalachian communities is the extensive bonding social capital that is likely to be present.

The need for preservation of social capital in the mountains is particularly acute in the face of the forces of modernity. Billings and Blee, for example, remark at the end of their study of one Kentucky county on "the need to preserve cultural strategies that sustain social capital" in poor areas, strategies such as stable ties to the land and to kin (2000:323). Sonya Salamon (2003) suggests a number of ways to sustain gemeinschaft community through the preservation of public spaces and "watering holes" where community members can gather; creating venues for ordinary social interaction and the incorporation of newcomers; the self-conscious development of community life where citizens have the opportunity to complain and argue and contribute, building a shared life and common identity. Salamon argues that building community also extends to adolescents who can be seen as either "weeds or seed corn." Communities with bonding social capital must recognize their wealth and work intentionally to conserve those assets.

Another challenge in Appalachian communities is the development of bridging social capital, which is the key to accessing external resources, for it is when bonding and bridging social capital are high that there is the best opportunity for change and development (Flora et al. 2003). In their book on rural community development, Cornelia and Jan Flora describe in detail the characteristics of communities high in bonding and bridging capital. In these kinds of communities, there is reciprocity across wealth and educational divides. There are lots of contacts outside the community to regional, state, and national resources and organizations. There are many opportunities for diverse leadership, and communities of interest grow with partnerships and collaborations. The continual exercise of existing social capital reinvigorates it and creates the opportunity for expansion. Excluded groups are approached for incorporation in community efforts. There is consideration of new ideas and a willingness to accept alternatives to old ways. Successful collective action for community betterment builds on the strong bonds within the community while initiating instrumental linkages to groups outside the community.

Comparative studies of community development analyzing the impact of social capital find that individual leadership is an additional factor that is essential for successful organizing. In some cases, these leaders are successful if they already have extensive external support through mediating agencies such as political parties or government offices or if they are young educated community members with mediation skills (Flores and Rello 2003; Krishna 2002; Molenaers 2003). In other cases, religious leaders have sufficient power and authority to leverage support for change (Purushothaman et al. 2004; Wallace 2004). Leadership development is another challenge facing rural Appalachian communities. Clearly, participatory approaches to development demand that local individuals be encouraged to develop leadership skills and find ways to lead collective action based on people's trust evolving from their strong social connections in the community.

Finally, Appalachian communities must create a new narrative to counteract the destructive narratives that others have imposed. A new storyline is needed based on mountain peoples' own identity (Hatch and Keefe 1999). This new cultural paradigm would appreciate mountain culture and recognize the assets of local people and communities. In the new narrative, Appalachian people are hard working and resourceful, generous and neighborly, and honest and trustworthy. They are rooted in the land; they respect their cultural traditions; and they cherish the memory of family members who have passed on. They have a strong religious faith that helps them to endure. And they have the capacity to address problems and to partner with others in solving them. Participatory development practices that build on these attributes have great promise in Appalachian communities.

Note

1. There is considerable literature developing on these various forms of capital. Human capital is a form of nonphysical capital that was identified by economists early in the twentieth century as more skilled workers became necessary in the industrial economy. It includes individual skills, qualifications, and educational training. Political capital is used by political scientists to refer to the political influence and power gained through the electoral process. "Cultural capital" is a term developed by Pierre Bourdieu to refer to the information and knowledge about how to behave appropriately assumed by growing up in an upper-class family (Bourdieu 1984, 1987). While Bourdieu was interested in the way elites use cultural capital to set themselves apart from subordinates, other writers have applied the concept to illuminate ways in which knowledge of ethnic minority (or alternative) cultural capital operates among such disparate groups as Nuyorican crack dealers (Bourgois 1996) and Zapotecan peasant migrant associations in Mexico City

(Hirabayashi 1993). Social capital refers to relationships of trust embedded in social networks and the resources available to individuals and groups that they do not have as isolates. It refers to the advantages of social connections and the investment in social relationships. Bourdieu saw this as an extension of cultural capital, in that it is the means by which cultural capital is reproduced, but the concept has been broadened by others (Coleman 1988; Putnam 2000). Symbolic capital, also identified by Bourdieu (1987), refers to the prestige attached to a family and a surname. For example, family name may get your foot in the door for a job interview. Psychological capital has been identified by Sherry Ortner (2002) as significant in determining social class outcomes for graduates in her study of a New Jersey high school class of 1958. This refers to certain positive personality traits, such as being an extrovert or a risk-taker or having charisma, which can improve one's chances for leadership, opportunities, and mobility. Finally, spiritual capital is used by Raquel Romberg (2003) to refer to access to supernatural power and the influence it gives to witches (*brujos*) in urban Puerto Rico. In her analysis, brujos are spiritual entrepreneurs who use their access to knowledge and power gained from the supernatural to advise clients on compliance with state laws and new economic opportunities, help lawyers win custody suits, and help sick employees to resolve labor disability claims.

References

Anglin, Mary. 1983. "Experiences of In-Migrants in Appalachia." In *Appalachia and America: Autonomy and Regional Dependence,* Allen Batteau (Ed.). Lexington: University Press of Kentucky. Pp. 227–38.

Appalachian Land Ownership Task Force. 1983. *Who Owns Appalachia? Landownership and Its Impact.* Lexington: University Press of Kentucky.

Arnstein, Sherry R. 1969. "A Ladder of Citizen Participation." *Journal of the American Planning Association* 35(4):216–24.

Banks, C. Kenneth, and J. Marshall Mangan. 1999. *The Company of Neighbours: Revitalizing Community through Action-Research.* Toronto: University of Toronto Press.

Baron, Stephen, John Field, and Tom Schuller (Eds.). 2000. *Social Capital: Critical Perspectives.* Oxford: Oxford University Press.

Batteau, Allen (Ed.). 1983. *Appalachia and America: Autonomy and Regional Dependence.* Lexington: University Press of Kentucky.

———. 1990. *The Invention of Appalachia.* Tucson: University of Arizona Press.

Beaver, Patricia D. 1986. *Rural Community in the Appalachian South.* Lexington: University Press of Kentucky.

Billings, Dwight B., and Kathleen M. Blee. 2000. *The Road to Poverty: The Making of Wealth and Hardship in Appalachia.* Cambridge: Cambridge University Press.

Billings, Dwight, Kathleen Blee, and Louis Swanson. 1986. "Culture, Family, and Community in Preindustrial Appalachia." *Appalachian Journal* 13 (Winter):154–70.

Bourdieu, Pierre. 1977. *Outline of a Theory of Practice.* Cambridge: Cambridge University Press.

———. 1984. *Distinction: A Social Critique of the Judgment of Taste.* Cambridge, MA: Harvard University Press.

———. 1987. "What Makes a Social Class?" *Berkeley Journal of Sociology* 22:1–18.

Bourgois, Philippe. 1996. *In Search of Respect: Selling Crack in El Barrio.* Cambridge: Cambridge University Press.

Bruce, Thomas A., and Steven Uranga McKane (Eds.). 2000. *Community-Based Public Health: A Partnership Model.* Washington, DC: American Public Health Association.

Bryant, F. Carlene. 1981. *We're All Kin.* Knoxville: University of Tennessee Press.

CBS News. 1965. *Christmas in Appalachia.* Narrated by Charles Kurault. Released by Carousel Films.

Cernea, Michael M. (Ed.). 1985. *Putting People First: Sociological Variables in Rural Development.* New York: Oxford University Press.

Chambers, Robert. 1983. *Rural Development: Putting the Last First.* London: Longman.

———. 1997. *Whose Reality Counts? Putting the First Last.* London: Intermediate Technology.

Cockcroft, James D., Andre Gunder Frank, and Dale L. Johnson (Eds.) 1972. *Dependence and Underdevelopment: Latin America's Political Economy.* Garden City, NY: Doubleday Anchor.

Coleman, James S. 1988. "Social Capital in the Creation of Human Capital." *American Journal of Sociology* 94 Suppl:S95–S120.

———. 1990. *Foundations of Social Theory.* Cambridge, MA: Harvard University Press.

Cooke, Bill, and Uma Kothari. 2001. *Participation: The New Tyranny?* London: Zed Books.

Cornwall, Andrea, and Rachel Jewkes. 1995. "What Is Participatory Research?" *Social Science and Medicine* 41(12):1667–76.

Couto, Richard A. 1999. *Making Democracy Work Better: Mediating Structures, Social Capital, and the Democratic Prospect.* Chapel Hill: University of North Carolina Press.

Couto, Richard A., Nancy K. Simpson, and Gale Harris (Eds.). 1995. *Sowing Seeds in the Mountains: Community-Based Coalitions for Cancer Prevention and Control.* Washington, DC: National Cancer Institute.

Cross, T., B. J. Bazron, K. Dennis, and M. R. Isaacs. 1989. *A Monograph on Effective Services for Minority Children Who Are Severely Emotionally Disturbed,* Vol. 1 of *Towards a Culturally Competent System of Care.* Washington, DC: Georgetown University Child Development Center, National Technical Assistance Center for Children's Mental Health.

Davies, Charlotte A. 1999. *Reflexive Ethnography: A Guide to Researching Ourselves and Others.* London: Routledge.

Depoe, Stephen P., John W. Delicath, and Marie-France Aepli Elsenbeer (Eds.). 2004. *Communication and Public Participation in Environmental Decision Making.* Albany: SUNY Press.

Durrenberger, E. Paul. 2002. "Why the Idea of Social Capital Is a Bad Idea." *Anthropology News* (December):6.

Edwards, Michael, and John Gaventa (Eds.). 2001. *Global Citizen Action.* Boulder: Lynne Rienner.

Ergood, Bruce, and Bruce E. Kuhre (Eds.). 1991. *Appalachia: Social Context Past and Present.* 3rd ed. Dubuque: Kendall/Hunt.

Escobar, Arturo. 1995. *Encountering Development: The Making and Unmaking of the Third World.* Princeton, NJ: Princeton University Press.

Fals-Borda, Orlando. 1991. "Introduction." In *Action and Knowledge: Breaking the Monopoly with Participatory Action-Research,* Orlando Fals-Borda and Muhammed Adisur Rahman (Eds.). New York: Apex Press. Pp. 1–13.

Field, John. 2003. *Social Capital.* London: Routledge.

Fisher, Stephen L. (Ed.). 1993. *Fighting Back in Appalachia: Traditions of Resistance and Change.* Philadelphia: Temple University Press.

Flora, Cornelia Butler, Jan L. Flora, Jacqueline D. Spears, and Louis E. Swanson. 1992. *Rural Communities: Legacy and Change.* Boulder: Westview Press.

Flora, Cornelia Butler, Jan L. Flora, with Susan Fey. 2003. *Rural Communities: Legacy and Change.* 2nd ed. Boulder: Westview Press.

Flores, Margarita, and Fernando Rello. 2003. "Social Capital and Poverty: Lessons from Case Studies in Mexico and Central America." *Culture and Agriculture* 25(1):1–10.

Foucault, Michel. 1977. *Discipline and Punish: Birth of the Prison.* New York: Pantheon.

———. 1980. *Power/Knowledge: Selected Interviews and Other Writings.* New York: Pantheon.

Francis, Mark, Robin Moore, Daniel Iacofano, Stephen Klein, and Lynne Paxson (Eds.). 1987. "Design and Democracy (Special Issue)." *Journal of Architectural and Planning Research* 4(4):271–360.

Freire, Paulo. 1970. *Pedagogy of the Oppressed.* New York: Continuum Publications.

———. 1998. *Teachers as Cultural Workers: Letters to Those Who Dare Teach.* Boulder: Westview Press.

Friedmann, John. 1992. *Empowerment: The Politics of Alternative Development.* Cambridge, MA: Blackwell.

Gaventa, John. 1980. *Power and Powerlessness: Quiescence and Rebellion in an Appalachian Valley.* Urbana: University of Illinois Press.

———. 1991. "Toward a Knowledge Democracy: Viewpoints on Participatory Research in North America." In *Action and Knowledge: Breaking the Monopoly with Participatory Action-Research,* Orlando Fals-Borda and Muhammed Anisur Rahman (Eds.). New York: Apex. Pp. 121–31.

———. 1993. "The Powerful, the Powerless, and the Experts: Knowledge Struggles in an Information Age." In *Voices of Change: Participatory Research in the United States and Canada,* Peter Park, Mary Brydon-Miller, Budd Hall, and Ted Jackson (Eds.). Westport, CT: Bergin and Garvey. Pp. 21–40.

Gaventa, John, and Helen Lewis. 1991. "Participatory Education and Grassroots Development: The Case of Rural Appalachia." Gatekeeper Series No. 25, Sustainable Agriculture Programme of the International Institute for Environment and Development, London.

Gaventa, John, Barbara Ellen Smith, and Alex Willingham (Eds.). 1990a. *Communities in Economic Crisis: Appalachia and the South.* Philadelphia: Temple University Press.

———. 1990b. "Toward a New Debate: Development, Democracy, and Dignity." In *Communities in Economic Crisis: Appalachia and the South,* John Gaventa, Barbara Ellen Smith, and Alex Willingham (Eds.). Philadelphia: Temple University Press. Pp. 279–91.

Gazaway, Rena. 1969. "Portrait of a Rural Village." In *Culture Change, Mental Health, and Poverty,* Joseph C. Finney (Ed.). Lexington: University of Kentucky Press. Pp. 42–57.

Geertz, Clifford. 1973. *The Interpretation of Cultures.* New York: Basic Books.

Giddons, Anthony. 1990. *The Consequences of Modernity.* Stanford: Stanford University Press.

Gittell, Ross, and Avis Vidal. 1998. *Community Organizing: Building Social Capital as a Development Strategy.* Thousand Oaks, CA: Sage.

Gramsci, Antonio. 1971. *Selections from the Prison Notebooks.* New York: International Publishers.

Gran, Guy. 1983. *Development by People: Citizen Construction of a Just World.* New York: Praeger.

Granovetter, Mark. 1973. "The Strength of Weak Ties." *American Journal of Sociology* 78:1360–80.

Green, Gary Paul, and Anna Haines. 2002. *Asset Building and Community Development.* Thousand Oaks: Sage.

Grootaert, Christiaan. 1997. "Social Capital: The Missing Link?" In *Expanding the Measure of Wealth: Indicators of Environmentally Sustainable Development.* Washington, DC: World Bank. Pp. 77–93.

Halperin, Rhoda H. 1990. *The Livelihood of Kin: Making Ends Meet "The Kentucky Way."* Austin: University of Texas Press.

———. 1998. *Practicing Community: Class, Culture, and Power in an Urban Neighborhood.* Austin: University of Texas Press.

———. 2006. *Whose School Is It? Women, Children, Memory, and Practice in the City.* Austin: University of Texas Press.

Hamilton, Peter. 1992. "The Enlightenment and the Birth of Social Science." In *Formations of Modernity,* Stuart Hall and Bram Gieben (Eds.). Cambridge: Polity with Open University Press. Pp. 17–58.

Hampshire, Kate, Elaine Hills, and Nazalie Iqbal. 2005. "Power Relations in Participatory Research and Community Development: A Case Study from Northern
England." *Human Organization* 64:340-49.

Harrington, Michael. 1962. *The Other America*. New York City: Scribner.

Hatch, Elvin, and Susan E. Keefe. 1999. "Exploring Mountain Identity." Paper presented at the annual meeting of the American Anthropological Association,
Chicago, November 18.

Higgs, R. J., A. N. Manning, and J. W. Miller (Eds.). 1995. *Appalachia Inside Out*.
Knoxville: University of Tennessee Press.

Hinsdale, Mary Ann, Helen M. Lewis, and S. Maxine Waller. 1995. *It Comes from
the People: Community Development and Local Theology*. Philadelphia:
Temple University Press.

Hirabayashi, Lane Ryo. 1993. *Cultural Capital: Mountain Zapotec Migrant Associations in Mexico City*. Tucson: University of Arizona Press.

Hoff, Marie D. (Ed.). 1998. *Sustainable Community Development: Studies in Economic, Environmental, and Cultural Revitalization*. Boca Raton, FL: Lewis.

Holland, Dorothy, William Lachicotte Jr., Debra Skinner, and Carole Cain.
1998. *Identity and Agency in Cultural Worlds*. Cambridge, MA: Harvard
University Press.

Hong, George K., Margaret Garcia, and Marcel Soriano. 2000. "Responding to the
Challenge: Preparing Mental Health Professionals for the New Millennium."
In *Handbook of Multicultural Mental Health: Assessment and Treatment of
Diverse Populations*. Israel Cueller and Freddy A. Paniagua (Eds.). San Diego:
Academic Press. Pp. 455-76.

Hooghe, Marc, and Dietlind Stolle (Eds.). 2003. *Generating Social Capital: Civil
Society and Institutions in Comparative Perspective*. New York: Palgrave
Macmillan.

Horton, Aimee I. 1989. *The Highlander Folk School: A History of Its Major Programs,
1932-1961*. Brooklyn: Carlson.

Horton, Billy D. 1993. "The Appalachian Land Ownership Study: Research and
Citizen Action in Appalachia." In *Voices of Change: Participatory Research in
the United States and Canada,* Peter Park, Mary Brydon-Miller, Budd Hall,
and Ted Jackson (Eds.). Westport, CT: Bergin and Garvey. Pp. 85-102.

Horton, Myles, and Paulo Freire. 1990. *We Make the Road by Walking: Conversations
on Education and Social Change*. Edited by Brenda Bell, John Gaventa, and
John Peters. Philadelphia: Temple University Press.

Jason, Leonard A., Christopher B. Keys, Yolanda Suarez-Balcazar, Renee R. Taylor,
and Margaret I. Davis (Eds.). 2004. *Participatory Community Research: Theories
and Methods in Action*. Washington, DC: American Psychological
Association.

Jewkes, Rachel, and Anne Murcott. 1996. "Meanings of Community." *Social Science
and Medicine* 43(4):555-63.

Keefe, Susan E. 1994. "Urbanism Reconsidered: A Southern Appalachian Perspective." *City and Society* 1:20–34.

———. 1998. "Appalachian Americans: The Formation of 'Reluctant Ethnics.'"In *Many Americas: Critical Perspectives on Race, Racism, and Ethnicity,* Gregory R. Campbell (Ed.). Dubuque: Kendall/Hunt. Pp. 129–53.

———. (Ed.). 2005a. *Appalachian Cultural Competency: A Guide for Medical, Mental Health, and Social Service Professionals.* Knoxville: University of Tennessee Press.

———. 2005b. "Introduction." In *Appalachian Cultural Competency: A Guide for Medical, Mental Health, and Social Service Professionals,* Susan E. Keefe (Ed.). Knoxville: University of Tennessee Press. Pp. 1–26.

Keefe, Susan E., Una Mae Lange Reck, and Gregory G. Reck. 1991. "Family and Education in Southern Appalachia." In *Appalachian: Social Context Past and Present,* Bruce Ergood and Bruce E. Kuhre (Eds.). 3rd ed. Dubuque: Kendall/Hunt. Pp. 345–51.

Kennedy, Rory. 1999. *American Hollow.* Moxie Films Production; Home Box Office.

Koch, Tina, and Debbie Kralik. 2006. *Participatory Action Research in Health Care.* Oxford: Blackwell.

Koontz, Thomas M., Toddi A. Steelman, JoAnn Carmin, Katrina Smith Korfmacher, Cassandra Moseley, and Craig W. Thomas. 2004. *Collaborative Environmental Management: What Roles for Government?* Washington, DC: Resources for the Future.

Korten, David C. 2001. *When Corporations Rule the World.* 2nd ed. Bloomfield, CT: Bloomfield.

Kretzmann, John P., and John L. McNight. 1993. *Building Communities from the Inside Out: A Path toward Finding and Mobilizing a Community's Assets.* Evanston, IL: Institute for Policy Research, Northwestern University.

Krishna, Anirudh. 2002. *Active Social Capital: Tracing the Roots of Development and Democracy.* New York: Columbia University Press.

Kumar, Somesh. 2002. *Methods for Community Participation: A Complete Guide for Practitioners.* London: ITDG Publishing.

LaLone, Mary B. (Ed.). 1997. *Appalachian Coal Mining Memories: Life in the Coal Fields of Virginia's New River Valley.* Blacksburg, VA: Pocahontas Press.

———. (Ed.). 1998. *Coal Mining Lives: An Oral History Sequel to Appalachian Coal Mining Memories.* Radford, VA: Department of Sociology and Anthropology, Radford University.

Landis, Suzanne, Thomas Plaut, June Trevor, and Judy Futch. 1996. *Building a Healthier Tomorrow: A Manual for Rural Coalition Building.* Dubuque: Kendall/Hunt.

Ledeneva, Alena V. 1998. *Russia's Economy of Favours: Blat, Networking and Informal Exchange.* Cambridge: Cambridge University Press.

Lennertz, Bill, and Aarin Lutzenhiser. 2006. *The Charrette Handbook: The Essential Guide for Accelerated, Collaborative Community Planning.* Chicago: American Planning Association.

Lewis, Helen M. 2001. "Participatory Research and Education for Social Change: Highlander Research and Education Center." In *Handbook of Action Research: Participative Inquiry and Practice,* Peter Reason and Hilary Bradbury (Eds.). Thousand Oaks, CA: Sage. Pp. 356–62.

Lewis, Helen M., Linda Johnson, and Donald Askins (Eds.). 1978. *Colonialism in Modern America: The Appalachian Case.* Boone, NC: Appalachian Consortium Press.

Light, Ivan H. 1972. *Ethnic Enterprise in America: Business and Welfare among Chinese, Japanese, and Blacks.* Berkeley: University of California Press.

———. 2004. "Social Capital for What?" In *Community-Based Organizations: The Intersection of Social Capital and Local Context in Contemporary Urban Society,* Robert Mark Silverman (Ed.). Detroit: Wayne State University. Pp. 19–33.

Lloyd, Cathy E., Stephen Handsley, Jenny Douglas, Sarah Earle, and Sue Spurr (Eds.). 2007. *Policy and Practice in Promoting Public Health.* London: Sage.

Lynch, Eleanor W., and Marci J. Hanson. (Eds.). 1998. *Developing Cross-Cultural Competence: A Guide for Working with Children and Their Families.* 2nd ed. Baltimore: Paul H. Brookes.

Mason, James L., Marva P. Benjamin, and Sarah A. Lewis. 1996. "The Cultural Competence Model: Implications for Child and Family Mental Health Services." In *Families and Mental Health System for Children and Adolescents: Policies, Services, and Research,* Craig Anne Heflinger and Carol T. Nixon (Eds.). CMHS Vol. 2. Thousand Oaks, CA: Sage. Pp. 165–90.

McKnight, John L. 1997. *A Twenty-First Century Map for Healthy Communities and Families.* Evanston, IL: Institute for Policy Research, Northwestern University.

McKnight, John L., and John P. Kretzmann. 1996. *Mapping Community Capacity.* Evanston, IL: Institute for Policy Research, Northwestern University.

McLean, Scott L., David A. Schultz, and Manfred B. Steger (Eds.). 2002. *Social Capital: Critical Perspectives on Community and "Bowling Alone."* New York: New York University Press.

Miller, Wilbur R. 1991. *Revenuers and Moonshiners: Enforcing Federal Liquor Law in the Mountain South, 1865–1900.* Chapel Hill: University of North Carolina Press.

Minkler, Meredith (Ed.). 1997. *Community Organizing and Community Building for Health.* New Brunswick, NJ: Rutgers University Press.

Molenaers, Nadia. 2003. "Associations or Informal Networks? Social Capital and Participatory Development Practices." In *Generating Social Capital: Civil Society and Institutions in Comparative Perspective,* Marc Hooghe and Dietlind Stolle (Eds.). New York: Palgrave Macmillan. Pp. 113–31.

Mora, Juana, and David R. Diaz. 2004. *Latino Social Policy: A Participatory Research Model.* New York: Haworth Press.

Obermiller, Phillip J., and Michael E. Maloney (Eds.). 2002. *Appalachia: Social Context Past and Present.* 4th ed. Dubuque: Kendall/Hunt.

O'Dell, Gary A. 2005. "Community Self-Help Activism in Water/Sewer Development: Case Studies from McDowell County, West Virginia, and Letcher County, Kentucky." *Appalachian Journal* 33, no. 1:54–76.

O'Looney, John. 1996. *Redesigning the Work of Human Services.* Westport, CT: Quorom Books.

Ortner, Sherry B. 2002. "Subjects and Capital: A Fragment of a Documentary Ethnography." *Ethnos* 67, no. 1:9–32.

Phillips, Lynne (Ed.). 1998. *The Third Wave of Modernization in Latin America: Cultural Perspectives on Neoliberalism.* Wilmington, DE: Scholarly Resources.

Plaut, Thomas. 1999. *People, Politics, and Economic Life: Exploring Appalachia with Quantitative Methods.* 2nd ed. Dubuque: Kendall/Hunt.

Portes, Alejandro. 1998. "Social Capital: Its Origins and Applications in Modern Sociology." *Annual Review of Sociology* 24:1–24.

Purushothaman, Saneetha, Simone Purohit, and Bianca Ambrose-Oji. 2004. "The Informal Collective as a Space for Participatory Planning: The Peri-Urban Interface in Hubli-Dharwad Twin City Area." In *The Power of Women's Informal Networks: Lessons in Social Change from South Asia to West Africa,* Bandana Purkayastha and Mangala Subramaniam (Eds.). Lanham, MD: Lexington Books. Pp. 105–20.

Putnam, Robert D. 1993. *Making Democracy Work: Civic Traditions in Modern Italy.* Princeton, NJ: Princeton University Press.

———. 2000. *Bowling Alone: The Collapse and Revival of American Community.* New York: Simon and Schuster.

Rappaport, Julian. 1994. "Narrative Studies, Personal Stories, and Identity Transformation in the Mutual-Help Context." In *Understanding the Self-Help Organization: Frameworks and Findings,* Thomas J. Powell (Ed.). Thousand Oaks, CA: Sage.

Robb, Caroline M. 1999. *Can the Poor Influence Policy? Participatory Poverty Assessments in the Developing World.* Washington, DC: World Bank.

Romberg, Raquel. 2003. *Witchcraft and Welfare: Spiritual Capital and the Business of Magic in Modern Puerto Rico.* Austin: University of Texas Press.

Rubin, Herbert J., and Irene S. Rubin. 2001. *Community Organizing and Development.* 3rd ed. Boston: Allyn and Bacon.

Salamon, Sonya. 2003. *Newcomers to Old Towns: Suburbanization of the Heartland.* Chicago: University of Chicago Press.

Sargent, Frederic O., Paul Lusk, Jose A. Rivera, and Maria Varela. 1991. *Rural Environmental Planning for Sustainable Communities.* Washington, DC: Island Press.

Sarnoff, Susan. 2003. "Central Appalachia—Still the *Other* America." *Journal of Poverty* 7(1–2):123–39.

Sassi, Paola. 2006. *Strategies for Sustainable Architecture.* New York: Taylor and Francis.

Schech, Susanne, and Jane Haggis. 2000. *Culture and Development: A Critical Introduction.* Oxford: Blackwell.

Schwarzweller, Harry K., James S. Brown, and J. J. Mangalam. 1971. *Mountain Families in Transition: A Case Study of Appalachian Migration.* University Park: Pennsylvania State University Press.

Scott, James C. 1976. *The Moral Economy of the Peasant: Rebellion and Subsistence in Southeast Asia.* New Haven, CT: Yale University Press.

Seligson, Mitchell A., and John T. Passe-Smith (Eds.). 1993. *Development and Under-development: The Political Economy of Inequality.* Boulder: Lynne Rienner.

Selznick, Philip. 1992. *The Moral Commonwealth: Social Theory and the Promise of Community.* Berkeley: University of California Press.

Shapiro, Henry D. 1978. *Appalachian on Our Mind: The Southern Mountains and Mountaineers in the American Consciousness, 1870–1920.* Chapel Hill: North Carolina University Press.

Shuman, Michael H. 1998. *Going Local: Creating Self-Reliant Communities in a Global Age.* New York: Free Press.

Smart, Alan. 1993. "Gifts, Bribes, and *Guanxi*: A Reconsideration of Bourdieu's Social Capital." *Cultural Anthropology* 8(3):388–408.

Smith, Jennie M. 2001. *When the Hands Are Many: Community Organization and Social Change in Rural Haiti.* Ithaca: Cornell University Press.

Stack, Carol B. 1974. *All Our Kin: Strategies for Survival in a Black Community.* New York: Harper & Row.

State of the World: A Worldwide Institute Report on Progress toward a Sustainable Society. 2001. New York: Norton.

Szreter, Simon. 2000. "Social Capital, the Economy, and Education in Historical Perspective." In *Social Capital: Critical Perspectives,* Stephen Baron, John Field, and Tom Schuller (Eds.). Oxford: Oxford University Press. Pp. 56–77.

Thiele, Leslie Paul. 1999. *Environmentalism for a New Millennium.* New York: Oxford University Press.

Titi, Vangile, and Naresh Singh (Eds.). 1995. *Empowerment for Sustainable Develop-ment: Toward Operational Strategies.* Winnipeg, Manitoba: International Institute for Sustainable Development.

Toennies, Ferdinand. 1957. *Community and Society.* Translated and edited by Charles P. Loomis. Originally published in 1887 as *Gemeinschaft und Gesellschaft.* East Lansing: Michigan State University Press.

Velez-Ibanez, Carlos G. 1983. *Bonds of Mutual Trust: The Cultural Systems of Rotating Credit Associations among Urban Mexicans and Chicanos.* New Brunswick, NJ: Rutgers University Press.

Veltmeyer, Henry. 2001. "The Quest for Another Development." In *Transcending Neoliberalism: Community-Based Development in Latin America,* Henry

Veltmeyer and Anthony O'Malley (Eds.). Bloomfield, CT: Kumarian Press. Pp. 1–34.

Wallace, Sherri Leronda. 2004. "Social Capital and African American Church Leadership." In *Community-Based Organizations: The Intersection of Social Capital and Local Context in Contemporary Urban Society,* Robert Mark Silverman (Ed.). Detroit: Wayne State University. Pp. 147–70.

Waller, Altina L. 1988. *Feud: Hatfields, McCoys, and Social Change in Appalachia, 1860–1900.* Chapel Hill: University of North Carolina Press.

Whisnant, David E. 1980. *Modernizing the Mountaineer: People, Power, and Planning in Appalachia.* New York: Burt Franklin.

———. 1983. *All That Is Native and Fine: The Politics of Culture in an American Region.* Chapel Hill: University of North Carolina Press.

White, Robert. 1994. "Participatory Development Communication as a Social-Cultural Process." In *Participatory Communication: Working for Change and Development,* Shirley A. White with K. S. Nair and J. Ascroft (Eds.). New Delhi: Sage. Pp. 95–116.

WHO Europe. 1999. *Health 21: Health for All in the 21st Century.* Copenhagen: World Health Organization.

Yang, Mayfair Mei-hui. 1994. *Gifts, Favors, and Banquets: The Art of Social Relationships in China.* Ithaca: Cornell University Press.

Yunus, Muhammad. 2003. *Banker to the Poor: Micro-Lending and the Battle against World Poverty.* New York: Public Affairs, Perseus Books.

A New Company in Town

LESSONS ON LOCAL IDENTITY
AND COMMUNITY DEVELOPMENT
IN THE MOUNTAIN SOUTH

Elvin Hatch

Community is alive and well in this case study by Hatch, who questions those who assert that mountain people are by nature too fractious and individualistic to come together for the common good. This ethnographic example from a western North Carolina county also demonstrates that local leaders are crucial for development. They come from the relatively small but significant middle class that developed in the county after World War II. Local leaders have a strong sense of local identity and high social capital, having been born and raised in the community. These assets are reinforced by local civic work, and they, in turn, provide strong motivation to participate in work that contributes to community survival. At the same time, Hatch suggests that there are local divisions between conservatives and progressives in many small rural communities that often cause development efforts to fail. Participatory development efforts will need to pay heed to the local political landscape in order to be successful.

This is a success story with a sad ending. In May 1993, in a small county in western North Carolina, a few civic leaders were quietly told that a large manufacturing firm might build a new, $40 million factory there. If all went well, the new facility would eventually add 750 jobs to the local labor market. County leaders then began negotiations with state officials, company executives, and members of their own community to put together a package of economic incentives to clinch the deal. The project was successful, and the festive ground-breaking ceremonies in October were attended by a large body of county members, company executives, the governor and some of his staff, and other state dignitaries. The following May—a year from the time the handful of civic leaders learned of the company's interest—the first shift went to work in the brand-new building.

Critics may argue that state and county resources should be put to better use than attracting factories, but I set that question aside here. The purpose of this essay is not to argue for or against the use of public money for economic development, but to suggest what lessons this case may offer to other localities that want to influence the course of their future, whatever direction they want it to take. I will also use this case as a basis for making suggestions about the characteristics of communities in the mountain South and about the problems and possibilities of their pulling together to achieve common goals.

Between 1996 and 2000 I spent a total of twenty-one months living in the county doing ethnographic and archival research. I was not in the county at the time that most of the events that I describe here took place. The following is based on both newspaper articles and interviews with people who were central to what happened.

The County

I refer to the county by the pseudonym of Bradford County, which is located in the Blue Ridge Mountains in North Carolina. The next county to the east is half in the mountains and half on the piedmont. Transportation in and out of the county was difficult as late as the 1950s because of poor roads, but today several paved highways intersect the region, and as a result travel in and out of the mountains is reasonably easy. Nevertheless, there is no interstate in the county, or even a four-lane highway. When the factory discussed here was built—I refer to the company as Albury Manufacturing—the county did not have a single mile of highway that met state standards for width. It also has a very small population, consisting of fewer than fifteen thousand people.

This is a place that has never been dominated by a single industry, such as coal mining or timber harvesting, and an index of this is that there has never been a railroad in the county. Nor is tourism an important component of the local economy; for example, the county has no ski resorts and only a limited amount of national park land. Recently, second homes have become a major development; at the time of writing, a majority of the land sales are to outsiders looking for summer homes. This is raising the value of land (to the point that anything more than a few acres is beyond the reach of most locals), increasing tax revenues, and providing some jobs in construction and service work. Eventually the second-home owners may radically change the nature of the county, although this has yet to happen. For example, nonlocals have a very limited presence in county politics. Local political dynamics reflect the schisms and interests of the locally born, not second-home owners, who tend to remain aloof. Nor have the part-time county residents had a significant impact on the social texture of the county, for even though the newcomers are physically present, for the most part they are socially unknown to the locals. As the number of newcomers who live in the county year-round increases, however, these people will begin to press for their own interests in county government and will surely alter the course of change in the region.

Until the late 1950s and early 1960s, a large majority of the households raised most of their own food, and very few people had regular jobs, although many worked sporadically to acquire cash (Hatch 2004a). Some men worked on the construction of the Blue Ridge Parkway in the 1930s and at the small, owner-operated sawmills in the county. And every year most local people sold a calf or two and perhaps a load of apples or other surplus subsistence goods. Cash played a highly limited role in the local economy, and the dominant economic activity was subsistence farming. A few families who were regarded locally as well-to-do made up what we would call today the upper-middle class. These included the banker, doctor, several merchants, and a handful of farmers who were active in the market economy primarily by buying and selling livestock. But the middle class was very small, and a large majority of the farmers seem to have regarded themselves as working people, although they did not conceive of themselves as poor or materially deprived.

By the late 1940s cash was beginning to play an increasingly important role in the local economy, and as it did so a crucial development occurred, which is that a substantial number of subsistence farm families moved into the middle class. Today many households in the county are in the working classes and are supported chiefly by fairly low-paying jobs, including factory work, as we will see, but the county also contains a sizable middle class that consists primarily of local people—people who were born in the county and whose parents and grandparents were born there. These locals explicitly identify themselves as mountain people, and they have a strong sense of identity with the county and with their forebears who were subsistence farmers.

After World War II, electricity was extended into the county and roads were improved, with the result that Grade A dairying became feasible. Consequently, a growing number of hard-working farmers with small to medium-sized farms were not only drawn into the cash economy but also became reasonably well-to-do by local standards. In recent decades the profitability of dairying has declined, and today only a handful of people make a living from full-time farming, yet many of those who once farmed are still reasonably well off in part because another cash crop, Christmas trees, has developed. The people who grow Christmas trees typically do not do the work themselves, however, for usually it is contracted out, and today most of the labor is done by Hispanic migrant workers.

Nonfarmers also participated in the growth of the home-grown middle class after World War II. The increasing role of cash in the local economy brought more and more business to the stores, and this, together with the general affluence of the postwar decades, enabled a number of townspeople to move up the rungs of the economic ladder. Not everyone became middle class, of course. Many working-class people today still own small farms and raise a portion of their own food, but the vast majority of them now are primarily wage earners with low incomes.

Electrification of the county and road improvements after World War II made possible not only the development of commercial dairying but factories as well. Most of these manufacturing plants produced clothes, such as tee shirts and trousers, and many of the people hired were women. In 1996 about a third of the labor force worked for these firms. While the county has a very rural appearance, during the period of my field research it in fact was strongly oriented toward factory work.

Bradford County, like many others in the mountain South, experienced a serious economic decline beginning in the 1980s, when several factories closed as a result of changes in the global economy. The county experienced the sense that it was entering into difficult times. At one level, the crisis was about the loss of jobs and the decline in general economic well-being, but at another it was about community and identity. I will have more to say about this shortly, but I want to emphasize here that many people whose economic well-being was not directly affected by the local economic problems became concerned that their way of life and their community were threatened. An important basis for the local support in attracting the new factory, Albury Manufacturing, was to strengthen the local economy in order to preserve the community. And among the supporters of the plan were some prominent people with high social capital.

Preconditions for Success

The story of the company's move to Bradford County begins even before the firm became interested in building there, for a number of earlier developments turned out to be crucial in paving the way. The first took place in the late 1980s, when the county commissioners voted to purchase an eighty-eight-acre tract of land on the outskirts of town as an industrial park. The thinking behind this was that the county needed to bring in new business ventures in view of the decline in factory work. Purchase of the industrial park was a risky move, however, for it was conceivable that the site would never attract enough businesses to be successful. The commissioners were severely criticized by some for spending county money on such a venture, while others regarded their actions as both visionary and courageous. In any event, the Albury factory was to be built in the industrial park that the county had acquired, and the availability of this land was an important inducement for the company to choose the county.

The way the industrial park was acquired is itself enlightening, for a key to its purchase was the assistance of an adventuresome second-home owner, a college president in a piedmont city. He and his wife have owned a summer home in Bradford County since the early 1970s, and in the 1980s, when news broke that a shoe factory in the county was closing, it occurred to him that he had met a part-owner of the shoe company—a wealthy philanthropist—in connection with his work at the college. He phoned her to explain the effect that the plant's closing would have on the local economy, and she was apparently moved, for she arranged for him to meet the chairman of the board, the president of the corporation, and the vice president the next day in New York City. At the meeting the college president pointed out that the plant had originally been built for about $200,000, that the property was now worth about a million dollars, and that if they sold the plant at full market value they would pay a large capital gains tax. He urged them instead to sell the property to the county at a much lower figure and to donate to the county the rest of the property's value as a tax-deductible gift. The company agreed. The county then applied for and got a federal matching grant to help pay for the factory, and then they began raising money locally. One of the first donors was the shoe company, which pledged $50,000 on top of its other contributions. The county, now the owner of the former shoe factory, spent several hundred thousand dollars refurbishing it and soon leased the plant to another firm that eventually bought the property. The proceeds from this sale provided part of the money to buy the land for the industrial park.

Another precondition for the success in attracting Albury Manufacturing was the development of a pattern of cooperation among local organizations, including the chamber of commerce, town council, county commission, and the two local utility companies, which are cooperatives. A number of people in these organizations—all of whom had high social capital—had worked together on a number of issues, and when the time came to negotiate with the state and Albury Manufacturing, they already had a good working relationship. It is important that this cooperation required a good deal of care, for these organizations were divided on a number of grounds. For example, the town councilors and county commissioners tend to be at loggerheads over the financing of mutual projects since the people in town pay both town and county taxes, while rural people pay only the latter. When the town and county contribute equally to a project, town residents pay through both systems of taxation, while rural people do not.

A third development that proved to be important in the county's later success in attracting the company was the cultivation of relations with state officials. The head of the chamber of commerce, the county manager, and other county officeholders had made a concerted effort to contact the members of the state department of transportation and others in order to make known the county's needs. For example, the group made video recordings while following behind trucks that were traveling at high speeds on the narrow highways in the county. The videos offered graphic evidence of the dangers the highways presented, and especially telling was footage of large rigs passing school buses coming in the opposite direction. One of the local people involved commented, "We started fanning out everywhere to meet our [regional state highway] board members, to go to [the state capitol] to walk the halls [contacting state officials]; to know our legislators better than any other county."[1] As a result of these efforts, county leaders knew who in the state government to call when the need arose, and they knew they would receive a sympathetic hearing.

Incentives

Albury Manufacturing produces an electrical component for household appliances, and its head office and main factory are located in a town several hours' drive from Bradford. In the early 1990s the firm decided to build a second factory, and by early 1993 it had narrowed its list of possible locations to two counties, one of which was Bradford, while the other was in a different state. When the civic leaders in Bradford were informed by North Carolina officials that the firm was looking at the county as a possible site for their new facility, a behind-the-scenes dialogue got under way among a small group of local men, the company executives, and members of the state department of commerce. Knowledge of these developments was restricted to a very narrow circle at this point, however, apparently at the company's request.

Three men in particular spearheaded the drive for Bradford County. These were the head of the Bradford Chamber of Commerce, the development manager of one of the utility cooperatives in the county, and a regional development official in the state department of commerce. A number of other people were also involved, though less centrally, including the county manager and several local elected officials. At an early stage of negotiations the three main participants traveled to the other site to see firsthand what their competition had to offer, and the experience was disheartening. One of the men reported to me that the other county is larger and has a more substantial labor supply and business base than Bradford County; that the proposed site there is located within one hundred yards of a four-lane highway (recall that Bradford County has none); and that the competitors' site already had adequate water and sewer facilities and electrical power, while the location in Bradford County was undeveloped. The other county also had a fund of nearly $8 million set aside for economic development, and the county there offered to construct the building for the company and to sell it to them at a price below market value. "They basically were going to give [the plant] to them, was what it boiled down to." The man remarked, "We thought, we're dead."

Yet the project seemed like a golden opportunity for Bradford County. For one thing, the number of jobs in the county was shrinking, as noted, and the jobs at Albury Manufacturing would be primarily for men, not women, which was regarded as particularly desirable. As other factories in the county closed, the tax base declined, and the new company would provide a major boost in this regard. These issues stimulated the resolve of those who were planning Bradford County's campaign. One of these people remarked, "I think part of the reason Albury [chose Bradford County] was [our] having a core group of individuals that worked on the project that flat would not take no for an answer. There were ten times a day every day when we could have, easily and justifiably, thrown our hands up and said it can't be done, it's not worth it, forget it. But we had a key core group that constantly was involved with the project, that just refused to give up on it. And every time there was a hurdle, we found a way to get around it." An example of the group's doggedness was one occasion when the signature of a state official was required, and the delay of even two days would have been disastrous. The official was attending a conference in a neighboring state, so one of the local leaders caught the next flight from a piedmont airport to get the signature.

The final package of economic incentives included, first, substantial North Carolina state funds for infrastructure needs. The state provided $10 million for road improvements, and another $1.6 million to expand the sewer and water systems. Loans were made available from a variety of sources, such as the Rural Electrification Authority, for site preparation. The county commission voted to give fifty acres in the industrial park to the company, and this was valued at about $300,000. The town council, county commission, and the two utility companies each pledged to donate $600,000. Perhaps most impressive is that local citizens pledged well over $600,000. One of the civic leaders told me that one anonymous donor, a native of the county, pledged $50,000 of his own money, and that one of the industries in the county pledged $25,000. Two professional men reported to me that they had pledged $10,000 and $1,000, respectively. The company was also given tax incentives, and for ten years the county would impose a wheel tax (an annual tax of $10 on every vehicle in the county) to help cover the county's donations.

What were the motivations behind these contributions? Consider first the state funds. I did not interview state officials, but in the early 1990s the growing disparity between the urban and rural areas became an important political issue at the state level. The decision to direct state funds toward Bradford County's infrastructure was probably stimulated in part by an interest in using the county as a model case. One of Bradford County's civic leaders remarked, "I think that they [the state officials] said that this is a chance literally for Bradford County to be a model for every rural county in the state. If they [Bradford County] can do it, anybody can do it."

The donations of the two utility companies were based on business considerations. The telephone cooperative calculated the increase in telephone use that Albury Manufacturing would bring, plus the executives of the new factory made a commitment to use the local company as its long-distance carrier for ten years. Similarly, the electric cooperative based its contribution on the increased revenues that the new factory would bring.

What stimulated the donations from local citizens? For one thing, the project made good economic sense. Private pledges were made to a nonprofit organization that was established for this purpose; consequently, contributions were tax deductible. The new factory would also improve the economic climate of the county, which in turn would put money in people's pockets, and the new company would increase the local tax base and ease some of the county's financial strain. The contributions offered by the state would also improve some of the main roads in the county and develop both the water and sewer systems that were insufficient even without the new factory. All of these factors were emphasized again and again by the project's proponents and were clearly important in attracting local support.

Yet it stretches the imagination to think that economic and practical interests such as these are sufficient fully to explain the private donations. An additional motivation was the desire to maintain the local way of life, for it was believed that the economic malaise was threatening the community's very existence. The single most frequent theme heard in relation to the Albury Manufacturing project was that the new factory would make it possible for young people to find jobs in the county and to continue living there—in other words, that the factory would help keep the community alive. This was epitomized by the statement that "our most important export is our children." A sense of the potential decline of the community as a distinctive place with its own personality and history—a history in which one's family had been a part for several generations—helps explain the anonymous contribution of $50,000, as well as the pledges by the two professional people mentioned above. But note that it was not *their* children—the children of the well-to-do—who would benefit from the new factory. It is most unlikely that these young people were anticipating a life of factory work.

A similar conclusion seems inevitable in looking at the list of local people who took strong positions of leadership in the project. To take a position at all was to open oneself to criticism, for at the beginning no one knew if this was going to be a controversial issue or not. In any event, if the primary motivation for the project was economic, we would expect that the leaders in the effort would be the ones who stood to enjoy the most economic gain from it, but this was not the case. For example, one outspoken proponent was the chairman of the county commission, a dairy farmer who could not conceivably benefit from the new factory. Another was a member of the town council, a former business owner who was retired and would not have benefited.

The community sentiment that appears to have been crucial in stimulating financial support for the project was manifest in the spirit that pervaded the public meetings that were called to discuss the incentive package. The meetings were mandated by law since public funds were to be used for industrial development, and the events attracted sizable crowds. One meeting in particular, held at the county courthouse, was key. A civic leader described the event for me:

> It was the most public process that you can imagine; everything was laid on the table. There were 300 people at least packed in the courthouse, standing room only. The presentation was made, [and] there were at least two standing ovations. The chairman of the county commissioners went down every row and asked every person that was in that courtroom to make any comments,

whatever they wanted to say. There was not one—virtually everybody spoke—there was not one negative word that was uttered. And I mean people cried. [This shows] what a state of euphoria that there was. It was a love fest, it certainly was. . . . And it *was* that [a love fest]. The company officials were in the audience that night [though very few people knew who they were]. . . . But that right there [the expression of community support] was what brought them [the company] here. There's no doubt in my mind.

The newspaper reports of the meeting substantiate the strongly positive response of the people who attended. For example, one of the newspapers quoted a man with particularly high standing (and high social capital) as saying, "If there's ever been a feel-good meeting in Bradford County, this is it."

One of the participants in the project gave me his analysis of people's motivations in the undertaking. He said that none of the people "were necessarily hoping to benefit other than [from] the impact that it [the new factory] would have on the community." He compared the efforts to bring Albury Manufacturing to the county with an earlier and equally successful effort to build a hospital in the county. He then expanded on this point:

But you'll find a number of projects, nothing of the magnitude of Albury Manufacturing, but you will find a number of projects in this county that people [have contributed to]—our Education Foundation [which provides scholarships], bringing the music symphony [to the county]. I remember a young boy coming here . . . who had lupus. . . . [T]hey detected it when they had been here awhile. And it was amazing to me; here was a total stranger, or basically a total stranger, that the community raised [so] much money for . . . to fight that disease. We led the state basically in the last ten years in the heart fund. We raise more money per capita than any other county in the state for the heart fund. And again, the magnitude of the pledges surprises me a little bit on Albury Manufacturing, but in terms of the community wanting to be involved, it doesn't, because of the past experiences that I've seen.

I don't suggest that there was complete unanimity about the project, however. It may have been unpopular to be against it, but objections were heard. For example, I was told that some people expressed concern that property taxes would go up, and others complained that the influx of new people would increase the rental price of land for raising cattle and growing Christmas trees.

While opposition to the project may have been limited at the time (the incentive package was approved in 1993), when I began my fieldwork in 1996 the grumbling was quite apparent, and I suspect that this represents an almost predictable pattern. Once the original enthusiasm subsided, more and more people became disenchanted. An index of this is that the dairy farmer who was chairman of the county commission at the time of the communitywide meeting was one of two board members who were voted out of office at the next election, and the analysis that he and other political leaders gave for this was that a growing number of voters were in revolt over the wheel tax. It seems that the first bills for the tax were placed in the mail shortly before the election. I asked one woman how she felt about Albury Manufacturing, and she replied, "Well, I hope they're going to do everything they say. I'm a little bothered by this ten dollar tax [the wheel tax] we pay, because I think it's kind of sad that people on welfare here would be paying a ten dollar a year car tax to this big company. I don't think that's quite fair. It's not that much money, but it's not really logical to me." The woman then raised another issue, which is that a substantial number of people may not have been fully informed about the public meeting in the courthouse. She continued, "some local people don't really read the papers. They were apprised of the meeting, the county meeting that they were going to have. I read [about] it [in the newspapers] and I didn't come. But I read [about it], they advertised that they were going to discuss this, and most people did not read that they were having this meeting, so they thought it was just kind of put over on them. But truly they did have a county meeting about that ten dollar tax. But it's caused a lot of resentment. I hope it [the factory] is going to be as great as they said it would."

A strong supporter of the project remarked, "After Albury was announced [in other words, after it was announced that the company had chosen Bradford County], I think there was a dawning on people. . . . Some of the old timers, they were very supporting during the process, [but] in the back of their minds they thought it would never happen. When it did start to happen I think then people started realizing that this is going to change our community. . . . And I think at that point in time people started getting a little scared."

During my fieldwork in the summer of 1996, the wheel tax was one of the most controversial issues before the county commissioners. Other complaints that were common were that the company was not hiring as many people as the agreement called for, wages were not as high as expected, and many of the jobs went to people from other counties who commuted to work. Yet the chamber of commerce, county manager, and county commissioners were adamant that the company was living up to its agreement and that its general benefits to the county were clearly evident. For example, the county then had an extremely low unemployment rate, and the county manager reported that jobs were available for anyone who wanted to work.

In January 2000, Albury Manufacturing held an open house that was described by the newspaper as being "for the people in the community," and the news account reported that between 900 and 1,000 people were there. The purpose of the event was to mark the factory's fifth anniversary. The factory director is quoted as saying that he hoped to see the plant double in size in the next five years.

But a year and a half later, in August 2001, the newspaper headlines announced that the plant was closing. The company's explanation was twofold: foreign competition—the product that was made at the plant could be manufactured more cheaply abroad—and "the general economic situation." The county was stunned. The town manager is quoted by the newspaper as saying that "this is just sheer devastation on an economy that has already been beat to death." Other plant closings the year before resulted in a loss of "10 percent of our workforce," and the closing of Albury Manufacturing would mean the loss of another 10 percent. A month after the newspaper announced that the plant would close, the commissioners voted unanimously to rescind the wheel tax, and at the next local election, in late 2002, two more commissioners were voted out of office. The election results were generally interpreted as a rebuke over Albury Manufacturing.

In the introduction to this volume, Susan Keefe underlines the need to frame a new narrative about Appalachian communities, one in which mountain people are portrayed not as victims who need the benevolence and enlightenment of outside experts, but as "plucky and hardworking self-starters." They have both the good sense and social assets to help themselves. I pursue this issue further here by focusing on two features of this new narrative: first, the ability of mountain communities to unite in the pursuit of common goals and, second, some of the obstacles that stand in the way.

What does stand in the way? More precisely, what underlies the discord that is so often associated with attempts by mountain people to cooperate among themselves? And what does the case of Albury Manufacturing suggest about the ability to cooperate?

A common theme in the literature on the mountain South is that the communities there are especially fractious, more so than other rural places in the United States. Some writers of an earlier generation who have addressed the refractory nature of mountain communities lay the blame on the passive and fatalistic characteristics of mountain people, attributes which in turn (it has been suggested) have led them to resist change and rendered them incapable of banding together to help themselves. The features of passivity and fatalism (it has been said) are among the main contributors to the region's continuing poverty.[2] In the 1960s a reaction against these ideas emerged among a growing body of Appalachian scholars who offered a different explanation for the region's continuing destitution: mountain poverty (it was now argued) was not the fault of the people or their culture, but was a product of outside forces, particularly the large corporations that for generations had exploited the area's resources, such as coal, timber, and cheap labor. The mountain South had become an oppressed colony within the borders of the United States, and this sapped the initiative of mountain people, leaving them largely incapable of helping themselves.[3]

But if it is true that mountain communities are too passive to mobilize for collective actions, how do we explain the success of Bradford County when it was courting Albury Manufacturing? Here was a body of mountain people who were hardly apathetic or fatalistic. One possible explanation is that Bradford was never colonized. Unlike communities in the coal fields, local affairs there were never dominated by large corporations with absentee owners. Consequently, a sense of oppression and poverty was never an important part of the local self-identity. Nor were the local politicians a tool of outside interests, and in general the people in the county did not regard themselves as disenfranchised or powerless.

But it is questionable that even the colonized communities in the mountain South are particularly passive, which is suggested by a number of recent studies. For example, in the 1980s Billings and Goldman (1983) argued that a school textbook controversy in Kentucky was at bottom a reaction among working-class people to the urban, middle-class domination of their schools. This was a case of mountain people standing together in opposition to what was perceived as a common menace. Other writers have documented the emergence of Appalachian citizens' organizations and local protests against strip-mining, among other things (see Fisher 1993b). And a recent study in West Virginia shows how one community sought to take charge of its fate by revitalizing its downtown (Hinsdale, Lewis, and Waller 1995). Bradford's ability to pull together in courting Albury Manufacturing was not as unique as one might think.

Another explanation for the fractiousness of mountain communities (in addition to the notion that mountain people are passive and fatalistic) is that mountain culture places a particularly strong emphasis on the values of individualism and independent-mindedness. The work of John Campbell (1921)—who in many respects was a sympathetic observer of mountain life during the early twentieth century—illustrates this form of explanation. Campbell suggested (93–94, 104–11) that the remote, frontier conditions of the mountains required such a strong sense of self-reliance that people never developed an orientation toward community cooperation. An extension of this argument is that the extreme individualism of mountain people has contributed to a propensity toward violence and feuds, or to a pattern of taking the law into one's own hands.[4]

Paul Salstrom (1994:xxvi, 55, 59), a historian, also draws a link between the fractiousness of mountain society and the values of independent-mindedness. According to Salstrom, during the period when most of Appalachia was engaged in subsistence farming, closely related households cooperated with one another by exchanging labor, tools, and equipment, but few cooperative relations extended beyond relatives to include neighborhoods or larger communities. Salstrom explains this as a rational adjustment to the requirements of subsistence agriculture in the mountains: close kin needed to stick together, even if it meant distancing themselves from other neighbors. An even more striking example of the idea that mountain individualism has inhibited community cooperation is Robert S. Weise's historical study of Floyd County, Kentucky (2001; see especially 56–60, 226–27). In the past, Weise argues, an ideology of what he calls household localism prevailed in Floyd County, whereby households were engaged in competitive struggles with one another over land, which was the primary basis of their livelihood. Neighbors were so heavily focused on land disputes that local cooperation and cohesion had little hope of developing.

Subsistence farming was the primary basis of the economic life of Bradford County until after World War II, and the values of independence and self-reliance are strongly entrenched there, which locals are quick to affirm. However, not only did Bradford have the ability to pull together in courting Albury Manufacturing, but major cooperative undertakings have taken place at various times in the past. The case of Bradford County raises serious doubts about the idea that subsistence farming made mountain communities too individualistic and fractious for cooperative activities to develop.

We have seen that the phase of courting Albury Manufacturing did not last long and that the entire project eventually became highly divisive, to the point that two county commissioners were soon voted out of office in apparent retribution for their support for the project. Several years later, two more were voted out. Is Bradford County a fractious place after all? More to the point, what explains the divisiveness that eventually developed in this case?

It seems unlikely that mountain communities are any more dispute ridden than other rural communities throughout the United States, and the California farm town that I studied in the 1960s (Hatch 1973, 1979) is illustrative. That community was divided into two somewhat amorphous factions that existed at least as far back as the 1920s. Virtually every local undertaking became entangled in this web of disagreement, which in turn made it difficult for the people to define common goals, and truly communitywide cooperation was limited. Not only does the divisiveness of mountain communities seem to be comparatively common for small, rural communities in general in the United States, but I suggest that the fractiousness of mountain localities may be explained in terms similar to those of other rural parts of the nation.

An important place to look in trying to understand the local dynamics of small communities is competing economic interests, for when collective undertakings favor one fraction of the community over another, disputes are bound to occur. I have said that economic interests by themselves cannot explain the cooperation that developed in Bradford County in its efforts to attract Albury Manufacturing, and economic principles seem to be no more successful in explaining the controversy that developed later. For example, many of the strongest supporters of the factory until the time its closing was announced—and whose support attracted growing criticism—had no direct economic interests in the company, while some of the bitterest opponents were people who were more likely to have benefited most from the jobs that it provided. What explains the controversies that later emerged, rather, were principles that are very similar to the ones underlying the factional division that I discovered in the California community. Put simply, both communities were caught up in cultural struggles.

In the past, cultural anthropologists typically assumed that cultures and societies are relatively homogeneous, and that most members of small communities adhere to the same worldviews and values. But in the last few decades notions of cultural consensus and homogeneity have been thrown into doubt. It is clear that even in small, seemingly homogeneous communities people conduct their affairs with conflicting moral beliefs, and some of the most intense struggles among locals are at bottom struggles over cultural orientations.[5] People strive to assert or insinuate their moral beliefs in local affairs, and seemingly minor issues may become major points of disagreement, because what is at stake is not the specific issue that the people are arguing about, but the underlying moral beliefs. Consider the wheel tax in Bradford County. To some, a ten-dollar tax per vehicle per year was a small price to pay to provide jobs and to help keep the community alive, while to others it was an economic giveaway to a corporation that was far wealthier than Bradford's taxpayers. Underlying this division of opinion was a difference in perspective between what are referred to in the county as progressives and conservatives, a somewhat fluctuating and unstable cleavage based on differences in views about how county government should be run and what the county should try to achieve. The vocal opposition to the wheel tax that emerged was not simply about the wheel tax itself, or about economic interests, but rather the dispute became the site, or a surrogate or synecdoche, for a much broader struggle over county governance and, beyond that, moral beliefs.

The distinction between what is referred to in Bradford as conservatives and progressives should not be confused with another, closely related one between conservatives and liberals. In particular, many who identify as progressives in the county also hold politically conservative beliefs on topics like gun control, abortion, health care, and consumer rights. Be that as it may, the division between conservatives and progressives rests on a number of disparate features, and an important one involves differences in belief about how the county should be run. For progressives, it should operate according to modern principles of business efficiency, whereas for conservatives it should be managed according to the informal, personalistic rules that have defined county affairs for generations. For example, progressives hold that the county tax records ought to be computerized and that the tax office should be run according to codified, businesslike rules that a desk clerk can interpret, whereas conservatives hold that taxation issues should be tempered by a knowledge of the personal circumstances of individual taxpayers. For the conservative, what some consider "progress" in the way the tax office has been run in recent years is not progress at all, for it robs the individual of his or her dignity—it reduces the complexities of real life to a body of abstract rules and denies the specificities of individual cases. Similarly, progressives believe that money should be spent to make county government more efficient, and that greater efficiency can be achieved by computerized tax records, raising the salaries of county employees, and upgrading county equipment. By contrast, conservatives believe that greater efficiencies are achieved by maintaining a lean county budget. Again, progressives believe that the county should aggressively promote economic development, which is what it did in acquiring the industrial park, whereas conservatives hold that the county should stay out of those kinds of affairs. Acquisition of the industrial park should be seen in this context, for it became a major topic of dissension between the two sides. The division is complicated by the fact that the same individual may be conservative in some respects and progressive in others, and that he or she need not be consistent from one situation to the next. In spite of these complexities, the distinction between conservatives and progressives has a long history in the mountain South (see Hatch 2004b), and it is apparently a common feature of contemporary mountain communities.[6]

The initial success in mobilizing local support to acquire Albury Manufacturing represented an achievement for the progressive point of view in the struggle to influence local opinion. People's concerns about losing their community were powerful enough at first to overcome the community's fractiousness—Albury Manufacturing provided a cause that a majority of local people could agree upon, and it also fit the progressive agenda. When I was told that it was not popular to oppose the project, an implicit meaning was that the conservative point of view was in retreat. But as time passed, the conservatives' criticisms left their toll, and a growing number of people began to doubt the wisdom of the project. Rumors circulated that the company was not employing as many people as promised, or paying the high salaries that that the company had said it would, that too many jobs were taken by people from outside the county, and that the progressive county commissioners had forced the project down people's throats. These rumors were mistaken, but they had an effect, and progressivism in the county suffered a setback. When the factory eventually announced that it was closing, the county commissioners who were voted out of office were closely associated with the progressive orientation.

I want now to look at the other side of the coin of community cooperation—not at the underlying bases of the county's fractiousness, but at what made it possible for people to pull together in the early phase of the project to attract the new factory. What explains the initial, widespread enthusiasm? Central to its early success was a strong sense of community—or, more precisely, county—identity.

Many Bradford people were born and raised there, they were baptized in the local churches, and they graduated from the local schools. As children they went to the movie theater on Saturdays, and when they could they played on the sidewalks and in the stores of the small downtown. Many of them later raised their own children in Bradford, and they buried their parents in the local cemeteries next to aunts and uncles, grandmothers and grandfathers, great grandmothers and great grandfathers. This is a place that they feel profoundly a part of. Even many of those who are relatively new—such as in-marrying spouses—soon occupy distinct places in the local social system, have individual identities within the community, and develop a commitment to it. A number of writers have noted that mountain people often exhibit a strong attachment to place (e.g., Beaver 1986; Halperin 1990; and Keefe 1998), and this is not simply to the rural neighborhood where the family farm and church are located, but to the larger locality as well, including, in Bradford, the county.

People's conceptions of who they are as individuals are constructed from a variety of elements, such as age, gender, race, and, as Keefe suggests in introducing this volume, locality. Among mountain people, local identity is an important component of the individual's sense of who he or she is. In this sense localities in the mountain South are like many other small, rural communities in the United States, where people's sense of who they are is based in part on the position they occupy in the local social order and on their relations with others in the community. This sense of local identity underlies the common reaction among many rural people to the threat that their local school—or post office or store—will close, and to the decay of the nearby town. Not only is the sense of self locally rooted, but so is the sense of self-worth, for conceptions of what constitutes an upstanding person are realized in the context of everyday social relations.[7] What powered the movement to acquire Albury Manufacturing in Bradford County was a concern that an important part of the people's sense of both self and self-worth were at stake.

One feature of the Bradford case may make the dynamics of this county somewhat unusual compared to other places in the mountain South. In the town revitalization project in the Virginia community that I mentioned earlier (Hinsdale, Lewis, and Waller 1995), the non-elites had to convince a socially and culturally distant—and possibly insensitive—group of leaders that improvements were needed. But in the case of Albury Manufacturing, the local leaders, people with high social capital, experienced the same concerns about the loss of community as everyone else. Bradford is smaller and may be more easily mobilized than most other mountain counties, and this may give it an advantage in pursuing common goals. But a major factor that propelled those with high social capital to assume positions of leadership in this case was their sense of local identity. This same factor is not wholly absent elsewhere in the mountains, and the likelihood of winning support from established leaders is enhanced when they experience a common sense of identity.

Another important dimension of the leader's role in small communities is the cultural ideal that the officeholder or other official should be a public-minded person who is concerned about and works for the larger good. Local influential people may seldom live up to this ideal in real life, but in the American, and especially Southern, imagination, the model of the public servant is prominent. In many cases, the sense of self-worth among people of high social capital—the sense of themselves as effective human beings and estimable individuals—is linked to the cultural expectation that the public leader should also be public spirited.[8]

Mountain communities, like rural communities throughout the United States, are often fractious places, but strong forces are available to people who want to strive for common goals. I've focused on two of these forces here, a sense of local identity and a willingness among those with high social capital to promote local causes. A number of traps exist in pursuit of these causes, however, including the process of globalization, which led to Albury Manufacturing's closing after only a few years. Local support for common goals may also be fickle, and a typical source of this in mountain communities, and a major challenge in arriving at goals that people can agree on, is the back-and-forth struggles between conservatives and progressives.

Notes

Different phases of the project were funded by the University of California–Santa Barbara Academic Senate and Interdisciplinary Humanities Center, and the National Science Foundation. I am very grateful for their support. I am also extremely grateful to the editor of the county newspaper who loaned me the complete file of clippings on Albury Manufacturing to help me in writing this paper. Finally, I thank the librarians in the Appalachian Collection at Appalachian State University in Boone, North Carolina, who are always enormously helpful in bringing their knowledge to bear in guiding me in my search for historical resources.

1. The quotations in this paper come from verbatim transcriptions of my tape-recorded interviews with local people. I have made a few minor changes in these quotations for the sake of readability.

2. For example, see Campbell (1921:chap. 11). See also Ball (1968); Cain (1970); Cressey (1949); Ford (1965); Pearsall (1959); Stephenson (1968); and Weller (1965).

3. See especially Appalachian Land Ownership Task Force (1983); Eller (1982); Lewis (1984); Lewis, Johnson, and Askins (1978).

4. Altina Waller's study of the Hatfields and McCoys (Waller 1988:6–8) refutes this image. Fisher (1993a) also notes that the news media, novelists, missionaries, and others have implanted in the national consciousness two conflicting images of Appalachians. On one hand, the people are portrayed as backward, unintelligent, and submissive; and on the other, as some of the most violent people in the United States.

5. An example of this type of analysis of local conflict is Altina Waller's *Feud* (1988). See also Billings and Goldman (1983).

6. For example, a central theme of John Stephenson's study of *Shiloh* (a small community in western North Carolina in the 1960s) is a division between what he calls the modern and traditional subcultures. His discussion focuses on values and attitudes relating to the lives of individuals, not to the management of county affairs; consequently, it is difficult to relate his analysis directly to mine. But it seems clear that his findings and my own correspond.

7. See my analysis of respectability in a small rural county in New Zealand (Hatch 1992).

8. Elsewhere I have discussed the relationship between leadership roles and personal reputations in the context of a small farm community in California (Hatch 1979:83–101, 109–10, 233–57, 262–65).

References

Appalachian Land Ownership Task Force. 1983. *Who Owns Appalachia? Landowner-ship and Its Impact.* With an Introduction by Charles C. Geisler. Lexington: Univ. of Kentucky Press.

Ball, R. A. 1968. "Poverty Cases: The Analgesic Subculture of the Southern Appa-lachians." *American Sociological Review* 38:885–95.

Beaver, Patricia D. 1986. *Rural Community in the Appalachian South.* Lexington: Univ. of Kentucky Press.

Billings, Dwight, and Robert Goldman. 1983. "Religion and Class Consciousness in the Kanawha County School Textbook Controversy." In *Appalachia and America: Autonomy and Regional Dependence,* Allen Batteau (Ed.). Lexington: Univ. Press of Kentucky. Pp. 68–85.

Cain, S. R. 1970. "Appalachian Analogue: Anthropology and Change." *Growth and Change* 1:31–36.

Campbell, John C. 1921. *The Southern Highlander and His Homeland.* New York: Russell Sage Foundation. [Reprinted in 1973 by the Univ. of North Carolina Press.]

Cressey, Paul F. 1949. "Social Disorganization and Reorganization in Harlan County, Kentucky." *American Sociological Review* 16:389–94.

Eller, Ronald D. 1982. *Miners, Millhands, and Mountaineers: Industrialization of the Appalachian South,1880–1930.* Knoxville: Univ. of Tennessee Press.

Fisher, Stephen. 1993a. "Introduction." In *Fighting Back in Appalachia: Traditions of Resistance and Change,* Stephen Fisher (Ed.). Philadelphia: Temple Univ. Press. Pp. 1–14.

——— (Ed.). 1993b. *Fighting Back in Appalachia: Traditions of Resistance and Change.* Philadelphia: Temple Univ. Press.

Ford, Thomas R. 1965. "The Effects of Prevailing Values and Beliefs on the Perpetua-tion of Poverty in Rural Areas." *Problems of Chronically Depressed Rural Areas.* Raleigh: North Carolina State Univ., Agriculture Policy Institute.

Halperin, Rhoda H. 1990. *The Livelihood of Kin: Making Ends Meet "The Kentucky Way."* Austin: Univ. of Texas Press.

Hatch, Elvin. 1973. "Social Drinking and Factional Alignment in a Rural California Community." *Anthropological Quarterly* 46:243–60.

———. 1979. *Biography of a Small Town.* New York: Columbia Univ. Press.

———. 1992. *Respectable Lives: Social Standing in Rural New Zealand.* Berkeley: Univ. of California Press.

———. 2004a. "Delivering the Goods: Cash, Subsistence Farms, and Identity in a Blue Ridge County in the 1930s." *Journal of Appalachian Studies* 9:6–48.

———. 2004b. "The Margins of Civilization: Progressives and Moonshiners in the Late 19th-century Mountain South." *Appalachian Journal* 32:68–99.

Hinsdale Mary Ann, Helen M. Lewis, and S. Maxine Waller. 1995. *It Comes from the People: Community Development and Local Theology.* Philadelphia: Temple Univ. Press.

Keefe, Susan Emley. 1998. "Appalachian Americans: The Formation of Reluctant Ethnics." In *Many Americans: Perspectives on Racism, Ethnicity, and Cultural Identity,* Gregory Campbell (Ed.). Dubuque: Kendall/Hunt. Pp. 129–54.

Lewis, Helen M. 1984. "Industrialization, Class, and Regional Consciousness in Two Highland Societies: Wales and Appalachia." In *Cultural Adaptation to Mountain Environments,* Patricia D. Beaver and Burton L. Purrington (Eds.). Athens: Univ. of Georgia Press. Pp. 50–72.

Lewis, Helen M., Linda Johnson, and Donald Askins (Eds.). 1978. *Colonialism in Modern America: The Appalachian Case.* Boone, NC: Appalachian Consortium Press.

Pearsall, Marian. 1959. *Little Smokey Ridge: The Natural History of a Southern Appalachian Neighborhood.* Tuscaloosa: Univ. of Alabama Press.

Salstrom, Paul. 1994. *Appalachia's Path to Dependency: Rethinking a Region's Economic History, 1730–1940.* Lexington: Univ. Press of Kentucky

Stephenson, John B. 1968. *Shiloh: A Mountain Community.* Lexington: Univ. Press of Kentucky.

Waller, Altina L. 1988. *Feud: Hatfields, McCoys, and Social Change in Appalachia, 1860–1900.* Chapel Hill: Univ. of North Carolina Press.

Weise, Robert S. 2001. *Grasping at Independence: Debt, Male Authority, and Mineral Rights in Appalachian Kentucky, 1850–1915.* Knoxville: Univ. of Tennessee Press.

Weller, Jack. 1965. *Yesterday's People: Life in Contemporary Appalachia.* Lexington: Univ. Press of Kentucky.

Rebuilding Communities

A TWELVE-STEP
RECOVERY PROGRAM

Helen Matthews Lewis

Helen Lewis uses the term "community building" to refer to participatory development work. Her work in Ivanhoe, Virginia (described in It Comes from the People *[1995]), is a prime example of the community developer role she advocates, one that emphasizes people development and grassroots organizing. In contrast with Elvin Hatch, Lewis focuses her attention in this chapter on those communities that have been devastated by industrial exploitation and abandonment, where local assets are diminished. Nevertheless, her twelve-step recovery program identifies actions that every community might consider in creating a plan for sustainable community development*

Rebuilding communities is essential work for the coming decades. With both industrialization and deindustrialization we have experienced the erosion and destruction of communities. Some of this destruction has been deliberate through so-called development programs: the building of TVA dams, sports arenas, urban renewal, interstate road corridors, world fairs, and Olympic

Games. Spurred on by our great faith in industrial progress, we have destroyed towns, homes, and social networks. Many progressive choices have led to the loss of community through the consolidation of schools and the cutting of new roads through neighborhoods.

With the growth of our national consumer-based economy, we have seen the local mom-and-pop grocery stores, cafés, and filling stations, which provided local gathering places, replaced by smart, modern outposts of distant firms located on the outskirts of town. I have heard that for every new Wal-Mart, twenty-one small stores close. Wal-Mart's television advertising claims they are the salvation of communities in which factories have closed, because they provide employment for the displaced workers. The negative impact to the local economy is more than the loss of small businesses. There is the loss of self-determination, social networks, local gathering places, community participation, and mutual aid.

The loss of community shows up in many other changes. Raymond Williams (1983), in a book about the year 2000, wrote that a major problem is the increasing privatization of life. Our increasing individualization is exemplified by the home entertainment center, home computers, the great growth in VCR rental stores, plugged-in lone runners, round-bale solo hay balers, and bowling alone. "Bowling Alone" is also the title of an article and book by Robert Putnam, a Harvard Professor writing and talking about the loss of civic participation (Putnam 1997; see also Putnam 1995). He writes: "Participation has fallen (often sharply) in many types of civic associations, from religious groups to labor unions, from women's clubs to fraternal clubs, and from neighborhood gatherings to bowling leagues. Virtually all segments of society have been affected by this lessening in social connectedness and . . . declining social trust" (Putnam 1997:27). Putnam uses the term "social capital" to describe the networks, norms, and social trust that make it possible for people to cooperate and work together for mutual benefit. In other words, he means *community*. Putnam links the loss and destruction of communities to many of today's problems and warns us of the decline of democracy, defined by a lack of civic engagement and political participation, which contributes to many of our social ills.

Much of the continuing loss of community is related to the deindustrialization and globalization of our economy. As the major manufacturing and mining base of our economy has declined, communities have been devastated by the loss of their economic base. This reshaping has transformed America's agricultural and industrial economy to a service and finance economy (Gaventa 1991). In the past fifteen years, this transformation has resulted in an enormous loss of manufacturing and production jobs, with the migration of workers and families in search of employment. The demographic profile of communities has changed, leaving behind the older, retired, or disabled residents.

While national in scope, such economic restructuring reflects itself unevenly in different regions of the country. In Appalachia and the South, a region that historically has provided the nation with its mines, resources, and low-wage, low-skill workers, the residents have been more dependent upon such traditional industries than in almost any other region. As the agricultural and manufacturing industries have been moved in large numbers to developing countries where they find cheaper labor and resources, the area has seen the devastation of many communities. Earlier, the Appalachian South benefited from such capital mobility as a place where runaway shops from the north came in search of low-wage labor, cheap resources, and community subsidies. Now the tide has changed, and plants in Appalachia and the rural South are closing and/or relocating overseas.

The new economic crisis in the region poses a dilemma for conventional economic development policy. Historically, the development model for the region has been based on creating a favorable "business climate," which in turn could be used to lure industry into the region. In the name of maintaining this business climate, workers received low wages, communities provided tax and other concessions to industry, and dissent and disagreement were silenced. Based on a traditional understanding of trickle-down economics, the assumption was that what was good for business was good for workers and communities. To some extent, within its own definitions of success, the business climate model of development worked. Thousands of plants came to the region and the overall standard of living grew. Along with the industrial park, tax incentives, low wages, and a nonunion labor force, the region offered large quantities of exploitable resources with few restrictions and low taxes. We offered up our coal, timber, water, air, people's labor and their health.

But soon greener industrial parks beckoned from overseas nations desperate for jobs and willing to offer lower wages, fewer environmental restraints, and untapped resources. The communication revolution and use of computers for management facilitated this transition, making it possible to coordinate and manage far-flung transnational businesses.

Economic growth in the South became limited to certain "hot spots," deepening the internal patterns of uneven development in the region. The movement of industry to Appalachia and the Southern states is limited to a few big deals in which states compete and offer very large packages of tax incentives and cash benefits in exchange for jobs. Benefits to the states take years to realize, if ever, and the social costs are never counted.

But we continue to rely on industrial recruitment as a main strategy for economic development. We continue to build industrial parks and shell buildings to attract an industry on its way farther south. The industrial recruitment model has become so ingrained in our planning and development policies that, even in the face of massive evidence of its inability to develop rural communities, it is still the major model of most planners and industrial and economic development bodies. There are strong economic interests and political power supporting the building of industrial parks and subsidizing factories to relocate in rural communities. Much like the cargo cults of the South Pacific, with natives who built airstrips in the jungle and lit torches to magically call down the planes that left after World War II, our industrial parks sit empty, hoping to attract a flying factory.

Our reliance on the industrial recruitment model seems almost like an addiction. Perhaps we need a twelve-step program similar to an Alcoholics Anonymous recovery program to recover from this addictive, nonfunctioning model of development and the codependent behavior that accompanies it. We need a model that builds communities rather than exploits and destroys them.

Social Infrastructure and Community-Based Development

In contrast to the industrial recruitment model for economic development, which concentrates on building physical infrastructure, a community-based model for economic development focuses attention on building community. This model claims the traditional industrial recruitment model has failed to develop rural areas. Rural communities, it is argued, can no longer depend upon recruiting outside industry as their road to development but must turn to a policy that facilitates development from within (Gaventa and Lewis 1989a, 1989b).

Putnam claims that economic development is related to the existence of social capital. In a twenty five year study of northern Italy, Putnam found the difference between prosperous and non-prosperous communities lay in the quality and intensity of citizen involvement (Putnam 1993). He concluded that these communities did not become civic simply because they were rich—they became rich because they were civic. They collaborated; they had trust, a social infrastructure, and social capital. Economic development therefore requires the building of community and the development of a social infrastructure.

In the industrial recruitment model, the role of the community is to make it ready to receive and to serve business, thus making community and worker interests subservient to the needs of maintaining a favorable business climate.

Development is done to and for local communities, not by the people themselves. While this model relies upon enterprising elites to bring in outside industry and capital that would create development, community-based development requires local community members to participate in the process.

Women and Community Development

In Appalachia much of the knowledge of community-based development has grown out of the work of grassroots community groups largely led by women in the region (H. Lewis 1996; H. Lewis et al. 1986). The organizations they found and the work they do differ from the more male-dominated emphasis on industrial development and recruitment. From their own economic experiences, the women tend to define development more broadly than jobs and income to include education, democratic participation, and dignity. Because women have been delegated to the fringes of the mainstream economy, their development work has been largely limited to community-based alternatives.

Women's experience in the domestic economy has given them a different perspective on development. Women's work, in contrast to men's jobs, is more life sustaining, life producing, family- and community-based. It is part of livelihood, reproducing and working for children and grandchildren, both for survival and for a better life to pass on. The domestic economy deals with people and their needs, treating people as human beings, not as raw material or commodities, not just as a labor force.

Women's development projects draw from these experiences and values as they recognize both community and individual needs, combining education and development to link personal and community growth. Their community-based organizations tend to be more democratic, more participatory, seeking to develop and use local skills and resources to involve everyone. They also include cultural expression like poetry, crafts, music, and religion. Some of these community groups have collected oral histories, written community history, and organized reunions, festivals, and parades. They have lots of potluck dinners and meetings with prayers, songs, and dancing that encourage broad participation. Art, theater, and music are used to challenge, interpret, and envision the future.

People's stories, experiences, and histories are brought forth, and they help to save and celebrate human qualities that are the lifeblood of community. Stories help build connections between people, provide ways to share knowledge, strengthen civic networks, and provide the tools to rebuild communities by creating and maintaining the social infrastructure, the social capital, which is essential in democratic community-based development. This infrastructure includes education for human development, cultural creativity, the recovery and understanding of history, democratic participation, and a consciousness of the community's religious and political symbols.

Economic Literacy

The separation of people from development is also paralleled in the production of knowledge and analysis about economic development. "The Economy" has become something external to everyday experience, something to be defined and analyzed by experts. It is left to the economists, the business analysts, and the developers, who measure and count the effect of changes on business and ignore the social costs and the impact on communities. Community-based development requires residents to undertake a process of education and participatory research through which they can assess their own situation and define and implement strategies for themselves (see Kobak and McCormack 1988; Lewis and Gaventa 1988; Luttrell 1988). People need to reclaim a knowledge and understanding of the economy in a way that can enhance effective citizen participation and strategy development.

Rural community groups, especially those at the grassroots level, have lacked the educational opportunities needed to analyze the economy, to define and to create development for themselves. Economic literacy enables and empowers local citizens to analyze their own economic problems and resources, to develop solutions to joblessness and poverty, and to gain the tangible skills they need to make rural community-based development happen.

The definition of successful development is thus expanded to include criteria broader than jobs and income, such as community participation, democratic participation, and sustainable communities. Emphasis shifts from the initial focus on job creation to broader social and cultural projects that help to provide the community with better educational opportunities, a sense of identity, and community pride.

Creating a Twelve-Step Recovery Program

The Twelve-Step Recovery Program grew out of the work in rural mountain communities where people were trying to revive their communities. Most of these communities had lost their economic base of mining, timbering, agriculture, or manufacturing. They were usually located on the back side of the mountain and the back side of the county, ignored by the county seat and bypassed by whatever development came down the new interstate highways. The communities were peripheral, marginalized, and left out of any economic development activity. Mines had closed or were mechanized so they no longer provided much employment; the resources of timber or minerals had been exploited and were used up or badly damaged; the factories had closed and moved further south to Mexico, Brazil, or Indonesia.

In many of these declining rural communities, in places like Ivanhoe, Virginia; McDowell County, West Virginia; Owsley County, Kentucky; Dungannon, Virginia; Rose's Creek, Tennessee; and Letcher County, Kentucky, people formed community development groups to try to rebuild their communities and their economies from the bottom up. They called it the "trickle up" theory of economic development. They say the "trickle down" never reached them and doesn't work.

The Twelve-Step Recovery Program is drawn from their work and provides some strategies for building social capital and developing socially responsible, democratic, sustainable communities. The twelve steps are not a straight-forward stairway to community revitalization. They are more like dance steps. Sometimes you go two steps forward and one step back to repeat number one. You tap-dance for the funders, foxtrot around the local authorities, and slow waltz into some of your projects. The metaphors are endless: you can rock and roll, do the twist, tango, or do a dip. Sometimes you go in circles; sometimes individuals come up with a creative improvisation and you keep repeating the steps. Sometimes participants run into major barriers, drop out of the dance, and again become wallflowers at the ball. The leadership model is that of the choreographer, who helps plan, train, and cheerlead, and who both participates in and watches the performance with pride.

Building Sustainable Communities: A Twelve-Step Recovery Program from Industrial Recruitment

There are some basic values and assumptions underlying the community-based model of development. First, it values *sustainability,* which means using resources today so there will still be resources in the future. It stresses the welfare of future generations. The process does not trade off the soil, water, and people for bad jobs and polluting industries. The industrial development model is a process of exploitation, not development, and communities realize they must stop recruiting and subsidizing folks to come in and exploit them. Secondly, the community-based model stresses *people development:* helping them to gain skills, education, pride, and confidence. People are a major resource and must be educated, encouraged, and nurtured. Third, this model is *culture based.* It does not destroy but encourages creativity and culture. It preserves important values and traditions. Fourth, the community-based model is *inclusive.* It is not limited to one elite group, one gender, or those who already have power and have always run things. Fifth, it starts with *local resources* and begins by looking at the glass half full rather than half empty. Instead of concentrating on deficits, it looks to available resources. It looks to the aspects of community that people want to preserve, and the resources, including people's knowledge and skills, from which they can build and maintain an economy. Finally, the model is *ecologically based*. It assumes the land, the water, and other resources must be cared for. It requires commitment to the long haul, planning for the future, the *long term*. It is based on the realization that there are no quick fixes. It aims to build a just economy, a moral economy.

The 12 steps in the recovery program are listed in Table 2. They are discussed in detail in the remainder of this chapter and illustrated with examples from the experiences of communities I have worked with over the years.

Table 2. A Twelve-step Recovery Program from Industrial Recruitment

1. Understand your history—share memories
2. Mobilize/organize/revive a sense of community
3. Profile and assess your local community
4. Analyze and envision alternatives
5. Educate the community
6. Build confidence and pride
7. Develop local projects
8. Strengthen your organization
9. Collaborate and build coalitions
10. Take political power
11. Initiate economic activity
12. Enter local/regional/national/international planning processes

UNDERSTAND YOUR HISTORY: SHARE MEMORIES

A conventional economic developer who goes into a community to work would start with a survey of needs, develop business plans, do feasibility studies, seek outside capital, and build physical infrastructure. As important as these steps may be, they do not build community. They do nothing to strengthen people's personal resources or sense of connection to one another. So with the twelve-step plan, you start by telling stories, understanding the past, and sharing memories. In *Habits of the Heart* (1985), Robert Bellah writes that community is made up of shared memories. People's stories, experiences, and histories help to save and celebrate the human qualities that are the lifeblood of the community. Stories build connections between people, provide ways to share knowledge, strengthen civic networks, provide the tools to rebuild communities, and produce the infrastructure, the social capital, that is essential in democratic community-based development. You need to get people talking, planning, and dreaming. As people begin telling stories of individuals and local places, as they share work histories, as they listen to stories from the elders who recall the good old days and the bad old days, community is rebuilt, pride develops, a sense of identity and roots are established.

In McDowell County, West Virginia, a summer youth program, in which young people collected oral histories and then turned them into dramatic presentations, brought people in various communities together, and they began to talk about current problems and issues and organized groups to deal with these problems.

Recalling past development histories is a way to begin planning and developing an understanding of the economic system and what has happened to produce current problems. When mines close or factories move, often the people feel they have failed, have caused the problems, and are not worthy people. Understanding the reasons for the moves, the economic benefits of leaving or closing, frees people to make changes and choose a different type of development.

In Ivanhoe, Virginia, members of the Ivanhoe Civic League, whose original goal was to recruit an industry, began an economics discussion group to understand why they were unsuccessful in recruiting an industry. They began telling and sharing work histories, stories of past development by former industries in their community. They reflected on how and why the industries used the community and why they left. They began to question their recruitment priorities, and they agreed that they did not want the type of jobs or development they had in the past, where workers were not treated fairly or respected or where the work was dangerous and unhealthy. They changed their vision and developed different strategies and development plans.

Past social movements or resistance history are often hidden away, not published, and need to be revived and restored as models for inspiration and present-day action. As communities regain their histories, they also develop an understanding of their community's role in the larger history of the region, the nation, and the world.

Mobilize/Organize/Revive Community

You need a gathering place to share stories. In many rural communities, the post office and the churches are the only viable institutions left where people can come together and talk. Unfortunately, churches tend to divide people by race, class, family, and community. Congregations can, however, come together and work to build community. There are some good examples in the mountains of cooperative church programs centered on housing, food pantries, and social services.

Ivanhoe took over the old commissary for a community education center; Dungannon, Virginia, moved an old depot to the middle of town for a community center; and Caretta, West Virginia, restored their old schoolhouse. The development of a place becomes a mobilizing effort in itself. Community clinics, volunteer fire departments, or local stores can be centers for meeting and talking, but a gathering place that is open to all and accessible is most important to begin a revival process.

You need unifying events. Meetings, reunions, festivals, parades, discussions, study groups, and celebrations are ways to make community-building fun. Music, dancing, and food bring people together and revive the spirit.

Ivanhoe revived the 4th of July parade and developed a recreation park in the empty industrial park with a community reunion and music festival that became an annual event. Quilting bees, craft exhibits, and local drama were used. McDowell County writers and musicians formed arts councils and developed community festivals.

Community building also requires an organization to coordinate actions, and it must include all segments of the community. If efforts are limited to one social class or age group or ethnic or racial group, the community will never be complete. Democratic participation is essential to a healthy community. Organizations already in existence (churches, 4-H clubs, fire and rescue departments, and civic clubs) can be encouraged to expand their work, be more inclusive, and become a force for community development.

PROFILE AND ASSESS YOUR LOCAL COMMUNITY

In order to build from within, the community needs to survey and map local resources and needs. Catalog people resources: skills, gifts, talents, and local expertise. Survey land resources: water, soil, timber, minerals, and natural beauty. It is important to draw on the resources rather than emphasize the deficiencies and needs. Look to businesses and organizations that are already in place. Do a study of existing groups, networks, and social capital. Outside resource persons to facilitate or help with research can be helpful, especially if they are committed to participatory research, but local members can do their own assessments and research. They can do a simple cost-benefit analysis of local industries and businesses to determine potential for growth or to understand whether it is exploitative rather than developmental. Participatory research provides data for future planning.

After a survey of the community, asking what people wanted to see happen and how they might help, the Ivanhoe community decided to develop an education program to develop literacy, the GED, and community college courses. The old company store became Ivanhoe Tech, an education center, meeting place, and hub of the community. The community developed a history project and published a two-volume history of the region which helped people rejoin their memories, their history, and regain pride in the contributions Ivanhoe had made to the development of the country. They planned together, developed music festivals, parades, parties, and celebrations. They rebuilt community. Only then were they ready to begin economic development, build coalitions, and enter the political arena.

ANALYZE AND ENVISION ALTERNATIVES

It is important to talk and plan together for the future, to have dreams and hopes and visions. This can be done in many ways: study groups, Bible study, civic group meetings, and so on. It is helpful to look back to traditional values to determine what the community wants to preserve, as well as look forward to what needs to change. Planning should involve studying together, visiting other communities, looking for models, alternatives, and new ways of development, and analyzing strategies for change. Outside facilitation and ideas can be helpful, but the community must always keep control. As groups concentrate on potentials and resources and what the community wants to preserve, the planning process should seek to balance needs and resources and involve people in making choices between alternatives. When the process is that of outside recruitment, then the outside industry makes the choices, and often the community trades health and environment for jobs without due consideration or democratic participation in the decision making.

The Owsley County Action Committee (in Kentucky) was formed to study and work for sustainable development in their county. Dungannon developed an education program in the depot community center, and as a result of one of their economics classes, they planned and developed a sewing cooperative that operated for five years providing work and training for a group of women in the community.

Ivanhoe organized a series of economic discussions in which the community studied, analyzed their situation, and, after a community survey, had a town meeting to review their findings and make plans for the future. Ivanhoe also used Bible study to link their faith and religious values with their development activities. In this process, they also questioned beliefs that prevented women's full participation and attitudes that support exclusion and racism. It served to foster an emergence, from silence, of a community of outspoken, knowledgeable citizens who demanded participation in the planning and direction of their community.

EDUCATE THE COMMUNITY

Personal transformation and community transformation should occur together. To develop new and better businesses, people need to develop new skills. The community organization needs to develop a leadership program—and people need to rethink leadership styles in order to allow for greater participation and the utilization of the many skills and talents in the community. The program should include education for democratic participation. In most rural communities there is a low level of education, so literacy/GED classes need to be organized and taught in ways to involve people in development work. Local community college classes, workshops, study circles, tutoring, and women's support groups all can be organized through the community group. Youth programs and senior citizen programs are also venues for educational programs. The community can recruit local young people to learn the skills needed in the community, to become doctors and teachers, and provide community scholarships so they will return. The process of education allows a community to develop understanding and awareness that can be used to plan, control, and monitor change. The questions become not only about what development policies shall shape the region, but also about who will participate in shaping the policies in the first place, and how to define success. Questions include "Development for whose interests?" but also "Development by whom?" and "Toward what ends?"

Participatory development requires educating for creativity, regaining popular knowledge and history, understanding democratic decision making, and consciousness of religious and political symbols. With this investment, people can become better equipped to rebuild their own communities and economies. They have the capacity and the social capital to access other resources, network, and collaborate with other groups to revitalize or develop their community.

BUILD CONFIDENCE AND PRIDE

Communities that have been dominated by one industry have a history of dependency and attitudes that must be changed. Regaining community history through oral histories, music, and theater helps build identity and pride. As the community rebuilds, people's work and the group's accomplishments should be recognized and celebrated. Graduations for GED completion and educational achievements and rewards for learning new skills help build community. Artists, writers, poets, and songwriters emerge and flower when a vital community development process begins. Spiritual growth should also be encouraged. Community rituals and ceremonies should be initiated to express the new spirit of development, both personal and communal.

Ivanhoe invited all former residents to return and support their revitalization projects by joining hands in a circle around the town. "Hands Around Ivanhoe" symbolized a new unity and support for renewal. Parades, graduations, Christmas and Thanksgiving gatherings with gift giving, prayers, poetry, theater, and music created new symbols and revived older ones.

DEVELOP LOCAL PROJECTS

As the group begins a planning process, it can link needs and resources and develop projects to bring them together: a volunteer child care center, tutoring for children after school, a craft cooperative, a recreation area, a park, activities like cleaning up the town, repainting, planting flowers or trees, honoring the ancestors with Christmas lights. Communitywide and small group projects increase participation and involve new and different groups in the community.

McDowell County developed a mini-grant program with small grants to community groups for projects to improve their communities. These acted as incentives for local community groups to organize and begin development activities. Projects were quite varied, ranging from developing a tutoring program to putting up a statue honoring former coal miners.

Often a community project, such as building a memorial park for veterans or coal miners who died in the mines, may not seem to outside resource persons as meeting essential needs, but these projects may be the way to mobilize, to build community, which has to precede other work. The community needs to encourage youth enterprises, look for local entrepreneurs, and celebrate each new project. Excitement becomes contagious.

STRENGTHEN YOUR ORGANIZATION

The community organization group needs care and nurturing. Although many communities have very strong charismatic leaders who get the process started, they cannot rely on one charismatic leader. Charismatic leaders can be most important in early mobilizing and continue to add spirit and enthusiasm to projects and activities, but broader, more diverse collective leadership is needed for long-term sustainability. Solo leaders burn out and organizations fold, unless there is broader leadership. Leadership development and staff training are important, and training is needed for special skills such as fiscal management, bookkeeping, and fund-raising. Everyone needs to be involved in strategic planning and evaluation. The organization may need to seek outside help with organizational development. They can learn from other groups and enlarge participation so that the organization does not evolve into another small clique pursuing its own self-interest.

Collaborate and Build Coalitions

Community groups need to make linkages and form networks and partnerships with other groups to gain strength, share resources, and learn from each other's efforts, successes, and failures. Small isolated community groups can become marginalized, be labeled as "trouble makers," and ignored. A coalition of groups can form a power base to influence or control local government. Community organizations should begin to make connections and linkages (local, regional, and national) to access resources. Using networks, the community group should work to get representation on boards: schools, libraries, county commissions, and economic development groups. Groups need not only to locate outside help but also to learn how to use and control outside resources and not be co-opted or controlled by them. Communities must set the agenda and make a contract with outside resource persons and organizations.

In McDowell County, through a creative program funded by the Benedum Foundation, efforts were made to develop local community development groups throughout the county and to link them together through a community board to give mutual support, share strategies and ideas, and develop political clout. Fifteen community development groups were organized and trained through a series of workshops and each developed community projects to improve life in their community. These included buying the local, abandoned school building and developing community recreation programs, child care programs, a CCC works project, a statue to honor the miners who had worked in the coal mines, a community library, and a tutoring program for children. The linked communities were able to share resources and information and, for the first time, to cooperate in planning, which resulted in the county being selected for a national Enterprise Community grant for sustainable community development. The Enterprise Community program has brought together grassroots community groups, service agencies, government and county officials, and decision makers to collaborate and plan together. In McDowell County, the grassroots community groups had strength enough to include their needs in the county agenda and keep control of the process when the county commission tried to take over the program.

With a coalition of groups, it is more difficult for the established power structure and decision makers to ignore or marginalize them. You cannot develop alone.

Take Political Power

Political activity becomes essential in order to challenge and change policies to redirect resources to the community. Community groups can encourage and support members of the community to run for political office. They can begin civic education, voter registration, facilitate participation, develop a local monitoring program by attending all council, commission, and board meetings, and get members on all the boards. Advocacy skills can be taught, and members can lobby elected officials, bringing them to the community, recognizing them when they make progressive moves, and educating them about community needs.

In Letcher County, Kentucky, local governance groups were organized to monitor and participate in local government. This resulted in a reform candidate for local judge executive and a citizen group appointed to the economic development board. They are now instituting a major project to provide county-wide sewerage and water and are beginning a sustainable development planning process.

Initiate Economic Activity

Community groups can encourage and begin development of home-grown businesses. They can seek capital for local projects, develop a revolving loan fund, establish a mini-grants program, and work with local banks to invest in community businesses. Groups can work to make policy changes in banks and economic development agencies. They can confront plant closures and try to recruit responsible outside industries and make community contracts with new industries. Communities also need to look for alternatives for survival, relearning older ways of self-sufficiency and survival from elders, such as raising and preserving food and home remedies. They can use the history of the region or the natural environment for historical or ecological tourism. Through the education program they can develop local job training and business development programs. Communities can establish an incubator for small local businesses. They can work with young people in the schools to develop entre-preneurial training and encourage small business development as a career.

In Owsley County, Kentucky, a group of women began an organization called Workers of Rural Kentucky that developed small businesses along with education and training programs. Small businesses included a cleaning busi-ness, a T-shirt silk-screening business, a bakery, and a thrift store. The orga-nization built coalitions and developed linkages with other development bodies to secure loan funds and technical resources.

ENTER LOCAL/REGIONAL/NATIONAL/ INTERNATIONAL PLANNING PROCESSES

Communities must recognize that they are part of a regional, national, and international economy, so they can understand how the global economy impacts the local community. They should join international movements that will help small communities worldwide. They can make international linkages with other grassroots community groups and rural communities. They can contribute to an international movement to develop a moral, just economy. In a global econ-omy, communities must also organize globally to make structural changes.

The Role of the Community Developer

The role of the outside helper, the development expert, in building social capital and community capacity is quite different than the role of the economic devel-oper in the conventional industrial recruitment model of development who comes with plans, feasibility studies, and the questions and the answers for the community. The participatory, collaborative research model better describes the work and process whereby the researcher/educator comes to the community at the invitation of the community to help them ask the questions and find their own answers. She may help facilitate their planning and development work by working as a resource person, sometimes as a teacher, a trainer of skills, and participant in the work. She must assist the group in their analysis and reflection, working to develop critical consciousness and an understanding of the historical background and root causes of their problems and pointing to alternative paths they may choose. The term "animator" describes an impor-tant part of the work, which is to encourage and help uncover creative talents and skills, to help people gain confidence in their own knowledge and abilities to solve their own problems.

As an outside "stranger," she is often needed to negotiate between conflict-ing interests. She becomes a buffer and a sounding board. She can help groups become more inclusive, pushing for more diversity and participation from all segments of the community. She can cross and sometimes break down barriers of class, race, and gender. She can recommend other resource persons when needed and share stories of other communities and link communities. She can be a catalyst for bringing about change. If her home base is a place such as the Highlander Research and Education Center in Tennessee, which has been working with grassroots in Appalachia and the rural South since 1932, she can serve an important role by bringing groups together to share their experiences and link them together to form a social movement. Such organizations remain when the community developer is gone and can continue to provide support, information, and resources to community organizations. If the community developer is from a university, she can often find useful university resources to help with technical problems or make other resources available.

But there are also difficulties if you are connected with a prestigious university. Judith Stacey concludes that the collaborative work of scholars with community subjects can give the appearance of respect and equality, but that it actually masks a deeper, more dangerous form of exploitation. Because the relationship also becomes a personal relationship, "engagement and attachment ... places research subjects at grave risk" of manipulation and betrayal by the ethnographer (Stacey 1991:113).

Participatory research encourages accepting, supportive, friendship, kin-type relationships. If the community development worker also tries to document, analyze, evaluate, and lead the community group to self-evaluation and self-criticism, the community may resist and define her work as betrayal. Yet, the community worker has the inescapable task of interpretation and evaluation. The difficult but necessary task is to involve the community in the analysis/evaluation process.

Researchers discover that the process of collaboration does not allow them full control. However, some of the interventions can be useful, offering practical help and emotional support, a chance to reflect and gain understanding of the process. Researchers can provide comparatively nonjudgmental acceptance and validation, recognition of the importance of what the community is doing. Though dangerous and painful, such collaborative methods provide greater depth and understanding of the process. Participatory development requires participatory evaluation.

A major goal of popular education and participatory research is to develop critical awareness, a critical consciousness that enables the learners to recover their experience, reflect upon it, understand it, and improve it. This requires the ability to be self-critical and to learn from the internal practices and organizational experiences as well as analysis of the outside economic and political system or the specific problem the group is seeking to change. Self-criticism and group criticism of the organizational structure and leadership practices are frequently the most difficult things for both grassroots groups and their leaders to do, and it is similarly difficult for social activist trainers, educators, and facilitators. But it is essential for developing strong, viable groups, good leadership, and democratic practices. Organization building requires the same type of analysis and action based on the research and reflection that the group uses to understand the social problem.

When working in communities, often the outside professionals who come to help the community, although technically qualified for the job, are not fully prepared for collaboration with community people. University and government assistants usually work on community or economic development from the centers of power, which are ruled by technicians, academics, and specialists who engage in development from the top down.

Nelda Daley and Sue Ella Kobak (1990) describe two types of outside helpers in one rural community: the "familiar outsider" and the "technical expert." The familiar outsider is permissive and emphasizes education, developing self-esteem, and critical consciousness. The technical expert emphasizes skill, discipline, and training for the staff and board to compete in the economic development world. This latter type can be interpreted as cold and condescending, a heavy taskmaster who makes the community group feel inadequate. The community learns to work with the technical experts because of the needed skills or the resources they control. The familiar outsider, on the other hand, emphasizes support, but does not leave the group with some of the needed skills.

The two roles complement each other and provide resources the community can use. But working together has to be learned. People and situations do not always fit the textbook examples. Despite the different ways of analysis by the community groups and outside experts, community groups sometimes learn that some of the things they want to do or the skills and understanding they need for certain projects require mutual commitment and cooperation between local members and the outside workers. Outside helpers must always remind themselves that this is not their community and avoid leading the community into confrontations or commitments they cannot deal with. For the outside helper can always escape, leaving the community folks to live with the situation.

When a community movement gets started and receives a lot of media attention, activists, educators, public interest groups, and social change organizations will offer resources and help. Other community groups want to share in the excitement of their activities and learn from it. Colleges want to send students to help or observe. Some helpers become "predators of communities," a term Wendell Berry (1987:52) uses to describe many professionals in our society who are rootless, without community, and who use other communities to fulfill their own needs for community.

Sometimes outsiders find it difficult to leave communities and the projects they have "delivered." They are tempted to remain to "protect" them, becoming watchdogs and adoptive parents. Both paternalistic or maternalistic attitudes can prevent autonomy from flourishing and impair the ability of the communities to take control of their own development.

In community work, everything is not always successful. There are ups and downs, sometimes quite serious, resulting from various crises and difficulties. Most community groups go through stages. At the beginning, there is often a movement based on the struggle for a specific demand. There is great excitement and energy. If the demands are not met early on, many drop out, and only the most dedicated or "hard-headed" stay with the movement for the long haul. Fals Borda describes how community "organizations and movements experience death and resurrection by turns, alternately bursting like a bubble and rooting themselves successfully in the ground like seeds" (1985:40). Death occurs "when the communities give in to the routine of exploitation and submission, when they return to the passivity of old, or forget . . . protest and vigilance" (40–41). They may be co-opted or become tired of fanatical, compulsive, overeager, or demanding outside helpers.

The Steel Ceiling

While grassroots community groups have succeeded in developing creative, innovative programs, they cannot become completely self-sufficient within the present system. It is almost as if they find a steel ceiling that limits how far they can develop. For some the ceiling seems higher, depending upon their resources and ability to manipulate the larger system, but for some of the poorest communities with the fewest resources, the ceiling is very low. The more capacity and social capital they have developed, the more resources they can access, and the higher their ceiling.[1]

Trammell, Virginia, a coal camp owned and operated by a single mine owner family was one of the poorest, most depressed communities in the coalfields. Recently, the family auctioned off the community and sold all the houses. An organized group of residents was able to raise funds to buy a group of the houses and begin a community renewal effort, which included building a water system. But the pervasive poverty and the low level of community resources were such that many residents could not afford the water bills. The basic economic situation went unchanged.

Rural communities find that they can develop community services, rebuild community spirit, and develop educational programs, but they still lack the access to capital and other resources needed to do substantial economic development. They remain outside the mainstream economy and unable to influence economic policies. Major changes in development policies, distribution of development money and resources must occur before rural communities can really develop economic security and substantially improve their income and economic well-being. Entering the political-policy development arena becomes essential. Coalitions must be formed and enough power developed to change the conventional industrial development model.

Dungannon Development Corporation bought land and developed roads and sewage and water systems for the whole community in order to develop a sewing factory. They built the factory and began operation with sixty women workers. They did not have enough capital to make a mistake, and when they underestimated the cost of a contract, the organization went bankrupt. At the same time the county had received a million dollars in development money and used it to buy a piece of land for another industrial park rather than help the community-based development operated by a group of women at the back side of the county.

Rural communities are still part of national and international economies, the agendas of which do not include preserving or reviving small rural communities. Until the needs and agendas of these communities are included in the national and international development plans, community efforts will be stalled and short circuited. Rural communities will continue to be disposable, and the creativity and participation that these grassroots movements encourage and develop will be ignored. That is why communities must also enter the policy arena, change development policies so that this vigor, energy, and social capital can be used to develop socially responsible, democratic, and sustainable communities throughout the world.

Notes

This chapter is based in part on a speech at Samford University, Birmingham, Alabama: "Community Development as Ministry," Dotson Nelson Lecture on Religion in Life, October 10, 1995. "The Role of the Community Developer" section is drawn largely from Hinsdale, Lewis, and Waller (1995). The chapter appeared in an earlier form as "Rebuilding Communities: A 12-Step Recovery Program" in *Appalachian Journal* 34 (Spring/Summer 2007): 316–25.

1. Anne Lewis of Appalshop Media Center, Whitesburg, Kentucky, has developed a video comparing Ivanhoe and Trammell, Virginia, and the community development process. *The Rough Side of the Mountain* (1997) can be obtained from Appalshop.

References

Bellah, Robert N., et al. 1985. *Habits of the Heart: Individualism and Commitment in American Life.* Berkeley: Univ. of California Press.

Berry, Wendell. 1987. *Home Economics: Fourteen Essays.* San Francisco: North Point Press.

Daley, Nelda Knelson, and Sue Ella Kobak. 1990. "The Paradox of the 'Familiar Outsider.'" *Appalachian Journal* 17(3):248–60.

Fals Borda, Orlando. 1985. *Knowledge and People's Power: Lessons with Peasants in Nicaragua, Mexico, and Columbia.* New Delhi: Indian Social Institute.

Gaventa, John. 1991. "Building a World Wide NGO Movement: People, Participation and Policy." Plenary speech to the Interaction Forum, Annapolis, Maryland, May 1.

Gaventa, John, and Helen Lewis. 1989a. "Rural Area Development: Involvement by the People." *Forum for Applied Research and Public Policy* 4(3):58–62.

———. 1989b. *Participatory Education and Grassroots Development: The Case of Rural Appalachia.* East West Center, Jan. 6. Published as Working Paper Series #18. New Market, TN: Highlander Research and Education Center.

Hinsdale, Mary Ann, Helen M. Lewis, and S. Maxine Waller. 1995. *It Comes from the People: Community Development and Local Theology.* Philadelphia: Temple Univ. Press.

Kobak, Sue Ella, and Nina McCormack. 1988. *Developing Feasibility Studies for Community-Based Ventures.* New Market, TN: Economics Education Project, Highlander Research and Education Center.

Lewis, Anne. 1996. *The Rough Side of the Mountain* (video). Whitesburg, KY: Appalshop Films.

Lewis, Helen M. 1996. "Women and Community Development: Growing Individuals and Communities." *Mountain Promise: The Newsletter of the Brushy Fork Institute* (Winter), Berea, KY.

Lewis, H. M., L. Selfridge, J. Merrifield, S. Thrasher, L. Perry, and C. Honeycutt (Eds.). 1986. *Picking Up the Pieces: Women in and out of Work in the Rural South.* New Market, TN: Highlander Research and Education Center.

Lewis, Helen, and John Gaventa. 1988. *The Jellico Handbook: A Teacher's Guide to Community-Based Economics.* New Market, TN: Economics Education Project, Highlander Research and Education Center.

Luttrell, Wendy. 1988. *Claiming What Is Ours: An Economics Experience Workbook.* New Market, TN: Economics Education Project, Highlander Research and Education Center.

MDC. 1986. "Beyond the Buffalo Hunt: Toward a Broader Definition of Economic Development." In *Shadows in the Sunbelt*. Chapel Hill: MDC, Inc.

Putnam, Robert D. 1993. *Making Democracy Work: Civic Traditions in Modern Italy*. Princeton, NY: Princeton Univ. Press.

———. 1995. "Tuning In, Tuning Out: The Strange Disappearance of Social Capital in America." The Ithiel de Sola Pool Lecture, American Political Science Association. *PS, Political Science & Politics* 28(4):664–84.

———. 1997. "Democracy in America at Century's End." In *Democracy's Victory and Crisis,* Axel Hadenius (Ed.). New York: Cambridge Univ. Press. Pp. 27–70.

Stacey, Judith. 1991. "Can There Be a Feminist Ethnography?" In *Women's Words, the Feminist Practice of Oral History,* Sherna Berger Gluck and Daphne Patai (Eds.). New York: Routledge. Pp. 111–20.

Williams, Raymond. 1983. *Towards 2000.* London: Chatto and Windus/Hogarth Press.

The Boundaries
of Participatory Research

Lessons Learned in the
Monacan Indian Nation

Samuel R. Cook

The concept of collaborative ethnography, as developed by Luke Lassiter, is founded on the principle of dialogue and joint participation by ethnographers and those with whom they consult. This form of participatory research addresses the goals identified by the community through research assisted by specialists. Cook explores his use of this form of participatory research with the Monacan Indian Nation in Virginia. It has taken him from a focus on basic research on Monacan history to collaboration on Monacan and greater American Indian goals in higher education at Virginia Tech University. Cook reminds us that, when taken seriously, the principles of participatory research lead the specialist to think differently about research agendas and career paths. In this case, collaboration results in benefits for both the tribe and the ethnographer.

On a hot Friday afternoon in early June 1996, I walked into an establishment called "The Indian Store," precisely six miles north of Lynchburg on U.S. Highway 29. So far, so good. I looked for an old acquaintance who was about to potentially make or break my fieldwork plans for the next few months. I had met George Whitewolf three years earlier in Tucson, Arizona. He was actually my advisor's best friend, and I was just beginning the early stages of my Ph.D. in cultural studies. George was then a prominent member of the Monacan Indian tribal council, and through my advisor's brokering he agreed to help me gain entry into the Monacan Nation to conduct ethnographic fieldwork for my dissertation.

George had asked me to meet him at his Native American arts store at 1 P.M. My apprehensions guided me there on time, and after George's wife Tracy called their house to remind him that he was supposed to meet me, George was prompt in keeping his word. He also wasted no time in subjecting me to open (albeit appropriate) scrutiny.

"Now, what exactly do you want to do here?"

I explained that I wanted to engage in ethnographic fieldwork by immersing myself in the community to the extent that anyone would allow me to do so, and to collect oral histories in the process. I explained that for the purposes of my dissertation I wanted to look comparatively at "variables of colonialism" within different Appalachian communities.

"You aren't going to be using words like that," George interjected. "You and I know what you're talking about, and how important it is, but a lot of these folks, especially the old folks, aren't going to know what the hell you mean by colonialism."

Of course, I knew very well that I was going to have to communicate in a profoundly different way in the Monacan community than I would in a graduate seminar on the political economy of Indian Country. However, I also understood that George was providing a sort of metanarrative concerning my entire experience. It was not just a matter of communicating with the Monacan people in their own style, but also a matter of understanding the historical forces that would complicate that process—forces that have often set certain limits on the extent to which non-Monacans have been truly accepted within the community.

Immediately following George's sage proclamation, we went to Bear Mountain, the heart of the Monacan community in Amherst County. As we rode down Father Judge Road toward the base of the mountain, George marveled at the approaching spectacle. "Now watch," he said. "From a distance you can see what a huge mountain it is, but as you get closer it just seems to get smaller and smaller. It seems so unthreatening and inviting. It's the most beautiful thing I've ever seen in my life."

We were heading to the tribal headquarters at Bear Mountain, where the tribe maintained a retreat cabin for tribal members and guests, usually visiting for the annual homecoming. This was to be my home for the next several months. Indeed, it was an impressive facility for an anthropologist expecting to rough it in the field. I thought that it was a tremendous convenience. George simply stated that he wanted me to get the true feel for the place. Some years later he laughed and admitted that he had arranged for me to stay up there to put me to the test. "I figured you were like all the rest of them academics and wouldn't make it in this community. But you hung in there and made it."

In this essay, I reflect on my eight years of involvement with the Monacan Indian Nation, both as a researcher and as a friend. My point is not so much to articulate a theoretical approach to participatory research, or to present an original model to such ends. Rather, I argue the obvious but easily forgotten point that participatory research must hinge on the agendas of the communities with which the academic researcher works. In a broader sense, then, this is a case study in cultural competency and the difficulties and rewards of participating in community endeavors. While my long-term work with the Monacans has been more concerned with community empowerment than development, I have been privileged to witness and take part in the redirection of older community institutions and practices to address contemporary economic issues.

Even the most open-minded of us in higher education have a propensity for letting our enthusiasm and ideals obscure the real concerns and goals of the grassroots communities with whom we work, thereby limiting our contributions in the long run. In working with the Monacans, I learned from the outset that my research agenda not only hinged on community support, but would to a large extent be determined by the community according to what the tribal council and its constituents regarded as critical and pertinent. After many lessons in humility and nearly a decade of experience, I have seen my research and methodologies evolve in a manner that prioritizes local concerns while embracing goals and issues of national and global significance. This is due, in large part, to the Monacans' position at the vanguard of American Indian political activism in Virginia and beyond. Ultimately, my role in this has become to simply serve as one of many agents linking indigenous social capital to outside resources (Flora et al. 2003).

My Initial Goals

As George Whitewolf said, I hung in there, but not without trial and enlightenment. The day after I arrived, George brought me to a community gathering at the home of Diane Johns Shield. Diane had only recently moved to the community—her family moved away before she was born for reasons stated below—but she had become such a selfless and active participant in tribal affairs (in less than a year she had amassed an incredible archive of tribal historical material and had initiated a community food bank), that she already wielded an impressive amount of respect from within the community. Possibly because she had had to contend with the status of "outsider" herself, Diane was very gracious and generous in helping me secure my footing in the community. However, her time was limited, and for much of those first days I had to fend for myself in community interaction, often through trial and error.

I had come to gather "raw data" for my dissertation, which ultimately formed the core of my book, *Monacans and Miners* (Cook 2000). As a native of the coalfields of southern West Virginia and Southwest Virginia, I was fueled by the type of political consciousness and idealism that has sustained the High-lander Research and Education Center for so many years. Indeed, although my literature review and methodology were much more complex, the philo-sophical model for my research was profoundly influenced by Friere's *Pedagogy of the Oppressed* (1970) and Gaventa's *Power and Powerlessness* (1980). However, like anyone who adheres to ideas, it is easy to enter the field with a certain degree of naïveté. Fortunately, I was able to transform mine into a positive learning experience, and to develop a more flexible approach to participatory research.

My initial plan was to conduct a comparative study of political economies in the Appalachian region through ethnographic and historical analyses of the experiences of two different communities—the Monacan Indian community in the Blue Ridge Mountains of Amherst County, Virginia, and a coal mining community in Wyoming County, West Virginia. I intended for my work to benefit the communities concerned, but in retrospect, I am not sure that I had given much thought to how this research would benefit either community beyond the possibility of making each of them more visible to an academic audience. However, the Monacans made it abundantly clear that I would have to adhere to two practical preconditions if I was to work within their com-munity: first, my research would be subject to review by the tribal council before publication; second, I had to make a good faith effort to conduct research that would aid the tribe in its pursuit of federal recognition. As I discuss below, these preconditions were conceived within a peculiar and turbulent historical context that defines the Monacan people as a unique ethnic entity. The param-eters within which I conducted my research, in turn, helped to shape my own understanding of the nature of participatory research, and have prompted me to pursue more collaborative, if not praxis-oriented, endeavors.

Historical Context

Most scholars who advocate a model of cultural competency for field researchers accentuate the importance of reflexivity in coming to understand contrasting cultural values and norms while keeping one's own cultural biases in check (Davies 1999; Lynch and Hanson 1998). This model has gained increasing visibility in the emergent field of collaborative ethnography, discussed later in this chapter. However, my conscious effort to hone my understanding of Monacan norms and values required a deeper understanding of the community's historical experiences vis-à-vis state and local policymakers, and of how these experiences continue to profoundly influence the way in which Monacans interact differentially with outsiders.

George Whitewolf had informed me, and I quickly confirmed, that the Monacan people were bound to be polite but extremely reticent in dealing with anyone who wanted to study the community. This reticence was not unwarranted.

The present-day Monacan Tribe of Amherst County, Virginia, is evolved from a once vast alliance of Siouan-speaking tribes that inhabited a territory occupying most of Virginia's piedmont in the east and spanning across the Blue Ridge, possibly as far west as the Big Sandy River in Kentucky at its peak (Hantman 1990).[1] From the time that Captain John Smith made contact with Tidewater tribes to the east in 1607, to the inception of the American republic, the history of most Monacan-allied peoples was one of tribal diasporas and continually shifting sociopolitical configurations. In fact, by the 1740s, most of the known Monacan allies had migrated northward and become incorporated into the Cayuga Nation of the Iroquois Confederacy (Dixon 2002; Hale 1885:1–3). Those who remained in the vicinity of present-day Amherst County were descended from Saponis and Tutelos (Monacan-affiliated tribes), and possibly some migrants from weakened Algonquian tribes of the Virginia tidewater (Cook 2000:51–53).[2] These Indians evidently made a concerted effort to enclave themselves in the remote Tobacco Row Mountains (a front range of the Blue Ridge) in order to avoid extensive contact with Euro-Americans. By 1750, a core community was present around Bear Mountain whose residents were the ancestors of the contemporary Monacan Nation.

As with most indigenous groups in the Southeast, contact with Euro-Americans was ultimately prolonged and often yielded both interracial tensions and unions. Prior to the Civil War this meant that Indians in Virginia and other Southern states were most often classified as "free people of color," which meant that they were not slaves, but barely citizens (Cook 2000:56–60; McLeRoy and McLeRoy 1993). Although the legal status of "free colored" theoretically became moot with the emancipation of slaves, Indians in Virginia found that the race-based legal structures of Virginia were creatively designed to deprive them of the right to self-identify as indigenous peoples, much less to be acknowledged as such in census data and courts of record. After the Civil War, miscegenation laws (laws prohibiting interracial marriage and often defining criteria for racial classification) became much more rigidly enforced in those states where they existed. Undoubtedly, this trend reflected fears of challenges to the status quo that would come following the (theoretical) enfranchisement of people of color (Saks 1988). It also coincided with the advent of the eugenics movement, which found one of its most dedicated proponents in Walter A. Plecker, director of the Virginia Office of Vital Statistics from 1912 to 1945.

Plecker, a physician by training, was obsessed with the notion of racial purity and eliminating or confining "inferior" human stocks. He single-handedly drafted and successfully lobbied for the passage of the 1924 Virginia Racial Integrity Law—possibly the most explicit articulation of miscegenation law to date—which essentially stated that there were only two "races" resident to Virginia: "White" and "Negro." Plecker was well aware that this would effectively make it illegal for anyone native to Virginia to claim to be "Indian." He devised a so-called scientific method for identifying people of color based on the occurrence of their surnames on nineteenth-century vital records—in other words, on records where Virginia Indians were most often legally classified as "colored" or "free colored." Plecker frequently enforced this system by hand-altering scores of vital records—notably, birth certificates—that had originally classified individuals as "Indian," to read "Negro" (Cook 2000:85–108). This meticulous but inherently flawed system of racial classification is best characterized by J. David Smith, who aptly refers to it as "documentary genocide."[3]

Although Plecker's policy targeted and negatively impacted all Virginia tribes, he seems to have developed a particular vendetta against the Monacans, who were the subject of countless hateful letters and memoranda penned by Plecker. Unfortunately, his campaign of "documentary genocide" provided a convenient excuse for local planters to exploit Indian labor as a means of compensating for postbellum economy.

Whereas Amherst County had been a major producer of tobacco prior to the Civil War, after the war many local planters turned toward a more cost-effective orchard economy on the slopes of the Tobacco Row Mountains to cut their losses. In the process they moved into lands that many Monacans lived on as virtual squatters (their historic status as "free colored" obscuring any indigenous title to the land), often pressing Indians into a quasi-feudal form of tenant farming. Monacans effectively found themselves integrated at the bottom of a local caste system. Not only were they providing cheap, if not virtually free labor for local orchard owners and farmers, but they were not allowed to attend county schools until 1963—not even those established for African Americans (Cook 2000:65–67; Houck 1984:95–104).

The Monacans' predicament in the early twentieth century was not simply a reflection of the local political economy but was reinforced by external forces with an international reach. By the 1920s the eugenics movement reached its zenith in America and Europe. The Unites States Supreme Court had essentially condoned eugenic policies by upholding the right of states to sterilize those deemed "unfit" (*Buck v. Bell*, 274 US 200 [1927]). The subject of this infamous decision, Carrie Buck, was a poor white woman from Amherst County who had given birth to a child out of wedlock after being raped, but was nonetheless deemed "unfit" (Smith and Nelson 1989). However, a year earlier an internationally distributed booked titled *Mongrel Virginians* (Estabrook and McDougal 1926) was published that had a direct and devastating impact on the Indians in the same county. Largely due to Plecker's public fixation on the Monacan people, eugenicists Arthur Estabrook and Ivan McDougal came to the community to conduct research on a group of people whom they termed the "WIN tribe"—a weak effort to protect the anonymity of Monacans through an acronym for "White, Indian, Negro." After gaining the trust of people in the community, the eugenicists produced the aforementioned book whose title speaks for itself. The report essentially characterized the Monacan people of being a chronically and irreversibly retarded community as a result of years of interracial unions. Needless to say, the Monacan people were deeply offended by this work and still remember it with extreme bitterness (Cook 2000:93–94, 106–7). To be sure, the publication of the book and the context within which it was produced resulted in a formidable obstacle to any subsequent scholars—myself included—hoping to do work in the Monacan community.

Gaining Entry

Elsewhere I have discussed the complex process and convergence of forces that enabled the Monacan community to break the bonds of colonialism and selectively assert its autonomy as a tribe (Cook 2000:116–33, 2002). Suffice it to say, the assumption of autonomy has hastened community vigilance in determining who may conduct research in the community.

Actually, local pediatrician and historian Peter W. Houck must be credited with helping to break the ice for contemporary scholars working with the Monacan community. In the early 1980s Houck, who had a number of Monacan children as patients, became concerned by the paucity of recorded historical material on the origins of the Amherst Indians (as they were known prior to the mid-1980s) and began to collect material linking the community to the "Monacan Confederacy" of precolonial times.[4] Houck's resulting book, *Indian Island in Amherst County* (1984), and supporting research provided a foundation for the Monacans' successful campaign for state recognition as an Indian tribe in 1989. Nonetheless, Houck's work did not erase the memory of *Mongrel Virginians*. In fact, whether he intended it or not, the practical manifestations of his book (namely, helping the tribe to secure state recognition) probably inspired the tribal council to set certain parameters within which outsiders may conduct research in the community.

Long before I arrived in the Monacan community I submitted a formal request to the tribal council asking for permission to conduct my research in the community. While this had not been an institutionalized practice for the council, my gesture was well received and set a precedent for subsequent researchers in the community. The tribal council granted me permission to work within the community with two major stipulations: (1) the council would have the right to review any of the research for inaccuracies and potentially damaging assertions; and, (2) I must make a good faith effort to use my research to support the tribe in its campaign for federal recognition as an Indian nation.

As I have argued elsewhere, the historical context of racial politics in Virginia in the late nineteenth and early twentieth centuries converged with indigenous experiences with these policies to essentially forge a praxis-oriented ethic among anthropologists and other researchers working with tribes in the state—an ethic that has demanded that we become, and that our work reflects our role as, Indian rights advocates (Cook 2003). More often than not, the tribes in the state have reinforced this ethic by placing certain stipulations on our research, especially in the wake of the eugenics era. However, this has never been a simple matter of gaining the approval of tribal councils. In my case, I had to run the polite but reserved gauntlet of community scrutiny to demonstrate my sincerity and commitment to honoring the people with whom I wanted to work.

Every anthropologist has a story concerning her/his climactic moment in gaining entry and acceptance in a specific community or group. While some are more exciting than others, all tend to be reflective accounts on what the researcher did right or wrong. In my case, the defining moment came about two weeks after arriving in the community. Although I had been invited to many community events as a matter of courtesy, most people were very generous in dealing with me but politely stand-offish. I probably made a somewhat positive impression among a certain segment of the community by making it a point to attend church services at St. Paul's Episcopal Mission. The church itself is no longer the lone focal point of spiritual activity in the community (if it ever was) because many Monacans have pursued a revitalization of indigenous spiritual traditions. However, the 7.5-acre mission complex is now the tribal center, and only the church building remains under the stewardship of the Episcopal diocese. Even attending after-church lunches could be awkward, for there was plenty of food but little conversation for one with a research agenda. I dealt with this by trying to keep my research agenda in the background and simply interacting with people in the community as a human being.

In fact, my climactic moment of gaining community acceptance was quite unintentional on my part—that is, I did not mean for the gesture to advance my research agenda. One evening in mid June of 1996, as I sat in the retreat cabin on the hill above the tribal center, the tail end of an unseasonable tornado rushed down the hollow. I heard a sequence of loud cracks below, and after the storm cleared I rushed to the bottom of the hill where I found Chief Kenneth Branham and a couple of other tribal members assessing the damage. Two large sycamore trees had been uprooted, doing some damage to the roof of the church, blocking thoroughfares on the tribal grounds, and creating a potential flash flood hazard in the creek beside the tribal center. Chief Branham decided that the problem could wait until morning. The next morning I went down and started clearing branches and debris from the creek, cutting larger branches with a crosscut saw that I had found in a tool shed. By 9 A.M. a few more men were on hand. This time, they were surprisingly gregarious. By noon, one of them who had seemed most suspicious of me had volunteered to give me an interview without my having asked.

Although that was a pivotal moment in my relationship with the Monacan community, both as a researcher and as a friend, I have had to continually demonstrate a willingness to get my hands dirty. I have also found that my acceptance in the community has not made my research subject to review and restrictions, but has garnered certain expectations from the Monacan people regarding my research. Acceptance is tantamount to bearing the responsibilities of being a part of a community, and my work with the Monacans on their terms has been at once humbling and enlightening. My entry and acceptance in the community necessitated a more reflexive approach to my research, and ultimately facilitated the evolution of my methodology and theoretical approach to practical problems toward a truly collaborative approach to ethnographic and related research. Interestingly, this transformation has allowed me and others to address multiple agendas while it evolved out of a concerted effort to aid the Monacans in one of the tribe's single most important goals—the pursuit and attainment of federal recognition as an Indian Nation.

Manifestations: Multiple Agendas and Collaborative Research

When an Indian tribe is federally recognized, it is acknowledged as being legally subject to the privileges, restrictions, and responsibilities of an anomalous political entity that is frequently—if somewhat misleadingly—referred to as a "domestic dependent nation."[5] This means that tribes theoretically enjoy a political status higher than states and are therefore often immune to state jurisdiction within the external boundaries of recognized Indian lands (reservations, allotments held in trust, and so forth) within certain constraints. This also means that tribes may assume and exercise a great deal of autonomy over controlling internal affairs. However, this tenuous sovereign status has frequently been the subject of inconsistent interpretation by federal authorities, particularly the federal courts, and has historically resulted in severe restrictions to tribal autonomy (see generally, Deloria and Lytle 1983; Wilkins 1997). Be that as it may, federally recognized tribes do have the ability to exercise greater jurisdictional, economic, and political autonomy within a legal framework that is not available to nonfederally recognized tribes.

The concept of federal recognition or acknowledgement of Indian tribes has its antecedent in pre-1870 channels for federal-tribal relations, such as treaties and executive orders. These were fundamentally "cognitive" forms of recognition based on Euro-American conceptions of "legitimate" Indians (Anderson 1978; Quinn 1990:351–63). With the cessation of Indian treaty making in 1871 (16 St. 566), policies toward American Indians vacillated between extremes of integration and segregation, further complicating the sovereign status of tribes and obscuring those lacking recognition. The first of these was a consolidated policy of assimilation (as embodied in the General Allotment Act, which sanctioned partitioning of reservations into parcels of private property 24 St. 388), which came to an abrupt halt during the New Deal with a consolidated federal policy aimed at tribal reorganization (as sanctioned through the 1935 Indian Reorganization Act, 48 St. 984, which sought to preserve the lands and cultures of previously recognized tribes). Riding the wave of post–World War II conservatism, federal policy makers essentially resurrected assimilation policy in articulating a new policy of termination (see HCR 108-67 St. B132), which sought to "emancipate" the Indian and to end the political relationship between tribes and the federal government once and for all. Thus, legal channels for recognizing previously unacknowledged tribes ceased to be a federal concern. By the mid-twentieth century, numerous American Indian communities existed who had never been federally recognized for a variety of reasons. Some simply lacked treaties, agreements, or other legal documents marking their legal existence in the eyes of the law. Those who had been parties to such agreements under colonial rule—such as most Virginia tribes—were most often perceived as being too weak to pose real threats to colonists, and thus were not treated as political entities. This was especially true in the East, where tribes such as the Monacans later fell prey to a variety of racially skewed policies that would further obscure their legal existence—policies such as Virginia's eugenic campaign of documentary genocide (Cook 2002:95–100).

Following a resurgence of American Indian political activity in the 1970s, numerous nonfederally recognized groups mounted pressure on the federal government for the acknowledgment of their sovereign status as tribal nations. While Congress was already vested with the power to acknowledge tribes through legislation (and, in fact, has set the new precedent by acknowledging various tribes of Maine in 1980 [94 St. 1785]), the Bureau of Indian Affairs (BIA) followed suit by establishing mandatory criteria for tribal recognition under this administrative agency. These included a tribe's ability to prove its existence as a distinct tribal entity from "historical times" to present; a historically identifiable tribal land base; the continuous existence of a tribal government exercising "authority" over tribal constituents, however defined; a constitution or similar organizing document; a membership roll meeting guidelines acceptable to the secretary of the interior (a reflection, in part, of stipulations produced in the 1930s that imposed federal "blood quantum" requirements for acknowledging individuals as "Indian"); and the condition that tribal members did not belong to any other tribe (25 CFR 83.7 [a]–[g], 1991). In 1994 the BIA loosened its requirements to emphasize proof of a tribe's existence as a distinct and continuous American Indian community since 1900, and to highlight the historical existence of a "distinct community" rather than the preservation of a land base consistently identified as "Indian" ("Procedures for Establishing That an American Indian Group Is a Tribe" 1994). Nonetheless, the burden of proof is always on the tribe, and scholars working with tribes east of the Mississippi River often find that their cooperation on federal recognition projects has become an almost universal precondition to their acceptance in the community (see e.g., Blu 2001; Campisi 1991; Greenbaum 1985; Paredes 1992).

Although the political preconditions for my entry into the Monacan community were not unique, the circumstances under which many Monacans had decided to pursue federal recognition were. In turn, these circumstances and interests had a profound impact on the course of my research. But before I discuss these circumstances and their outcome, it is important to note that although a number of anthropologists have been involved in varying degrees as consultants for Virginia Indians seeking federal recognition (besides myself, Jeffrey L. Hantman at the University of Virginia has lent his support to the Monacans), most of us have done comparatively little in light of the degree of work that tribal historians themselves have put into the process. This is largely a reflection of a contemporary, if not unprecedented current of political solidarity and activism among Virginia's Indian nations.

While Indian tribes typically pursue federal recognition on an individual basis, since early 2000 six of Virginia's eight Indian nations have taken a most unusual approach to their common goal of attaining federal acknowledgment—they have sought to secure it through a single act of Congress. Several bills have been introduced and died in Congress, largely due to fears among conservative congressmen that federal recognition for Virginia Indians might bring Class III casino-style gaming to the state (Hardin 2000a, 2000b, 2000c). In response to these frustrating obstacles the six tribes formed a lobbying organization known as the Virginia Indian Tribal Alliance for Life (VITAL), retaining an attorney to guide their campaign, and ultimately striking a compromise with influential policymakers such as Senators George Allen and John Warner (both Republican) in which the tribes agreed to legislative language restricting their capacity to pen gaming operations (http://www.vitalva.org 2004).[6] While anthropologists Danielle Moreti-Langholtz (William and Mary) and Helen C. Rountree (emeritus, Old Dominion University) have served as scholarly spokespeople for the current campaign, much of the research has been conducted and organized by tribal leaders and historians themselves. Indeed, scholars such as myself spend most of our time in this endeavor writing letters of support. Remarkably, the current rendering of the recognition bill (Senate Bill 1423) has matriculated beyond the Senate Committee on Indian Affairs and awaits discussion on the floor.

On a strictly political level, my advocacy of the Monacan people in their pursuit of federal recognition has moved slightly beyond civic-minded letter writing or the drafting of memoranda to be filed away in the corner of congressional committee halls. Although I would be the first to question my right to be called a Monacan "expert," the publication of my book (Cook 2000) did provide the Monacans with a level of visibility among an international (and predominantly scholarly) audience, which, at the very least, helped to facilitate a more serious consideration of the Monacans' cultural and political existence from many audiences. I also offered a scholarly assessment of argument for the sovereign status of the tribe, federal recognition notwithstanding (Cook 2002). However, I believe that my most important contribution to the Monacan community came through the dialogues concerning federal recognition—dialogues that continue to shape my approach to research in a way that strives to place community voices and interpretations of reality at the forefront, and my own assessment of community affairs in the background.

Indeed, the political implications or manifestations of the pursuit of federal recognition are of secondary concern to many of the Monacan people. One of these is Phyllis Hicks, who was instrumental in helping the tribe to secure state recognition in 1989.[7] Inspired by Houck's research on the Monacan people, Phyllis successfully spearheaded this campaign in the late 1980s, largely under the auspices of the St. Paul's Vestry. However, she did not think of it as a political battle, and she expressed strong reservations concerning the prospect of federal recognition: "In a way I think it would be great for our people, and in a way I don't . . . Federal recognition scares me because I think—I'm afraid it's going to change our people . . . I'm at the age now where I don't want to see us change. I want us to grow, but I don't want us to change from who we are" (Hicks 1996). In fact, most of the Monacan people concur that the greatest benefit of *pursuing* federal recognition has been the necessary research that is helping to fill in the gaps of tribal history. Former Council Chief John L. Johns, who also chaired the federal recognition research committee for a number of years, added a crescendo to these sentiments: "We are who we are because that's who we are. And nobody has to tell us that's who we are. The only people that can really give us sovereignty are ourselves" (Johns 1996). These words, and my participation in dialogues where such sentiments provided views contrary to what one might expect of the constituents of a tribe pursuing federal recognition, helped me to pursue a more reflexive and collaborative approach to my research, and guided me toward becoming active in recent theoretical and methodological debates in anthropology.

In theory, modern anthropology has always espoused models for interpreting culture that reflect an *emic*, or "inside" point of view. However, approaches have varied over the years and have frequently been critiqued for obscuring the true emic perspective because the traditional authority—the anthropologist—has assumed the ultimate ethnographic authority through her/his *interpretation* of culture (see, e.g., Clifford 1988; Geertz 1973). In recent years, a growing number of anthropologists have sought to perfect a *collaborative* model for anthropological research that "fully embraces dialogue in both ethnographic practice *and* ethnographic writing" (Lassiter 1998:10). Such an

Samuel R. Cook 101

ethnography strives to be "multivocal" (Tedlock 1995) insofar as anthropologists attempt to use *dialogue* with members of the communities on which they focus as the mainstay of text in an effort to check the anthropologist's interpretation of reality (see, e.g., Lawless 1992; Tedlock 1983). Recently, Luke E. Lassiter (2003, 2005) has issued a call for a collaborative ethnographic practice that is truly *public* application—one "that has among its purposes and goals the need to place the people with whom we work above the discipline, and above generalizing, hierarchical discourses" (Lassiter 2003:6).

In fact, this principle has virtually become a precondition for scholars working with Virginia Indians, as recent political trends among the state's tribes have beckoned an unprecedented solidarity in reclaiming their respective histories and the right to articulate these historical experiences on their own terms. The current legislative campaign for federal recognition would seem to mark the focal point of this movement, but there are several important corollaries. First, the founding of the Virginia Indian Tribal Alliance for Life (VITAL) in 2000 has prompted unified efforts to advance important goals other than, but related to, federal recognition and sovereignty. Among these goals is the improvement of educational opportunities for Virginia Indians, who were for so long denied access to even the most rudimentary public education programs. Clearly, Virginia's tribal leaders and activists see the holistic link between education and tribal autonomy and have called on scholars and institutions within the state to respond accordingly. Responses have been diverse and positive. William and Mary anthropologist Danielle Moretti-Langholtz, for instance initiated a long-term collaborative oral history project with Virginia Indians that has so far resulted in a highly acclaimed book on Virginia tribes that is geared toward the general public (Waugaman and Moretti-Langholtz 2000), and a video on Virginia Indian history and culture that accentuates the contemporary existence of these tribes (Moretti-Langholtz 2002; http://www.wm.edu/airc). Likewise, University of Virginia Archaeologist Jeffrey Hantman has worked collaboratively with the Monacan people to reclaim and repatriate ancestral remains on numerous occasions. He has subsequently presented at conferences and authored collaborative works with Monacan representatives (e.g., Hantman, Wood, and Shields 2000).

Following the cue of my indigenous and nonindigenous colleagues, I used copresenting, researching, and authoring with Monacan community members as an entry point for collaborative work (e.g., Cook, Johns, and Wood 2005). However, my roll as a collaborative researcher and academic activist has taken some rather unexpected turns in relation to the waxing tide of Virginia Indian activism over the past few years. Significantly, the Monacans have been at the forefront of these movements that have influenced the direction of much of my research and outreach endeavors. This became abundantly clear in the summer of 1999 when the Monacan tribal council sent a letter to Virginia Tech President Paul Torgersen and several other key administrators and state legislators suggesting that Virginia's land grant institution consider establishing an American Indian studies program. In that letter, the Monacans provided a basic blueprint for a program that would not only educate the general public on American Indian history, cultures, and issues in a culturally sensitive way, but one that would—first and foremost—exist in service to indigenous peoples. They envisioned a program that would not treat Indians as subjects, but as partners and colleagues in collaborative efforts to develop curricula, to engage the state's (and ultimately other) indigenous communities in joint ventures that would bolster their cultural, political, and economic autonomy, and to create a wider awareness and space in the academic canon for the legitimacy and value of indigenous knowledge (Monacan Indian Nation 1999).

I was not unaware of the Monacan Council's intention to send this inquiry, since various tribal members had contacted my colleague Jeff Corntassel (Cherokee) in Virginia Tech's Political Science Department and myself requesting that we attempt to initiate the development of such a program. However, as junior faculty at an institution about to experience a major budget deficit, we found ourselves lacking the influence to beckon a positive response to the idea. Interestingly, the Monacan letter arrived on the president's desk at a time when the university was being subjected to intense scrutiny over diversity issues. Thus, coincidence or not, the administration opted to act immediately. In the fall of 1999 Provost Peggy Maeszaros organized a meeting between Monacan representatives and interested administrators, faculty, and staff at Virginia Tech to discuss the Monacans' query. The end result was strong encouragement from the administration to proceed with development of the program with one significant stipulation—it must be done without additional resources from the university.

The group had very little difficulty in determining that the program should be located in the Center for Interdisciplinary Studies (CIS), a unit within the College of Arts and Sciences that serves as a home for several ethnic studies and humanistic interdisciplinary programs, including Black Studies, Women's Studies, Religious Studies, and Humanities. While none of these programs constitutes an independent department, each offers minors and provisional majors under the degree program in Interdisciplinary Studies.[8] Theoretically, this unit also serves as a point of incubation for programs that might be well situated to become independent departments.

At that point I was serving as a non–tenure track instructor in CIS, teaching Appalachian Studies courses. However, I was also the only faculty member within that department with an extensive knowledge of regional indigenous cultures and issues, and by the fall of 2000 the coordinatorship of the developing program fell on me. Elsewhere I have discussed in detail the process of bringing Virginia Tech's American Indian Studies program to light (Cook 2004). For the purposes of this venue, I would like to emphasize the collaborative nature of this process—a collaborative venture in which my colleagues on the American Indian Studies Steering Committee worked, and continue to work, with the Monacans and other tribes in the state and region as *colleagues* rather than research subjects. Consequently, I must credit the Monacans and other tribes to a large extent with defining the parameters and mission of our program.

While American Indian Studies is by no means immune to the intense criticism to which most interdisciplinary fields in the humanities and social sciences are subjected, the field has come of age since the emergence of the first professed program in the 1960s. The most salient programs and scholars in the field recognize that such programs must be holistic in orientation. They must recognize the validity of traditional tribal knowledge while seeking to reconcile the tension between these and traditional academic worldviews; they must be fueled by interaction with tribal communities, not merely as acts of outreach to communities, but through the formation of meaningful partnerships between these communities and academic institutions; and they must be devoted to the common goal of nation-building—one that applies all modes of knowledge to the enhancement of the ability of tribal communities to articulate their own concerns and to manage their own affairs as sovereign Indian nations (Champagne and Stauss 2002; Mihesuah 1998). Without being as bold as to suggest that we have developed a model that has succeeded in advancing the aforementioned goals, I would point out that the philosophy behind such a model is at the very essence of the initial mandate for our program as outlined in the letter from the Monacan Tribal Council. Likewise, the Monacans' substantive involvement in the development of the program was not only a reflection of our institution's willingness to collaborate with indigenous peoples, but of the Monacan's understanding of the relationship between sovereignty and education. Indeed, Monacan leaders have been at the forefront of political campaigns and events that concern all tribes in Virginia, and frequently those beyond. As coordinator for American Indian Studies, I found that the Monacans' influence on my research agenda would not only guide my work toward practical ends, but also reflect a knowledge of the interrelatedness of tribal concerns and goals in the state.

My colleagues and I realized early on that we had to get all of the tribes in Virginia involved as partners and colleagues in our program (and eventually, to move out in concentric circles and involve other tribes in the same manner). With the help of our Monacan colleagues—notably Council Chief John L. Johns and Tribal Director for Social and Economic Development Karenne Wood—we began to foster diplomatic ties with these communities. Thus, in the spring of 2001 we hosted the first Virginia Indian Nations Summit on Higher Education (VINSHE). The purpose of this gathering was to break the ice—to dissolve barriers between our institution and the state's Indian nations (many of whom were openly suspicious of any state institution in light of Virginia's previously mentioned track record of dealing with indigenous peoples). We invited representatives from each of the eight tribes to come to our campus at our expense and to engage in two days of informal and open dialogue. Although many tribal representatives were initially reserved, they were not afraid to express their concerns and to adopt a wait-and-see approach. However, the end result was overwhelmingly positive. An important component of the summit—one that has become a recurring part of this annual gathering—was a public forum called "What It Means to Be a Virginia Indian in the 21st Century." During this session tribal representatives were invited to speak from the heart about their lives, cultures, and histories, and to convey to the general public what they thought was truly important to know about Virginia Indians and indigenous people in general. This forum gradually evolved into a frank conversation between tribal representatives and audience members, and constituted a remarkable ethnographic moment.

Besides opening an important channel for dialogue between Virginia Tech and the state's Indian nations, the first VINSHE yielded two important and very positive results. First, we established a standing tribal advisory board consisting of representatives from all of the tribes in the state, as well as a few at-large members from other tribes. Members of the advisory board serve as liaisons between their respective nations and Virginia Tech while exercising a certain degree of oversight in monitoring activities directed by the American Indian Studies program. It has not been easy to sponsor this group and the joint initiatives that we have pursued with our advisors, especially since most of our funding has come from external grants or from hard-sought, internal soft monies. Likewise, many of our tribal advisors are active members of VITAL and must devote much of their time to lobbying activities. However, all of our advisors devote a tremendous amount of their time, energy, and money to our program, even if it is spread thin. In fact, they see the development of this program as complementary to, and part of, their larger political agenda. Indeed, the pressure these advisors have exerted—as a group and as individuals—on university officials has constituted a crucial element in sustaining our program thus far. Indeed, without their support our program would be nothing more than a struggling academic minor at best.

A second important initiative stemming from the first VINSHE is the Virginia Indian Pre-College Initiative (VIPCI). At that first summit, tribal representatives expressed a qualified enthusiasm in assessing our desire to see more of their youth enter higher education. The main concern was that while higher education may empower individuals, as with Western education in general, it had historically been a primary means of destroying indigenous communities. The representatives at the summit insisted that if Virginia Tech (and other state instructions) works with tribal communities in promoting higher education, it should do so in a manner that recognizes the importance and legitimacy of indigenous knowledge. By the same token, they were concerned that while some of their students needed long-term guidance in preparing for college, all should be encouraged to make the most of whatever education they receive, regardless of whether they attend college or not. Thus, the VIPCI emerged as a two-tiered mentoring program in which Virginia Indian youth in grades eight through twelve are invited to our campus two weekends each year, along with parents and elders, to take part in specific programs that exhibit the possibilities afforded through education. Such programs have included tours of our university's state-of-the-art virtual reality facility, natural resource management hikes at a remote wildlife preserve maintained by Virginia Tech, and an indigenous art exhibition. The presence of elders is crucial to this program, because their presence conveys a message to the youth—namely, that the university values their knowledge and input. Indeed, these elders have been both enthusiastic participants and substantive critics of our program. At least five Virginia Indian students have entered Virginia Tech after having taken part in the VIPCI since its inception two years ago—a rather impressive ratio given the small number of Virginia Indians and the historical odds they have faced in pursuing higher education. In fact, one of these was the first Monacan student to ever attend Virginia Tech. While some might argue that the VIPCI is an outreach program that belongs in a nonacademic unit, we regard it as an integral part of the American Indian Studies mission, regardless of whether participants are involved in the minor program or not.

Our latest initiative—one that was conceptualized during the second VINSHE—is tentatively referred to as "Virginia Indian Nations 101" (VIN 101). This is a multifaceted project intended to provide various media through which Virginia Indians can educate both a general public and educators on Virginia

Indian cultures, histories, and realities. In the future, we hope to develop summer symposia for school teachers in which Virginia Indians and other indigenous representatives serve as the primary instructors in collaboration with scholars who have worked closely with these tribes for years. Currently, we are working with the tribal advisory board to develop a uniform set of standards for public school educators to follow in teaching about Virginia and other American Indians. Our immediate goal is to develop a set of textbook/binders for school teachers at various levels, with sections for each tribe in the state containing information prepared in collaboration with (or by) members of each tribe. Finally, we expect to have an online course in place by the fall of 2008 that will be taught by Virginia Indians but will afford school teachers necessary credit for their careers.

If, as Ivan Light has suggested, social capital is "a store of value that facilitates action" (2004:19), the tribal advisory board has optimized its resources to reap an impressive profit. It is worth noting that the representatives on this body come from an amazing range of educational and occupational backgrounds, including schoolteachers, steel mill workers, bus drivers, and a Ph.D. candidate in linguistic anthropology (Karenne Wood entered that track two years ago and is expected to earn the degree by spring 2008). Karenne Wood, in fact, has become the de facto chair of this advisory board, as she is recognized and respected for her skills and temperament—traditional criteria for many American Indian leaders. What is most impressive, however, is that this group has evolved of its own volition. My colleagues and I at Virginia Tech merely extended an invitation and provided an initial space and means of communicating with each other and, ultimately, with outside resources. The tribal advisory board, in fact, has initiated the most recent ventures, including expanding our partnership to include the University of Virginia in forging a cross-institutional program in indigenous studies and collaboration. This inclusion has been extended, of course, with the same degree of caution on the part of our indigenous hosts as was exercised during the first VINSHE. My role as an organizer of this event and related endeavors, then, has diminished inasmuch as the advisory board now sets the agenda and takes care of much of the logistical planning. To the extent that I have been an integral part in this process, I have long since handed over the proverbial "stick," as Chambers (1997) would put it, to tribal representatives. We have reached a point, I believe, where our institutions are not only prepared to assist the Monacans and other tribal entities in empowering their respective communities with the paramount guidance of indigenous knowledge, but to actually begin to "indigenize the academy" (Mihesuah 2004).

Lessons Learned

The field of Appalachian studies emerged from a regional scholarly cognizance of skewed power relations within the region and between Appalachia (however defined) and governmental or corporate entities from beyond the region. However, it is hard to resist the temptation to treat the region and communities therein as isolated entities in order to get our bearings. While we understand that local concerns are, ultimately, global concerns, we are obliged to realize that the people in the communities with which we work in a participatory capacity have the same understanding. I certainly knew this from the beginning, as I recalled my coal miner uncle who faithfully watched the *MacNeil-Lehrer Report* and urged his children, nieces, and nephews to learn something about the world instead of "Watching all that other trash" on television. However, my work with the Monacans gave me my first practical—and ongoing—experience with working with community-defined agendas in a participatory framework.

The greatest lesson I learned was that when one engages in participatory research, the community agenda cannot be constructively manipulated by the outside scholar. For instance, after about three years of working to establish myself as a "fixture" in the Monacan community, I conjured up the nerve to submit a proposal to the tribal council to establish a "peacemaker court." This would essentially consist of a small group of three or four community members who were uniformly respected in the community, and who might resolve differences between tribal members who might otherwise end up battling each other in local municipal courts. The council politely tabled the idea indefinitely, probably on the grounds that it would be hard to find at least three individuals who wielded the universal degree of respect that would be required of a mediator.

I also learned that the community's most salient collective goals were fundamentally political and farther reaching than I could have ever conceived when I first started working with the Monacans. Indeed, I first came to Bear Mountain at a time when the Monacans were spearheading an effort to lobby the Virginia state legislature to authorize corrections on Indian birth certificates that had been altered during the heyday of eugenic policies in the state, a campaign on behalf of *all* Indians in Virginia. Following this successful campaign the Monacans devoted greater energy to preparing documentation for federal recognition. I realized that I may contribute to that process as a researcher, fact checker, or, more directly, by using my credentials as a cultural anthropologist to add a perceived (in the eyes of the law) air of legitimacy to the tribe's claim to be an Indian nation. However, I did not realize that I would be working to enhance such pursuits on behalf of other tribes in the state by helping to create conduits for empowerment through higher education. Admittedly, I initially assumed I would be working solely with the Monacan community as an isolated entity. Long before I came to the community, Monacan tribal leaders had realized that their pursuit of community autonomy paralleled that of other tribes in the state and had acknowledged the importance of building intertribal solidarity in pursuit of these goals. By 2000, then, when I became coordinator for American Indian Studies at Virginia Tech, it became clear to me that I would not be labeled just a "Monacan anthropologist."

Notes

1. For a basic description of precontact Monacan society and territory (ca. 900–1600 A.D.), see Jeffrey Hantman (1990). Some of the better-known indigenous entities in the alliance were the so-called Monacans proper (settled near the falls of the James River at the time of European contact in 1608), Tutelos, Saponis, Occaneechis, and Manahoacs.

2. Peter Houck's (1984) suggestion that the settlers from the east were predominantly white traders (who brought with them English surnames such as Johns and Brenham, which became common among Monacans) has been commonly accepted until recently. However, the author and others have recently found documents linking the ancestors of certain Monacan families to Tidewater Indians in the eighteenth century (e.g., Heinegg 2001:718–20).

3. For an excellent discussion of the eugenics movement in Virginia, including Plecker's role in the international movement and his obsession with Amherst County, see J. David Smith (1993). Edwin Black (2003) offers a compelling and comprehensive examination of the eugenic movement in America with a considerable focus on its manifestations in Virginia.

4. James Mooney (1894) originally referred to three different "confederacies"—the Monacan, Manahoac, and Tutelo—in his ethnological survey of Siouan tribes of the East. Subsequent scholars—notably Hantman (1990)—have argued that archaeological evidence suggests such a large degree of cultural homogeneity existed between all of these groups that they probably constituted a single "Monacan Confederacy." However, I choose to use the term "alliance," since it better reflects the sociocultural and political fluidity that seems to have characterized relations between these groups.

5. Chief Justice John Marshall coined the term "domestic dependent nations" in the 1831 case of *Cherokee Nation v. Georgia* (30 U.S. 1), in which the Cherokee Nation challenged the state of Georgia's assertion of state laws into its territory on the grounds that the former constituted a "foreign nation" by the terms of the U.S. Constitution. While Marshall threw the claim out, he devised the notion of

"domestic dependent nation" as a means of balancing between states' rights interests and concerns about the extent of federal powers. The term has been variably
interpreted to suggest that relations with tribes are the exclusive concern of the
federal government, or that tribes are "wards" of the federal government (a prob-
lematic rendering where tribal sovereignty is concerned). For a more detailed discussion, see Deloria and Lytle (1983:30–33, 198).

6. Many scholars (myself included) working with Virginia Indians on federal
recognition pointed out that this compromise was legally unnecessary, and that
opposition to the initial legislation was unwarranted since the 1988 Indian Gaming
Regulatory Act (Public Law 100–497) already requires tribes to enter into compacts
with the states within which they reside before opening casinos. However, leaders
from the six tribes vying for recognition wisely opted to "let sleeping dogs lie."

7. The process of attaining state recognition varies from state to state, and in
many states there exist no established procedures. In some instances, it is as simple
as having the state's governor write a letter acknowledging the existence of a tribe,
which can be arbitrary and confusing. Virginia actually has one of the most rigor-
ous processes of any state for granting state recognition to tribes. Before the general assembly approves such recognition through legislation, the petitioning tribe
must first gain the approval of the Virginia Council on Indians, which consists
of representatives from all of Virginia's recognized tribes (there were seven at
the time the Monacans petitioned—the Monacan Nation is the eighth). Petitioning tribes must also demonstrate that they have an organized governing body.
See http://www.indians.vipnet.org. Virginia's eight state-recognized tribes are
Chickahominey, Eastern Chickahominey, Mattaponi, Upper Mattaponi, Monacan, Nansemond, Pamunkey, and Rappahannock.

8. CIS has subsequently been reorganized to constitute the Department of
Interdisciplinary Studies (DIDST) within the newly formed College of Liberal
Arts and Human Sciences. See http://www.idst.vt.edu

References

Anderson, Terry. 1978. "Federal Recognition: The Vicious Myth." *American Indian
    Journal* (May):7–19.

Black, Edwin. 2003. *War against the Weak: Eugenics and America's Campaign to
    Create a Master Race.* New York: Four Walls Eight Windows.

Blu, Karen I. 2001. "Region and Recognition: Southern Indians, Anthropologists,
    and Presumed Biologies." In *Anthropologists and Indians in the New South,*
    Rachel Bomey and J. Anthony Paredes (Eds.). Tuscaloosa: Univ. of Alabama
    Press. Pp. 71–85.

Campisi, Jack. 1991. *The Maspee Indians: Tribe on Trial.* Syracuse: Syracuse
    Univ. Press.

Chambers, Robert. 1997. *Whose Reality Counts? Putting the First Last.* London:
    Intermediate Technology.

Champagne, Duane, and Jay Stauss (Eds.). 2002. *Native American Studies in Higher Education: Models for Collaboration between Universities and Indigenous Nations*. Walnut Creek: Altamira Press.

Clifford, James. 1988. *The Predicament of Culture: Twentieth Century Ethnography, Literature, and Art*. Cambridge: Harvard Univ. Press.

Cook, Samuel R. 2000. *Monacans and Miners: Native American and Coal Mining Communities in Appalachia*. Lincoln: Univ. of Nebraska Press.

———. 2002. "The Monacan Indian Nation: Asserting Tribal Sovereignty in the Absence of Federal Recognition." *Wicazo 'Sa Review* 17(2):91–116.

———. 2003. "Anthropological Advocacy in Historic Perspective: The Case of Anthropologists and Virginia Indians." *Human Organization* 62(2):191–201.

———. 2004. "Developing an American Indian Studies Program: A View from Ground Zero." *American Indian Culture and Research Journal* 27(4):133–45.

Cook, Samuel R., John L. Johns, and Karenne Wood. 2005. "The Monacan Nation Pow Wow: Symbol of Indigenous Survival and Resistance in the Tobacco Row Mountains." In *Pow Wow: Native American Performance, Identity, and Meaning*, Luke E. Lassiter (Ed.). Lincoln: Univ. of Nebraska Press. Pp. 201–23.

Davies, Charlotte A. 1999. *Reflexive Ethnography: A Guide to Researching Ourselves and Others*. London: Routledge.

Deloria, Jr., Vine, and Clifford M. Lytle. 1983. *American Indians, American Justice*. Austin: Univ. of Texas Press.

Dixon, Heriberto. 2002. "A Saponi by Any Other Name Is Still a Siouan." *American Indian Culture and Research Journal* 26(3):65–84.

Estabrook, Arthur H., and Ivan McDougal. 1926. *Mongrel Virginians*. Baltimore: Williams and Wilkins Co.

Flora, Cornelia Butler, Jan L. Flora, with Susan Fey. 2003. *Rural Communities: Legacy and Change*. 2nd ed. Boulder: Westview Press.

Freire, Paulo. 1970. *Pedagogy of the Oppressed*. New York: Continuum Publications.

Gaventa, John. 1980. *Power and Powerlessness: Quiescence and Rebellion in an Appalachian Valley*. Urbana: Univ. of Illinois Press.

Gaventa, John, and Helen Lewis. 1991. "Participatory Education and Grassroots Development: The Case of Rural Appalachia." London: Gatekeeper Series No. 25, Sustainable Agriculture Programme of the International Institute for Environment and Development.

Geertz, Clifford. 1973. *The Interpretation of Cultures*. New York: Basic Books.

Greenbaum, Susan D. 1985. "In Search of Lost Tribes: Anthropology and the Federal Acknowledgement Process." *Human Organization* 61:288–98.

Hale, Horatio. 1885. "The Tutelo Tribe and Language." *Proceedings of the American Philosophical Society* 21(114):1–49.

Hantman, Jeffrey L. 1990. "Between Powhatan and Quirank: Reconstructing Monacan Culture and History in the Context of Jamestown." *American Anthropologist* 92(3):676–90.

Hantman, Jeffrey L., Karenne Wood, and Diane Shields. 2000. "Writing Collaborative History: How the Monacan Nation and Archaeologists Worked Together
to Enrich Our Understanding of Virginia's Native Peoples." *Archaeology*
53(5):56–61.

Hardin, Peter. 2000a. "Groups Oppose Sovereignty for Tribes: Elks, Petroleum
Marketers Cite Potential Economic Effect." *Richmond (VA) Times-Dispatch*,
Nov. 5.

———. 2000b. "Indians Asking Gilmore for Help: 'Sovereign Nations' Status Is the
Goal." *Richmond (VA) Times-Dispatch*, July 31.

———. 2000c. "Virginia Indians Bill Is Introduced: Eight Tribes Seek U.S. Recognition." *Richmond (VA) Times-Dispatch*, July 28.

Heinegg, Paul (Ed.). 2001. *Free African Americans of North Carolina, Virginia, and
South Carolina from the Colonial Period to about 1820.* Baltimore: Clearfield
Publishing.

Hicks, Phyllis. 1996. Recorded conversation with Samuel R. Cook. Bear Mountain,
VA, June 26.

Houck, Peter W. 1984. *Indian Island in Amherst County.* Lynchburg: Lynchburg
Historical Research Co.

Johns, John L. 1996. Recorded conversation with Samuel R. Cook. Bear Mountain,
VA, July 7.

Lassiter, Luke E. 1998. *The Power of Kiowa Song.* Tucson: Univ. of Arizona Press.

———. 2003. "American Anthropology, Local Publics, and Collaborative
Ethnography." Unpublished manuscript.

———. 2005. *The Chicago Guide to Collaborative Ethnography.* Chicago: Univ. of
Chicago Press.

Lawless, Elaine J. 1992. "'I Was Afraid Someone Like You . . . An Outsider . . . Would
Misunderstand': Negotiating Interpretive Differences between Ethnographers
and Subjects." *Journal of American Folklore* 105:301–14.

Light, Ivan H. 2004. "Social Capital for What?" In *Community-Based Organizations:
The Intersection of Social Capital and Local Context in Contemporary Urban
Society,* Robert Mark Silverman (Ed.). Detroit: Wayne State Univ. Pp. 19–33.

Lynch, Eleanor W., and Marci J. Hanson. (Eds.). 1998. *Developing Cross-Cultural
Competence: A Guide for Working with Children and Their Families.* 2nd ed.
Baltimore: Paul H. Brookes.

McLeRoy, Sherri S., and William R. McLeRoy. 1993. *Strangers in Their Midst: The
Free Black Population of Amherst County, Virginia.* Bowie: Heritage Books.

Mihesuah, Devon (Ed.). 1998. *Natives and Academics: Researching and Writing about
American Indians.* Lincoln: Univ. of Nebraska Press.

———. 2004. *Indigenizing the Academy: Transforming Scholarship and Empowering
Communities.* Lincoln: Univ. of Nebraska Press.

Monacan Indian Nation. 1999. Letter to Dr. Paul Torgersen, President of Virginia
Polytechnic Institute, June 6.

Mooney, James. 1894. *Siouan Tribes of the East.* Bureau of American Ethnology Bulletin 22. Washington: Smithsonian Institute.

Moretti-Langholtz, Danielle (Dir.). 2002. *"In Our Own Words": Voices of Virginia Indians.* Video Documentary. Williamsburg: College of William and Mary American Indian Resource Center.

Paredes, J. Anthony. 1992. "Federal Recognition and the Poarch Creek Indians." In *Indians in the Southeastern United States in the Late Twentieth Century,* J. Anthony Paredes (Ed.). Tuscaloosa: Univ. of Alabama Press. Pp. 120–39.

"Procedures for Establishing That an American Indian Group Is a Tribe." 1994. *Federal Register* 59 (Feb. 25). Washington: Government Printing Office. Pp. 9295.

Quinn, William. 1990. "Federal Acknowledgement of Indian Tribes? The Historical Development of a Legal Concept." *American Journal of Legal History* 34:351–63.

Saks, Eva. 1988. "Representing Miscegenation Law." *Raritan* 8:39–69.

Smith, J. David. 1993. *The Eugenic Assault on America: Studies in Red, White, and Black.* Fairfax: George Mason Univ. Press.

Smith, J. David, and K. Ray Nelson. 1989. *The Sterilization of Carrie Buck.* Fort Hills: New Horizon Press.

Tedlock, Dennis. 1983. *The Spoken Word and the Work of Interpretation.* Philadelphia: Univ. of Pennsylvania Press.

———. 1995. "Interpretation, Participation, and the Role of Narrative in Dialogic Anthropology." In *The Dialogic Emergence of Culture,* Dennis Tedlock and Bruce Manhelm (Eds.). Chicago: Univ. of Illinois Press. Pp. 253–87.

Waugaman, Sandra F., and Danielle Moretti-Langholtz. 2000. *"We're Still Here": Contemporary Virginia Indians Tell Their Stories.* Richmond: Palari Publishing.

Wilkins, David E. 1997. *American Indian Sovereignty and the U.S. Supreme Court: The Masking of Justice.* Austin: Univ. of Texas Press.

Participation versus Mobilization

Cultural Styles of Political Action in an Appalachian County

Lesley Bartlett and Jefferson C. Boyer

Bartlett and Boyer present further evidence to counter the stereotype of fatalism in the mountains with this description and comparison of two community groups involved in civic action in Watauga County, North Carolina. They identify two distinctive types of political engagement differing in crisis-orientation and preference for public contestation. The "mobilization" type, emerging in response to specific neighborhood problems, adopts formal organization and elected leaders, uses overt confrontational tactics, and easily incorporates newcomers living on the outskirts of town as members. In contrast, the "participation" type relies on influence through long-established social networks connecting local formal leaders with community activists concerned with maintaining the face of public harmony. This emphasis on long-term community goals, cultural heritage-based mobilization techniques, and traditional social affiliations, as neighbors and church members, appeals especially to natives engaged in what the authors call "commons-making" in this old rural community. Noting strengths and limitations of both styles of political engagement, Bartlett and Boyer suggest that building coalitions at the regional level and beyond might make either type of activism more sustainable, but local values and tactical styles must be reflected in these coalitions to make them appealing.

Current discussions about forms of political engagement in Appalachia reveal a gathering consensus that, indeed, democracy in America is under siege (Anglin 2002; Couto 1999; Holland et al. 2007; Reid and Taylor 2000). Global economic forces and the neoliberal policies that ensure market triumph over governmental regulation call into question three core values that uphold democracy: liberty, equality, and community. With regard to the first value, today's dominant discourses narrowly define liberty as merely the freedom of the market from government interference while neglecting other forms of political tyranny. The core value of equality, or widespread access to and participation in decisions about the allocation of public resources, is undercut when corporate lobbyists and wealthy elites control such crucial access. Similarly, democracy's third core value of community—the voluntary, communal bonds and common concerns that transcend individual self-interest—are under assault by the continual penetration of such large private interests into daily personal lives and community spaces, institutions, and practices (Holland et al. 2007:3–5). Communities throughout Appalachia, America, and the world either struggle against these global forces, accommodate and sometimes succumb to them, or very often attempt complex and contradictory efforts at both resistance and accommodation. Bartlett's chapter in *Local Democracy under Siege* (Holland et al. 2007) is a study of the political dynamics in Watauga County, in the Blue Ridge Mountains of western North Carolina and southern Appalachia. In this article, we contrast styles of political action in two Watauga communities during the 1990s and reflect on changes in those styles more recently in one of those communities.

Theorizing of Appalachian politics has dispelled the twin myths of the fatalistic and the angry, rebellious mountaineer (Anglin 2002; Couto 1999; Hinsdale, Lewis, and Waller 1995; Reid and Taylor 2000). Collections such as *Fighting Back in Appalachia* (Fisher 1993) examine the variety of political involvement under way throughout the region. While highlighting contemporary resistance movements, they question the extent to which local debates challenge the economic and political structures shaping disputes. These writings raise several interesting issues, including the conditions under which tradition alternately stalls and impels political action. In this article, we adopt and extend these questions as we analyze two contemporary case studies. We emphasize the diversification of southern Appalachian economies in recent decades, the emergence of a consumption-based economy in some areas, and the influence of such an economy on local politics.

We use case material to distinguish between two types of political involvement: participation and mobilization (see Calhoun 1982, 1983). By participation, we mean the ongoing pattern of engagement in political life. Participatory activities are not restricted to overt, strategic power contestations, but include civic involvement and even informal communication. Participation implies a history of relations over a long period of time. Participation's legitimacy as democratic process is fostered by the actor's connection through extensive social networks to fellow citizens (Buell and DeLuca 1996). By contrast, mobilization signals the rallying of people and resources in response to a problem or crisis. It has a definite and finite life span. It generally requires a command center with the capacity to orchestrate actions. Participation and mobilization represent distinct phases of the political process: participation in everyday social networks provides the necessary energy and contacts for mobilization, while mobilization often recruits people into political activities who may or may not decide to become more long-term participants. By exploring these types of involvement in the two cases that follow, we suggest some conditions necessary to foster involvement in Appalachia that stands a greater chance of meeting sustainable development goals. But first we examine the economic context shaping these political debates.

Economic Transformation and the Landscape of Consumption

Like many areas of the southern Appalachian region, Watauga County's economy has in the past few decades undergone significant transformation. From the 1970s through the 1990s, its already slim manufacturing base withered and the number of small family farms declined. The intensified promotion of tourism during the same period induced the disproportionate development of service and retail sectors. Likewise, tourism fed the growing second home industry, importing a flood of wealthy retirees and aggravating the already sizable division between the wealthy and the poor.

We argue that these changes resemble those characterized as a shift to a landscape of consumption by Sharon Zukin in her monograph, *Landscapes of Power* (1991). For Zukin, the concept signifies the reconfiguration of "material and social practices and their symbolic representation" around the provision of consumable goods and services. Moreover, the landscape itself, once valued for its food productive capacity, is now consumed as a visual commodity by the increasing number of people visiting or relocating to the area.

The economic development of Watauga has long been restricted by powerful forces attracted to its beauty. Tourism began as early as the 1800s, when wealthy Americans summered in the area. With the establishment of a teachers' training school (later a public university) in the county in 1899, principal administrators jealously protected the mountains from industrial development, preserving their scenery for students, their families, and tourists. The completion of the Blue Ridge Parkway in 1939 attracted an increasing number of middle-class tourists. This limited natives to two primary economic avenues: if they inherited land, they could farm; if not, they could work off the mountain in the furniture factories thirty miles south. The maintenance of an agricultural economy well into the twentieth century differentiates Watauga and the surrounding area from the rest of the Appalachian region.

These patterns continued unabated until the 1950s and 1960s, when a group of prominent businessmen recruited light industry from the Midwest and North. Small- and medium-sized plants manufactured wood products, textiles, shoes, saw blades, and electronic equipment. In 1970, manufacturing employment peaked at 22 percent of the total workforce. However, with the globalization of trade, steady automation and competition from products and cheaper labor markets undercut the fledgling manufacturing sector (Zelenko 1992:28). Concomitantly, the growth of tourism and the related expansion of residential relocation spiked the cost of land, pricing manufacturers out of the market. From 1970 to 1990, manufacturing plummeted to a mere 10.3 percent of the total workforce.

From the mid 1960s to the 1990s, several other factors augmented the county's transformation into a landscape of consumption. Tourism exploded, making the area one of the state's most popular destinations. The Blue Ridge Parkway has long attracted visitors to the area in the summer and fall seasons. The introduction of winter skiing in the 1960s made Watauga a four-season tourist destination. At its peak in 1987–88, the industry registered 606,000 skier visits, a figure that has declined somewhat in recent years due to warmer winters (Boyer, Monast, and Moretz 1993:29). By 1990, the U.S. Travel Data Center estimated four-season travel expenditures in the county topped $82 million. Travel and tourism account for nearly 2,595 jobs, or 15.4 percent of the county's workforce, according to local economic officials (30).

In addition to tourism, the rapid expansion of the university and the presence of students with expendable resources encouraged the growth of low-paying, low-skill service and retail jobs that were filled mostly by poor natives or students. From 1970 to 1990, the percentage of the workforce employed in retail nearly doubled. The service sector did not expand as quickly, though in the same twenty-year period it provided much more than double the number of jobs. By 1990, service and retail combined accounted for nearly 65 percent of all employment in the county. The university (long the county's largest single employer), the public schools, and the county government have been important sources of stable employment with opportunity for advancement in an otherwise insecure, low-pay job environment.

The landscape of consumption fueled the conversion of productive farms to residential lots. The advent of agro-business and shifting government policies eroded the ability of family farms to compete. The number of farms in the county declined from 1,564 in 1964 to 673 in 1992, according to the U.S. Department of Agriculture and the North Carolina Department of Agriculture. Sales of burley tobacco, long the staple crop in the region, declined more than 50 percent from a high of $5.6 million in 1982 to $2.7 million in 1993 (Boyer, Monast, and Moretz 1993:19). For many, farming became at most a part-time occupation, with the average farm realizing a post-expenses profit of only $3,867 in 1987 (17). Many stopped farming altogether; between 1970 and 1990, Watauga's farming population dropped from 4,142 to 1,269 (Region D Council of Government 1992). Some farmers were relieved to finance their retirement by selling parcels of land. Natives with large landholdings made a handsome profit. The estimated 500 percent increase in farm taxes from 1980 to 1997 in rural areas forced poorer natives to sell (see Bartlett and Boyer 1997:10). Seasonal residents and speculators bought much of the land. By 1990 seasonal housing accounted for 27 percent of total housing stock, and by 1997, 50 percent of land parcels were owned by people living outside the county (interview with county registrar of deeds, May 1997). New permanent residents likewise greatly contributed to the change in land tenure. By 1990, they constituted 37 percent of county population (Watauga Economic Development Commission 1992).

This shift to a service economy and influx of seasonal and permanent residents profoundly affected social divisions, increasing the unequal distribution of wealth. The county has experienced extraordinary economic growth, with per capita income rising from 61 percent of the state average in 1970 to 82 percent in 1990. The large presence of university students skews the poverty data, which shows that the number of families in poverty declined slowly while the number of persons in poverty increased. However, the Gini coefficient (a measure of variability used to assess income inequality across political entities) reveals the steady growth of the divide between rich and poor in North Carolina. Whereas in 1970 Watauga had the thirty-second highest level of inequality among the one hundred counties of the state, by 1990 it ranked twenty-third. Based on the data, the growth of the service and retail sectors, and the steady decrease in the unemployment rate, we argue that while absolute poverty steadily declined in the area, an increasing number of people are underemployed, working longer hours for lower wages. The recent state reform in social services resulting in a drastic cut in the number of food stamp recipients is likely to have a significant impact on poverty across the state. This divide between rich and poor can only increase with the establishment of a 6,000-acre transcendental meditation resort attracting the wealthy from all over the country. Once again, native people are being displaced.

In sum, in recent decades Watauga County has witnessed a structural transformation of the local economy around the commodification of the land. From its long tradition of reliance on family farms and food production, Watauga has in the past thirty years been converted into a landscape of consumption, wherein economic activity is organized around the promotion through the tourist, recreation, and second home industry of the land itself as a commodity. This phenomenon is occurring in much of the surrounding area in North Carolina, Tennessee, Virginia, Georgia, and South Carolina, particularly in those communities that became retirement meccas due to their natural beauty and initially low land prices. It also characterizes many of the counties and small towns bordering the Blue Ridge Parkway, which last year drew an estimated 13,088,370 visitors to the North Carolina segment of the road alone. Tourism- and recreation-dependent areas are undergoing cultural and political changes resulting from changing patterns of land use, population increases, and the cultural diversity of new residents. The deindustrialization and commodification of land are local manifestations of transformations currently under way throughout the Southeast, the nation, and areas of the world. These are the very processes fueling greater economic maldistribution and intensification of environmental crises globally, which are creating crises of sustainability for communities everywhere.

Political Engagement in Watauga County

These economic transformations set up certain political constraints in Watauga County. As more and more tourists clog the roads to the High Country, pollution threatens the hardwoods on the mountainside (Tursi 1997). At the same time, residents grumble about traffic lag time and demand the construction of more roads. Road construction simply invites more travel, setting up an unsustainable spiral. It also encourages the establishment of new asphalt plants in a rush to secure profitable paving contracts. As we see in the first case study, communities across the state are dealing with the threat of environmental hazards locating next door. In our second case study, economic transformation and rocketing land values due to residential development gut the community's capacity to maintain their productive farming activities and strip them of their identity, which they struggle to re-create through local planning efforts. The first example portrays a case of mobilization; the second illustrates phases of participation. However, neither case excludes the other process. Rather, divergent histories and institutional, cultural, and economic processes give rise to these differing patterns of mobilization and participation.

CASE #1: CITIZENS UNITE

Our first case concerns a debate over the location of an asphalt plant in an area several miles east of Boone.[1] In the early 1960s, a local family bought most of the verdant valley bisected by a fork of the New River. They established a dairy farm and cultivated vegetables on the side. When Watauga's housing boom began in earnest in the 1970s, they sold much of the hillside to local developers and subdivisions sprouted around them. By the mid 1980s, the family discontinued the dairy. Over the next decade, the land was solicited by several commercial enterprises. Eventually, the family agreed to lease a parcel to an annual county fair and later to a weekend racetrack. The newcomers in the subdivisions ringing the valley objected to the visual pollution and to the increase in traffic and noise, taking their complaints to local public meetings. But the county government's existing ordinance against carnivals did not apply to fairs, and an attempt to develop a noise ordinance was defeated by the local National Rifle Association. Residents resigned themselves to what they viewed as a disturbance of the peace and tranquility they had sought in the mountains.

However, a greater threat was looming. The passage of several generous road bonds and the commitment by the state's Department of Transportation to bring a four-lane highway within ten miles of 90 percent of the state's population set the stage. When the state scheduled a highway bordering the valley to be four-laned, a contractor approached the family and secured a lease to locate an asphalt plant in the bottomland, less than one hundred feet from the river. With no zoning in the county and no requirement to notify adjacent landowners, residents heard about the plans only when they were leaked informally. By that point, the company, which we call Pace, lacked only an air quality permit from the state and a local health permit for any sanitation requirements.

Drawing on networks established in the previous debates, the neighborhood and surrounding area immediately mobilized. In-migrant newcomers constituted the leadership and the overwhelming majority of the group's membership, although a few locals joined as well. They attended a county commissioner's meeting to present the issue to local leaders, who regretfully informed the group that none of the existing ordinances governing the plant or the area would allow them to intervene. The group hired the directors of Environmental Organization (EO), a statewide network of grassroots environmental groups, for assistance in organizing and strategizing. On their advice, the group selected a formal name (which we call Citizens Unite, or CU), elected leaders, and divided into subcommittees such as research, media and public relations, and fund-raising. They also convinced the state to grant a public hearing on the air permit, which offered them a chance to influence the state's decision and bought them some time to organize.

In the intervening months, CU worked hard to develop local support. They held a press conference and wrote letters to the editors of two local papers focusing on the environmental and health aspects of the issue. Their success in redefining the issue as one of environment and health, instead of zoning, was critical; it drew support from regional environmental organizations and allowed them to rely on the political rhetoric and tactics of other environmental groups. Several members used the Internet and other sources to learn about the regulation of asphalt production in other states. They circulated petitions and raised funds to pay for ads in the local papers, to mail newsletters, and to provide a stipend to the environmental organizers. Either the entire group or a smaller steering committee met weekly to share information and revise plans.

During the course of these events, the group tried unsuccessfully to gain strong support from the county government. One example will suffice to illustrate the interactions. CU attended a meeting and asked the board to take an active role, but the commissioners responded that they could do nothing about the situation. The CU steering committee, made up entirely of newcomers, accepted the advice of environmental organizers and student activists that they incorporate some visual protest into their next presentation. At the following county commissioner meeting, approximately fifty members filled the courthouse with their faces covered by painter's masks. They asked the commissioners to support four specific resolutions, including a moratorium on state air permits until the state decided whether to apply toxic emissions regulations to asphalt plants. The commissioners refused to respond immediately, wondering aloud if the actions were legal. The following month they declined any action beyond the resolution they had previously drafted as a board in support of CU.

The commissioners were unhappy with what they viewed as a provocation. One characterized the group as "demanding" and "adamant." Another complained, "[CU] springs stuff on us and hasn't even given us time to look at it ahead of time. I like to have things ahead of time so I can read and digest it. I'd rather have it in black and white." From the perspective of local leaders, CU was pushy and confrontational. They felt that CU was trying to force them into favorable decisions by not submitting their requests before the meeting and by showing up in such large numbers. The commissioners felt "threatened" by the political tactics of CU.

Several also chafed at the group's media orientation. A prominent community member said CU "hit the paper with the issue" before developing a relationship with the commissioners, which "backs [the board] into a corner." Instead, they should have sent a few spokespeople to talk privately with board members before approaching them in a public forum, he said. One board member reported that people in the area ridiculed CU's "media plays." He said, "They've conducted more of a media campaign. . . . They were wearing gas masks and doing all that kind of stuff. And people would mention that to me and they would just laugh about it. I think that kind of thing did leave a bad taste, when they were picketing out in front of the courthouse wearing the black robes and those kinds of things. Here again, a lot of people thought that was just a hoot." The commissioner dismissed the group because their activities did not meet standard community patterns of political participation.

Mountain norms of conflict avoidance in the public sphere are well documented (Beaver 1992; Foster 1988; Hinsdale, Lewis, and Waller 1995:66; Wagner, this volume). If maintaining ties for the long term is taken seriously, as is the case in traditional communities, then the time-honored strategy of nurturing harmony at overt, public levels while allowing disagreements and conflicts to simmer privately and through "rumor mills" makes instrumental sense (see Calhoun 1982, 1983; Schmidt 1977). CU's newcomer status politically handicapped them. They were unfamiliar with the cultural preference for friendly relations governing interaction between citizens and local politicians. As the debate raged on throughout the year, CU leaders became more attuned to local expectations and cultivated more amicable relations with county politicians.

However, precisely because CU's early actions were provocative, the media ran their image and story on the front page. The extensive use of the media through such visual stunts as wearing painter's masks and black robes while picketing, planning press conferences, and writing numerous letters to the editor of local papers raised awareness of the issue across the county and contributed greatly to the landmark turnout of more than four hundred people at the state-sponsored public hearing held in town later that year. So while some locals found the confrontational style distasteful, it succeeded in piquing interest in the issue.

State bureaucracies would largely decide this local issue, so CU successfully used it to challenge larger processes. During the public hearing, they convinced the Division of Air Quality to declare a moratorium on the construction of asphalt plants across the state until models and permits accounted for the never-before-measured fugitive emissions. Thus, CU helped shape state policy regarding the regulation of plants. (However, many other factors contributed to this decision, including particularly the simultaneous initiation of a study of fugitive emissions by the federal government.) Second, the group continues to monitor state air policy. At the prompting of EO, they recently caravanned to the state capital to protest a proposed weakening of the state's Air Toxics Program.

Further, genuine changes in political orientations emerged from this experience. Several members reported being politicized by the issue. As one said, "I'll never again trust the government to do what's best for me." Some members attended meetings coordinated by EO of environmental groups from across the state, where they heard about other environmental issues like hazardous waste and hog farms. Also, as they gradually came to consider themselves environmentalists, they modified the sometimes reactionary image they had maintained of environmentalists, facilitating further collaboration. They also paid more attention to the national environmental agenda. Apart from raising awareness, many members became more active in formal politics. One switched parties and started attending party-sponsored sessions on political organizing. Two are considering a run for state and local office.

We suggest that politicization around local issues can provoke a reconceptualization of the importance of political action among participants, who then become more active in local, state, and national issues. However, this case illustrates the importance of several factors. First, the orientation toward the state in this debate makes it more likely participants will continue to be involved in state issues. The now familiar activities of writing letters to the governor, visiting legislators in the state capitol, and calling various bureaucrats in the Division of Air Quality will be much less intimidating in future ventures. Second, the positive experience with the regulation of the asphalt plant has encouraged further activity. Finally, we cannot overemphasize the importance of political infrastructure. The community organizers with EO tutored CU members in all aspects of political engagement. They continued to involve CU with state-level debates by serving as watchdog for environmental issues and mobilizing the membership of affiliated grassroots groups on appropriate occasions. These professional environmental activists are crucial to the continued, effective, and informed involvement of local groups isolated from the discussions and decisions of state-level politicians and industry lobbyists.

Case #2: Laurel Valley

In contrast to CU's neighborhood's recent emergence as a bedroom community of Boone, Laurel Valley is one of the oldest communities in the county. The first settlers of Scots-Irish and English extraction took up residence on the banks of the Laurel Valley–Watauga River confluence west of Boone around the time of American Independence. Some German immigrant families joined this emerging rural society. By 1800 the community had a Baptist church. Due to the considerable bottomland, small farmsteads appeared along streams and branches of the western Watauga watershed. During the Civil War, the permanent camp for the county's Confederate Home Guard was located in Laurel Valley (Arthur 1992).

The writings of Watauga County historian John Preston Arthur illustrate Laurel Valley's extensive history. Arthur's inflated rhetoric about the materially progressive and civic-minded Laurel Valley citizens, so typical of its times, is fascinating in what it chooses to exaggerate:

> From [Linwood, the heart of the community] to the Tennessee line, [Laurel Valley] is so thickly settled as to be almost one continuous village. . . . For [Laurel Valley] is recognized as the Egypt of Watauga County. It contains some of the most fertile land in the State. Its people are progressive and cooperate in all public enterprises. Beginning . . . near the Tennessee line, there is a succession of villages. . . . Two large flouring mills are on the creek, while there is the first cheese factory ever established in the county in flourishing condition at [Linwood]. Churches, schools and Masonic lodges dot the hillsides. Hospitality reigns in every household. The people are prosperous and happy and helpful. . . . The town of [Linwood] and vicinity is lighted up with electric lights. Bathtubs supplied with clear spring water are found in many of the dwellings. . . . Automobiles and the latest improved farm machinery show the temper and spirit of the people. In short, there is no forward step which can be taken at this stage of its growth that [Laurel Valley] has not taken. (1992:210)

This is intentional myth-making at its best, linking the civic and productive aspirations of at least the wealthier families in this corner of southern Appalachia at the turn of the century. The passage highlights pride in agricultural and small industrial production. The emphasis upon voluntary participation in church and civic life is also clearly evident. It is impossible to judge the extent of internalization of such ideals for all Laurel Valley residents. However, both our research (Bartlett and Boyer 1997; Boyer, Monast, and Moretz 1993) and the literature (especially Beaver 1992) confirm that active churchgoing and daily visiting of kinfolk and neighborhood friends has been normative for all families since the community's inception. We may assume that participation in civic affairs was more frequently an activity of those families with the material means to afford the time away from the demands of livelihood. Yet no evidence suggests that the early-twentieth-century material progress of Laurel Valley's wealthy minority ruptured reciprocal ties; quite the opposite, as it often entailed material obligations to poorer relatives and neighbors. In this way, the basis for everyday engagement in the dense networks of rural community life was maintained (see Calhoun 1982, 1983). These extensive kin- and friendship webs critically mark the type of political activity in this area.

Unfortunately, Arthur's vision of twentieth-century prosperity and progress for rural western Watauga County was overtaken by harsher economic realities. These include the Great Depression, agricultural decline, and considerable out-migration. Boone's emergence as the primary urban center for Watauga and adjoining mountain counties eclipsed Laurel Valley's commercial and urban impetus. This was due to several factors, including the establishment much earlier of county government and services and the founding of Appalachian State University in Boone.

Several postwar infrastructural and institutional losses have exacerbated Laurel Valley's decline. The 1950s bypassing of the community center with the construction of a new highway west of Boone meant the failure of local businesses, including general stores and service stations, which followed the earlier closings of the flour mills and cheese factory.

Laurel Valley also lost what in this area is the chief symbol of community identity—the school. In the 1960s, their high school was consolidated with the town of Boone, and recently the elementary school was relocated four miles east of the community's center. One informant reported, "I don't think we have the feeling of community spirit that we did have when we had a high school." Another described the elementary school as "the hub, the center of attraction in Laurel Valley. [Its removal] gutted the community." Residents focus particularly on the absence of athletic teams: "We used to have a lot of pride in our local, community school. We had the high school and that was a real attraction to people, and the families would come together and they had competitive spirit with other schools in the county. There was a real competition and it was quite a thing people talked about. Now they don't have that identity or that concern they once did in their local community." The sense of loss is reflected in this recent "obituary" by Ralf Stokes:

> Looking at [Laurel Valley] now and comparing it with the rich heritage of
> yesteryears, I see a sad obituary. . . . Changes are usually for the betterment of
> the majority but with the benefits come the losses and it's the losses I address.

We lost when Watauga's first fair moved on after years of tenancy. Gone are the schools with all their laughter and excitement. The mill wheel no longer turns and the thoroughfare between Mountain City and Boone has been replaced by a bypass.

Gone are the pioneers and patriots, making room for us to fill their places as the last generation. (1997:47)

Their sense of lost heritage is palpable.

Small wonder, then, that the federal government's announcement in 1993 of intent to close the Laurel Valley Post Office triggered an outcry and an organized resistance. During a widely attended public meeting, post office officials argued that the consolidation of two county post offices would save taxpayer money and increase efficiency. This reasoning totally ignored residents' reasons for attachment to the post office, which had long been an important site of social interaction, fostering the circulation of community news. As one resident remembered, "they didn't want to hear our history." The government responded to opposition by threatening to eliminate both rural post offices. This angered people even further. Community members organized through local civic organizations. They formed committees, publicized the issue, collected two thousand signatures on a petition, and began a letter-writing campaign to state and federal representatives. Eventually, they created enough furor to convince the government to "back off."

From the post office mobilization emerged a small group of people concerned about the future of their community. Inviting leaders of the local Grange, Ruritan Club, Volunteer Fire Department, and Parent Teacher Service Organization to join, they formed Laurel Valley Preservation and Development, Incorporated (LVPD). The group included newcomers from other areas of the United States, natives who had significant work and life experiences outside the mountains, and natives who had lived their entire lives in the area.

Members of the group met with county planners to discuss a new, decentralized planning process called community councils that the commissioners had instituted. The intent of the councils was to give citizens greater voice in local affairs, devolving upon them the power to engage in land use planning and natural resource protection. After much discussion, in 1996 and early 1997 the Laurel Valley Community Council formed with fifteen members. Talks between Laurel Valley leaders and Appalachian State University's Sustainable Development (SD) Program led to a 1997 grant from the Z. Smith Reynolds Foundation for a sustainable communities coordinator based in Laurel Valley. The founding SD Program director, Jeff Boyer, purposely hired Bill Smythe, a senior native to the mountains with a proven track record in community revitalization, rather than a younger person with academic qualifications but with less experience or personal ties to the region.

The community council began the long process of debating what mechanisms might encourage community revitalization. The majority favored strict land use planning. However, they feared a backlash among the residents in the area, many of whom resist government interference with property rights. In order to build support for their efforts, they decided to make the widely beloved historic school the centerpiece of their plans. They leased the property from the county government, organized work parties to clean it up, and began raising funds for essential renovations.

The council called a community meeting for residents to undergo a SWOTS analysis (strengths/weaknesses/opportunities/threats) led by county planners. The turnout was disappointingly low, consisting mostly of council members and ASU affiliates. In an effort to receive more input, SD director Boyer suggested a community needs assessment; the council agreed, and the county offered to pay for the costs.

With the help of the council, community members, county planners, Bill Smythe, and four ASU students, we conducted a study of 101 persons in June and July 1997. Seventy-seven were surveyed during visits to their homes; 24 participated in one of the four focus groups we hosted. The assessment revealed unexpected support for land use protections, and most of all support for "the preservation of [Laurel Valley's] rural character." Fully 89 percent of those surveyed agreed that there is a need to better protect waterways and floodplains. Fewer natives (48 percent) than newcomers (72 percent) responded that development will threaten farmland; however, in a later question natives showed wide support for farmland protection, ranking it above all other natural resource protection strategies. In fact, farmland protection tied for first place with preserving the old high school when respondents were asked to name the second most important strategy to preservation of rural heritage. Almost all of those surveyed (96 percent) agreed that there is a need to "maintain rural character" (Bartlett and Boyer 1997:4, 9–10).

After presenting these findings to the community council, Boyer pointed out to them the similarity between their concerns and the Sustainable Communities Movement agenda (Barber 1996). He suggested that the council formally join the movement and include information about it in the document we were producing for the broader community. They declined, because they were anxious that the plan be seen as the truly local effort that it was, not as something imposed by "outsiders." One council member suggested that the efforts be recognized as sustainable in some formal presentation after they had established the plan.

While we were engaged in compiling the survey data, community organizer Bill Smythe, council members, and representatives of other civic organizations were busy planning a huge community event. The intent was to revive the county fair that had lapsed in the 1930s. Farm Heritage Days, a two-day event, drew an unprecedented three thousand people. The first day of celebration emphasized family, kids, and community, with an antique car parade, horses and tractor pulls, history and storytelling, butter churning, cider making, and games for children, all held at the historic high school. The second day featured tours of ten Laurel Valley farms. The event rejuvenated community enthusiasm and pride. For weeks afterward, community members bragged about the success of Farm Heritage Days, which was better planned and attended than the street fair held the next week in the town of Boone. The community received public accolades for the noncommercial nature of the event. One month after Farm Heritage Days, the main planners met to review their achievement, concluding it had been "a big hit, a huge success!" They immediately began planning for the next year.

Perhaps more important, the success of the event emboldened community council members. After Farm Heritage Days, council discussions became more animated and more focused. The event gave council members confidence that they, indeed, are capable of carrying out the more politically risky activity of drafting a substantive community plan. Such a plan may well result in farmland and waterways being protected from encroaching suburban development and in community-based economic development that should "preserve rural character." Further, the council hopes to install community services, such as a health clinic and a day care center, in the historic high school.

The desire for heritage preservation, while widely expressed and embraced in the abstract, was not strong enough to command attendance at community planning meetings. In contrast, there was widespread attendance of diverse populations at the Farm Heritage Days, which essentially was an affirmation of but not a political struggle for community. In an area renowned for front porch visits and covered dish gatherings, we suggest that public meetings are not always the most culturally appropriate mechanism for promoting community discussions. We view Farm Heritage Days as a form of community mobilization that was a necessary step in the process to build political will (see Lewis, this volume). These types of events are critical sites for the discussion of issues, the dissemination of information, and the opportunity to build consensus as well as extend the invitation to become more involved. The more lasting success for sustainable development in this grand celebration of tradition is the enactment of community as something worth preserving.

"A Different Way of Asking": Comparing the Cases

In many ways, the current political process in Laurel Valley is not as dramatic as in the case of CU. Rather than recruiting and organizing supporters around a single goal or politically charged event, Laurel Valley residents are addressing the rather amorphous issue of undesired community change. They do so at a more leisurely pace. Further, they rely on extensive social and kin networks to accomplish political tasks. They build support for issues during informal social interactions such as visiting, phoning, running into other people at the local store or post office, and attending church gatherings. The group also maintains an ethic of shared control. Among the leadership, no individual has emerged as the discernible central figure. The modus operandi seems to be management by committee.

Contrary to the charges of fatalism often leveled at Appalachians, it is not true that natives never engage in political controversy. The post office incident illustrates the often heated opposition that emerges. This is confirmed by numerous other examples, such as Ashe County's opposition to the damming of the New River and Ivanhoe's response to the flight of their industrial base (Foster 1988; Hinsdale, Lewis, and Waller 1995). But what one informant called "abrasive" politics are easier when the opponent is unknown, as in the case of the federal government. Anger directed at removed targets does not threaten community harmony.

There is a clear cultural preference for amicable political relations within the county. The middle-class members of the council are uncomfortable with controversy or public confrontation. Their avoidance of disagreement has kept the Laurel Valley Community Council from recruiting poorer families into the planning process, just as their fear of a possible backlash has prevented them from drafting more stringent land-use regulations or satisfactorily publicizing key community meetings. This reticence to engage in public conflict is perhaps best seen in council members' approach to county politics. Most of the interactions we have observed between Laurel Valley members and county (and state) officials are friendly and respectful, particularly when they request external support. Or, as one council member advised, one should always be "polite, considerate, and tactful" when dealing with the county commissioners. While a few council members came out to support CU at the air quality hearing in Boone, most shied away from the controversy. This response once again affirms the need to maintain ties for the long term—in this case, vertical clientelist ties with public authorities who are sources of needed material resources, both now and in the future.

At the local level, amicable political relations over the long term are rewarded. This accounts for some of CU's difficulty in gaining full cooperation from local officials. While they had mobilized previously around the fair and racetrack issue, CU members had not demonstrated a continuing civic interest. And they used confrontational tactics. The following extended quote from an interview with a county politician illustrates this point:

> It's not good sense to want things just for a local community. In other words, the group right now [CU], they are never politically real active unless something comes up that directly involves them, like this asphalt plant. Then is when they get demanding. [The Laurel Valley group] will be more of a long-standing group, will always want something but will never be demanding. They are an on-going active group, except, well, for example, they have accepted the responsibility of keeping up the old school building, which I think is very good. They have tried to get us to do some things that we did not want to do but we have finally done it because we felt like it was the best thing to do after looking at it the second time. CU is more apt to say if you don't do this and this and this, you are jeopardizing the health and welfare of Watauga County. There's a different connotation there. Sort of a guilt type portrayal, it makes you feel guilty if you don't. That's the best way I can describe it. [The Laurel Valley group,] they let you know their desires, and they'll ask you for things, and I expect they will continue to ask us for things, but it's in an entirely different tone. [It's] conciliatory, "if you can, we'd like this.' The other group [CU], "we are the only ones that know what's going on.' That's the way they come across. "You don't know a thing about the environment. And we're the ones that keep up with all this. You don't know a thing about it. We're telling you that you need to do this.' It's a different connotation altogether. A different way of asking.

This passage indicates just how crucial long-term, ongoing political relationships are in this local context.

Case Analyses and Suggestions for Community Practitioners

While small communities alone cannot challenge the hegemonic forces of global capital and complicit governmental policies, they can develop unconventional alternatives for resource use and allocation that contest the dominant paradigm. Each of the communities we examined has made progress in that regard. Members of CU have forced the state to regulate asphalt plants more strictly and have become watchdogs for state air policy in general. Their actions broadened local understandings of power, including industry's influence in politics. And this issue has encouraged several to become involved in the environmental movement. Laurel Valley's foray into its own land-use planning is remarkable in a region renowned for opposition to zoning. Because Laurel Valley residents got involved in the issue before too much development had occurred, their proactive planning stands a good chance of preventing some of the natural resource degradation other areas of the county have experienced. Further, their initial intent to avoid a tourist orientation, to search for community-based economic development, and to make community services the center of their efforts could serve to increase the economic viability of the area. This represents an attempt to craft a landscape of sustainable production. It certainly meets the sustainability goal of economic localization.

One way in which these isolated incidents might challenge larger power structures would be for them to ally through the Sustainable Communities Movement. Practitioners could facilitate such affiliation if they recognize that both participation and mobilization are essential to political work and judiciously select moments to encourage appropriate tactics. As phases of political engagement, mobilization and participation each have their limits. Because mobilization targets a delimited goal or crisis and its duration is finite, involvement in it is easier. Mobilizations often involve a broader segment of the community, including those who lack the leisure time to dedicate to long-term participation. However, the exhausting intensity of engagement sometimes discourages people from making a bigger commitment to public issues. Because of the huge time demands over long periods, participation can become an elitist activity. We should encourage selective mobilizations in order to diversify political actors, encouraging the sharing of responsibilities in order to avoid burnout.

As community practitioners, we must also attend to cultural codes governing the public spheres in our various sites. We should be aware of and responsive to community dynamics. As the foregoing indicates, small communities often prefer to avoid conflict. Mobilization frequently (but not always) takes an oppositional stance. It can confront structural issues that cannot be addressed through conciliatory channels. Moreover, the historic record is full of Appalachian communities mobilizing and fighting back when their vital interests and survival are threatened (Anglin 2002; Couto 1999; Fisher 1993). However, rapid intercommunity mobilizations with a single-issue focus can disrupt the social community ties so integral to everyday life. Again, attention to the limits of both participation and mobilization helps activists determine which battles are worth fighting publicly and which political tactics might be used to challenge but not confront the opposition.

Another mentioned cultural factor affecting politics in Appalachia is the extent to which political participation is rooted in the everyday interactions of social life. As activists, we should integrate into the community when possible; we must learn to work through social networks to build wider community and regional coalitions. It includes taking the time to stop and talk with neighbors, "doing a lot of porch settin,'" as Bill Smythe calls it. This also requires learning local and family histories and communicating through the informal networks of family, neighborhood associations (including churches), and other organizations. This is patient work, requiring great sensitivity to events, symbols, and feeling structures that may not be overtly political but nevertheless affirm community (Williams 1977). In the case study above, the time intensive engineering of Farm Heritage Days provided huge payoffs in support for community planning. However, practitioners must be cautious not to devote all their energy to nonsubstantive issues. One caution is a sole engagement with the participatory styles of established leadership without including the less powerful members of the community. This strategy risks stifling often important internal dissent while reinforcing appearances of harmony. In short, we should realize that, in Appalachia, the social interaction of everyday life, in its widest sense, contains the seeds of political engagement. We must allow adequate time to nurture those ties without becoming lost in their cultivation, especially for those more visible groups and interests at the expense of those less visible and too often left out. Practitioners should also search for culturally relevant ways in which to introduce such opportunities. For example, most residents in communities where we work appreciate public awards ceremonies such as the Farm/ City banquet, where people are recognized for such things as service to the dairy industry or for community beautification. Recognition of Laurel Valley's sustainability efforts by Appalachian State University's Goodnight Family Sustainable Development Program has been very helpful in this regard.

Integrating with the community is important for another reason. The region's long history of outsiders attempting to organize Appalachians for spiritual, economic, or political reasons has resulted in a well-founded suspicion of newcomers and their agenda (Whisnant 1994). Sustainable development could easily become the latest fad. Practitioners must begin with what people know and work on projects that address residents' pragmatic interests. We should strive to provide useful information from prior organizing experiences with other communities. Affiliation with the sustainable development movement will require the gradual introduction of information about the larger movement and its goals over time. In our case, Jeff's attempt to convince leaders to include the United Nations' Local Agenda 21 sustainable development criteria in their public planning document would have been more successful if we had laid more groundwork and made more consistent links to other communities working on sustainability in the United States (see Barber 1996).[2] Moreover, world sustainability movements from below have become frustrated with "official sustainable development" as the intergovernmental process at the United Nations is increasingly dominated by large corporate interests, the World Trade Organization, and free trade agreements. Clearly, any viable Local Agenda 21 must safeguard local traditions, institutions, and those aspects of economy based on community reciprocities and commonly held resources, cultural and material (Bruno and Karliner 2002; Schroyer and Golodik 2006).

In the intervening years since we first drafted this essay, CU predictably faded away as an organization after their successful bid to halt the location of the asphalt plant in their midst. Some of its members continue to be active in local community events and politics and remain proud of their past accomplishment. Just as predictably, Laurel Valley community development efforts have not only continued but have expanded, mostly through the efforts of the LVPD. The total renovation of the historic stone construction high school, now as a multiple community service center, includes a state-of-the-art geothermal heating system. A Chinese School of Medicine and community clinic, with medical students from all over the country, occupy more than a third of the building. A day care and early childhood development program, the Doc and Merle Watson Folklife Museum, and an excellent conference room are also found there, as is Bill Smythe's Outreach office. Other businesses have leased space in the building but did not survive the economic downturn of the late 1990s. Nevertheless, the Farm Heritage Days celebration continues each year, and a summer bluegrass and country music festival, often featuring the world renowned Doc Watson himself, draws thousands of fans. To a remarkable degree, the community has managed not to halt the residential, suburban development emanating from Boone, but to keep its distinctive identity as a struggling but viable rural community, at least for those who can afford to remain there.

Our cursory poststudy period assessment is that Laurel Valley's longevity is due to a combination of maintenance of traditional forms of community participation together with a hardheaded entrepreneurial attitude about the projects it engages. This increasingly means less of a generalized spirit of community cooperation in its widest sense and more of an expectation of returns on investments of time, labor, and capital. Many of the LVPD leaders, retired business people themselves (Smythe included), seem to have adapted well to the ubiquitous corporate business model that penetrates and shapes most forms of development and contemporary social life. A detectable proprietary outlook has emerged in community initiatives in negotiating the terms for leasing the renovated community center and for rental fees for the use of its facilities and grounds for annual celebratory events. The leaders, of course, must attend to LVPD's expenses and bottom line. One of them recently reminded me of the more than $1 million expenditures in grants, loans, and volunteer labor incurred in the remodeling of the community center, as we discussed the effect that a debt burden has on narrowing the organization's focus and priorities. Nevertheless, the seemingly constant need to secure and maintain the community center's financial base seems to take precedence over the wider needs of poorer Laurel Valley residents concerned about outsourced jobs, the end of tobacco subsidies, skyrocketing land taxes, and the lack of affordable health care and housing. To LVPD's credit, and with Smythe's pushing, they have attracted some jobs with the medical school and day care center, and they do look for business firms to locate in the community center in order to increase employment opportunities. But a concerted focus on meeting basic human needs for all community members is less visible, and the harried leadership seems to have little time to seek out and involve lower income members in LVPD decision making.

While acknowledging the widespread use of the social capital construct, Boyer elsewhere has criticized its use as reductionist of the community and communal skills of sharing, reciprocity, and widespread participation in social life (2006).[3] Donald Nonini (2006), Boyer (2006), and others suggest that scholars consider a conceptual alternative: the commons and the related processes of commons-making in community life: "What is now at stake at this point in world history is control over 'the commons'—the great variety of natural, physical, social, intellectual and cultural resources that make human survival possible. By 'the commons' I mean those assemblages and ensembles of resources that human beings hold in common or entrust to use on behalf of themselves, other living human beings, and past and future generations of human beings, and which are essential to their biological, cultural and social re-production" (Nonini 2006:164).

The writers of this series of articles specify varieties of commons. Tracing the rich history of land-based commons and community commons-making in Appalachia, Boyer defines commons as "a communally shared system of resources and services" and commons-making as "processes of social reciprocity and sharing by individuals and communal groups" (2006:217–18). Appalachia built on its earlier "open range" land commons and the reciprocal kin and rural community ties to create coalitions of community-regional organizations, including labor unions, to resist various forms of externally imposed exploitation and subordination.

While some commons-making through the processes of participation and mobilization was clearly evident in both CU and Laurel Valley, the more critical edge of these constructs makes it clear that much more could and can be done to cross class divides to become more equitable and democratic. In the former community, it seems clear that that mobilizing to save the neighborhood from the proposed asphalt plant's environmental and health threats was a form of commons-making, albeit limited by the focus on its mainly professional middle-class residents and its episodic, single-issue time frame. Laurel Valley's participation began as more of an all-inclusive process, led mostly by its more middle-class elites but open for input, in a very Appalachian way, to poorer natives. Several years after saving the old high school building and converting it to a multiple service center (and business incubator) and turning the annual festivals into moneymaking events, participation by Laurel Valley elites has increasingly narrowed to protect their significant capital and volunteer labor investment, trading on images of the imagined rural mountain community for financial return. Their expressed concerns for lower income residents are much less salient, and widespread involvement in community decision making has clearly waned. At this writing, the cycle of participation as an all-inclusive process of commons-making has declined.

We conclude that new perceived systematic threats to the survival of Laurel Valley as a community, as well as major economic opportunities, could trigger a renewed process of both widespread participation and mobilization potentially involving the older seasoned leaders and new recruits. Threats include massive suburban development emanating from Boone and the challenge to shift to renewable energy and relocalized mountain food systems because of global peak oil, climate change, and health threats. Opportunities include the creation of new livelihoods in such a transforming economy. As we work to strengthen the five-year-old Appalachian Coalition for Just and Sustainable Communities (http://www.appcoalition.org), we must take into serious account the local dynamics and distinctive modes of political engagement at the grassroots. Crucial is the lesson too easily deferred for more immediate political or material advantage: until poor and working people see themselves reflected in changing institutions and processes, they will not participate. And, until civic leaders are accorded respect for local priorities and concerns from increasingly undemocratic state and national authorities, they will not participate either.

Notes

We gratefully acknowledge the Z. Smith Reynolds Foundation and the National Science Foundation for funding the research that informs this essay.

1. We have used pseudonyms for the names of individuals, communities, and citizens groups.

2. The United Nations (1994) Local Agenda 21 includes the following subject areas: commerce and trade; combating poverty; changing consumption patterns; population growth and stabilization; human health; housing; transportation; energy use; air quality; water quality; land and soils; forest protection; sustainable agriculture; biodiversity; chemicals and waste; partnerships with civic organizations, governmental authorities, and business seeking to promote sustainable development; corporate responsibility and accountability; financing for sustainable development; utilizing appropriate technologies and scientific methods; community and organizational capacity building; supportive legal instruments and mechanisms; public education about sustainable development; and enhanced citizen decision making.

3. Boyer elaborates that inevitably these skills and capabilities, such as participation and mobilization, become reduced to capitalism's incessant processes of individualization, differential accumulation, and, of course, the materialistic commodification of virtually all social relations and life experience. Our view, shared by others (Gibson-Graham 2006:58–59), is that the current intellectual and practical use of social capital, often innocently enough in Appalachia, does not "accidentally" accompany this unprecedented period of global capitalist advance. It can include the mentioned use of corporate business practices and thinking for community development (and we could include similar debasements of public education and other aspects of public and private worlds). Richard Couto's major work on social capital (1999) insists upon stringent limitations for this construct's use. He found that such public goods and moral resources for much of the twentieth century have varied primarily with the market's need to produce and sustain laborers, and has often diverted such resources from the tasks of building viable communities. To "make democracy work better" (Couto's suggestive title), he argues that social capital can only be liberating and empowering when poor and working people are able to access and constructively use these resources, as opposed to just the professional, well-educated middle class and elites.

References

Anglin, Mary. 2002. "Lessons from Appalachia in the 20th Century: Poverty, Power, and the Grassroots." *American Anthropologist* 104(2):565–82.

Arthur, John Preston. 1992. *A Family History of Watauga County.* Johnson City, TN: Over Mountain Press.

Barber, Jeffrey. 1996. "The Sustainable Communities Movement." *Journal of Environment and Development* 5(3): 338–48.

Bartlett, Lesley, and Jeff Boyer. 1997. "[Laurel Valley] Resolves: A Community Assessment of Needs and Priorities." Boone, NC: Appalachian State Univ. Sustainable Development Program.

Beaver, Pat. 1992. *Rural Community in the Appalachian South.* Prospect Heights, IL: Waveland Press.

Boyer, Jeff. 1990. "Charisma, Martyrdom and Liberation in Southern Honduras." *Comparative Social Research Supplement I.* Pp. 115–59.

—— 2006. "Reinventing the Appalachian Commons." *Social Analysis* 50(3):217–32.

Boyer, Jeff, Jonas Monast, and Ray Moretz. 1993. "Toward a Sustainable Economy in Western North Carolina: Ashe and Watauga Counties." Boone, NC: Appalachian State Univ. Sustainable Development Program.

Bruno, Kenny, and Joshua Karliner. 2002. *Earthsummit.biz: The Corporate Takeover of Sustainable Development.* Oakland: Food First Books.

Buell, John, and Tom DeLuca. 1996. *Sustainable Democracy: Individuality and the Politics of the Environment.* Thousand Oaks, CA: Sage Publications.

Calhoun, Craig. 1982. *The Question of Class Struggle: Social Foundations of the Popular Radicalism during the Industrial Revolution.* Chicago: Univ. of Chicago Press.

——. 1983. "The Radicalism of Tradition: Community Strength or Venerable Disguise and Borrowed Language." *American Journal of Sociology* 88(5):886–914.

Couto, Richard A. 1999. *Making Democracy Work Better: Mediating Structures, Social Capital, and the Democratic Prospect.* Chapel Hill: Univ. of North Carolina Press.

Fisher, Stephen (Ed.). 1993. *Fighting Back in Appalachia: Traditions of Resistance and Change.* Philadelphia: Temple Univ. Press.

Flavin, Christopher. 1997. "The Legacy of Rio." In *State of the World,* Lester Brown (Ed.). World Watch Institute. New York: W. W. Norton.

Foster, Stephen. 1988. *The Past Is Another Country.* Berkeley: Univ. of California Press.

Gibson-Graham, J. K. 2006. *A PostCapitalist Politics.* Minneapolis: Univ. of Minnesota Press.

Hinsdale, Marianne, Helen M. Lewis, and Maxine Waller. 1995. *It Comes from the People: Community Development and Local Theology.* Philadelphia: Temple Univ. Press.

Holland, Dorothy, Donald Nonini, Catherine Lutz, Lesley Bartlett, Maria Frederick-McGathery, Thaddeus Gulbrandsen, and Enrique Murillo Jr. 2007. *Local Democracy under Siege: Activism, Public Interests and Private Politics.* New York: New York Univ. Press.

Nonini, Donald. 2006. "Forum Introduction: The Global Idea of the Commons." *Social Analysis* 50(3):164–77.

Region D Council of Government. 1992. In-house report. Boone, NC.

Reid, Herbert, and Betsy Taylor. 2000. "Embodying Ecological Citizenship: Rethinking the Politics of Grassroots Globalization in the United States." *Alternatives* 25(Dec.):439–66.

Schmidt, Steffen (Ed.). 1977. *Friends, Followers, and Factions.* Berkeley: Univ. of California Press.

Schroyer, Trent and Golodik, Thomas (Eds.). 2006. *Creating a Sustainable World: Past Experiences/Future Struggles.* New York: Apex Press.

Stokes, Ralf. 1997. "First Power Mower on [Laurel Valley]." Unpublished pamphlet. Laurel Valley, NC.

Tursi, Frank. 1997. "Creeping Death." *Winston-Salem Journal,* July 20, 1997.

United Nations. 1994. Agenda 21. New York: United Nations.

U.S. Dept. of Agriculture and North Carolina Dept. of Agriculture and Consumer Services. Various dates, 1964–92. North Carolina Agricultural Statistics. Raleigh: North Carolina Dept. of Agriculture.

Watauga Economic Development Commission. 1992. "Economic Trends in Watauga County." Unpublished report. Boone, NC.

Whisnant, David. 1994. *Modernizing the Mountaineer: People, Power and Planning in Appalachia.* Knoxville: Univ. of Tennessee Press.

Williams, Raymond. 1977. *Marxism and Literature.* New York: Oxford Univ. Press.

Zelenko, Laura. 1992. "Down Mexico Way." *North Carolina Business* (International Business Report) (Nov.): 25–35.

Zukin, Sharon. 1991. *Landscapes of Power: From Detroit to Disneyworld.* Berkeley: Univ. of California Press.

Playing the Power Game

THE LIMITS OF
PARTICIPATORY DEVELOPMENT

Melinda Bollar Wagner

This case study examines the struggle between rural residents and one of the largest energy companies in the world seeking to construct a power line along a route from West Virginia to Virginia. Working with residents in several counties, Wagner and her students set a precedent in the field of environmental impact assessment by establishing the significance of cultural attachment to land as a significant issue. Participatory research involving citizens in data collection and management was essential in completing the final report submitted to the State Corporation Commission. Wagner elaborates on the significance of three types of social capital (bonding, bridging, and linking) in the decision-making process. While social capital may have empowered citizens engaged in the process to protect their land, she concludes that powerful adversaries like the power company (who ultimately were granted construction rights) may inevitably trump citizen activists who scramble to get into the game. Furthermore, she points out that decisions made at the federal level to further centralize decision making in these issues do not serve participatory goals.

The introduction to this book tells us that "the purpose of intervention through participatory development is to strengthen stakeholders in contesting power holders' authoritative control of cultural meaning." This chapter reports on an attempt to do just that. But it also delineates the limits of participatory development. This case study of citizens' protest of a proposed 765,000 volt power line confronts this issue: "Who ought to sit at the table when the big decisions get made? . . . Whose values should inform the choices?" (Liebow 1998/99:18).

The power line project began in the spring of 1993 when Radford University's Appalachian studies seminar examined an ongoing controversy between the utility company and citizens' protest organizations. The Appalachian Power Company (American Electric Power)—"one of the largest energy companies in the world," with "one of the world's largest transmission systems—224,000 miles of transmission and distribution lines—and one of the highest volume power trading operations anywhere"—proposed building another 765,000 volt power line (http://www.AEP.com). It would carry electricity one hundred miles from coal-fired power plants in West Virginia to a substation in Virginia. From there the power could be used locally and also be sent or "wheeled" to other utility companies in the southeastern United States. The 765s, as they call them, are the huge power towers that are eight stories high—132 feet—with 200-foot-wide rights-of-way. This line would have 333 towers. The decisions regarding whether to build the power line, and if so, where, rested in the hands of state government bodies regulating utilities, labeled the Public Utilities Commission in West Virginia and the State Corporation Commission (SCC) in Virginia. Because the proposed route of the power line crossed federal land, an environmental impact assessment was required, with the U.S. Forest Service as the lead coordinating agency. Cultural attachment to land—along with many other aspects of the ecology and geology of the area—became a so-called significant issue in this assessment.

In some cases the desire to preserve natural resources and to conserve cultural resources are at odds with one another. For example, it may be that to preserve a fragile riverine ecosystem, farmers who have lived near it for generations would have to be moved off of the nearby land. But in the power line case, preservation of natural resources, conservation of cultural resources, and protection of future economic resources would all be served by the same "no build" decision. The natural resource of water running through karst topography would best be preserved by not putting a power line corridor requiring use of herbicides on top of it. Conserving the cultural trait of the use of springs as the primary water supply would be served by the same decision. Conserving folklore that has the power of the area's many bold springs as its locus would be served by the same decision. The natural beauty of the area would be preserved by not dotting it with power towers. Conserving the cultural attachment to the land that has this natural beauty as one of its pillars is served by the same decision. Protecting the economic aid promised by nurturing tourism in the area is served by the same decision.

Cultural Identity: Cultural Attachment to Land

Recognition is growing that environmental actions change the culture as well as the ecology in which human beings live. Folklorist Mary Hufford (1998:8, 10), studying in West Virginia, suggests that cultural activities that have the local landscape as their focus—talk about native plants and places, suppers that use a native plant, and roaming the mountains—function "as touchstones to a shared past, and as thresholds to a future. . . . [They] are resources for holding together a way of life that is continually dismantled by plans for progress."

Common knowledge of place, common talk of place, and activities in common places have helped residents to confront perceived threats. The proposed power line was seen as a threat to beauty and historic continuity. "Seeing the same things the ancestors saw" would be no more. It would tear at the serenity residents praised and thus be "just too costly in the human spirit." Anthropologists suggest that this resident's plaintive testimony was not an overstatement. Indeed, "without place conservation, the contents of culturally meaningful behaviors and processes of place-making disappear, cutting us off from our past, disrupting the present, and limiting the possibilities for the future" (Low 1994:66; see also Allen 1990; Downs and Stea 1977; Halmo, Stoffle, and Evans 1993; Relph 1976; Ryden 1993; Simonson 1989).

Cultural Intrusion

The sense of place versus the place of progress came head to head in the residents' and power company's perspectives on the power line. Residents aired their concerns at SCC hearings. The hearing examiner encapsulated their thoughts when he wrote that they "viewed the proposed transmission line as a symbol of corporate greed imposed at the expense of the cultural attachment of the people to their land and the scenic beauty of the region" (Anderson 2000:3). "As Bill Mitchell, a retired railroad engineer put it, "it's nothing but an electric interstate in the sky that's going to dump cheap Midwest electricity into the East Coast market" (Pritt 1995:23). Residents who came to the Appalachian studies seminar said, "We are a thinly settled rural relatively poor area lying between surplus generation in the west and growth area in the east." "It's the large corporation seeking to increase or maintain profits . . . they try to roll over poor rural people . . . destroy people and environment for a profit. They're making us a national sacrifice area." "They're going to peddle power over us."

The Project

In the Appalachian studies seminar we studied this controversy as an example of protest in the Appalachian region. Activists from this and earlier environmental controversies, power company executives, and academic experts on social movements and culture change visited the classroom and served as resource persons for students who interviewed them (Wagner, Scott, and Wolfe 1997).

Subsequently, citizens who had helped with this project asked us to undertake an anthropological ethnographic study of cultural attachment to land in their county. The ethnographic research methods of anthropology have been described as a "disciplined attempt to discover and describe the symbolic resources with which members of a society conceptualize and interpret their experience" (Basso and Selby 1976:2). Ethnographic methods are well known for eliciting information from the insider's/native's point of view. Ethnographer's label this an "emic" perspective and lay it alongside an "etic," or an outsider's/analytic perspective. So, ethnographic methods are particularly well suited to social impact analysis that requires an internal view of the affected community.

To answer the question of whether there is cultural attachment to land here, and if so, on what it is based, anthropological ethnographic interviews were conducted. From this talk, anthropologists learn what is salient in a culture. In ethnographic interviews, the ethnographers are careful not to ask leading questions or make leading comments. (For example, questions and comments like, "Would you say you loved your land?" or "I'll bet you love your land" would never be used.) There were no answers implied in the questions that we asked; there were no multiple choice answers supplied. The questions were used when necessary to elicit talk. Over 300 slides and more than 150 photos of areas that residents pointed out to the researchers were taken (in some cases, the residents were handed the cameras and framed the pictures themselves). We also attended church services, subscribed to the local newspapers, and collected archival materials such as booklets of local history and the like that residents gave us.

Long-standing anthropological theory contends that cultures contain themes that organize their rules for behavior and the meanings these behaviors have. Anthropological methods have demonstrated that behavior and language provide clues to a culture's themes and values. For example, an often stated motto would be a clue to a culture's overarching themes. Ortner (1973:1339) says that these key symbols (or cultural themes) "will be signaled by more than one of these indicators: (1) the natives tell us that X is culturally important; (2) the natives seem positively or negatively aroused about X, rather than indifferent; (3) X comes up in many different contexts. . . . X comes up in many different kinds of action situation or conversation, or X comes up in many different symbolic domains (myth, ritual, art, formal rhetoric, etc.); (4) there is greater cultural elaboration surrounding X, e.g., elaboration of vocabulary or elaboration of details of X's nature, compared with similar phenomena in the culture; (5) there are greater cultural restrictions surrounding X, either in sheer number of rules, or severity of sanctions regarding its misuse."

The first things people talk about, and the first things people show, as well as repetitions and patterns, are markers for their culture's themes. Thus, analysis of the text of interviews discovered what is salient to people by finding what they talk about *first,* what they talk about *often,* what *kinds* of things they talk about, what things they talk about with much *detail,* what *stories* they tell, what *metaphors* they use, and what kinds of things they *could* talk about but *do not.*

The residents' talk captured in the interviews was subjected to a threefold examination utilizing thematic analysis of content, linguistic analysis of speech, and analysis of the stories told. A triangulation of the three analysis tools revealed overall patterns in the data gleaned from the interviews. For example, cultural knowledge of the environment—discerned in thematic analysis—was also discovered by noting an elaboration of vocabulary used in describing the environment, and by tabulation of a large number of coded stories that utilized this knowledge.

As other counties that lay in the path of various proposed routes for the power line called on us, study of cultural attachment to land expanded to include eleven semesters, more than 100 undergraduate students, and 223 residents of ten communities in five counties. It resulted in over four thousand pages of transcribed interviews ranging from twenty minutes to six hours in length, and over three thousand pages of computerized linguistic analyses of these data, along with some two thousand pages of thematic content analyses. (See Wagner [1999, 2002] for more discussion of the methodology used.)

Social Capital

The term "social capital" is now being used to describe connections that can be useful and empowering.[1] The ultimate battleground for the power line controversy was the SCC of Virginia, a three-judge panel charged with the responsibility of making decisions concerning utilities, among other things. What role did social capital play in the citizens' actions in these legal-like proceedings?

A broad definition of social capital is "resources that stem from relationships." It is "the connections among individuals—social networks and the norms of reciprocity and trustworthiness that arise from them." The terms that define different kinds of social capital—bonding, bridging, and linking—refer to which groups are connecting (Furbey et al. 2006; see also Woolcock 2001; Gilchrist 2004). The power line protest included all three types of social capital.

BONDING SOCIAL CAPITAL

Bonding social capital occurs "within communities of substantially similar people," between "close-knit groups," such as family or friends who have "multifaceted relationships" (Furbey et al. 2006:7). One of the areas we worked with, Clover Hollow and its neighboring community, Plow Screw, in Giles County, Virginia, has around three hundred residents on about ten square miles of land. Some 70 percent of the land is still in the hands of the descendants of six families who settled there between the 1790s and the 1880s. The original power line protestors already had relationships like these described by Doris Lucas Link, a sixth-generation resident of Plow Screw: "My mother, my brother, I, and 90 percent of our neighbors have been on this land continuously," down through generations ever since the ancestors arrived (Link, Brady, and Givens 2002:139). When the community met for the first time about the power line, it met "at Marty Farrier's farm at the head of the Hollow." At first, not everyone in the community took up the battle cry. Doris tells that on her first attempt at fund-raising, an old-timer said, "There's no use to fight AEP [American Electric Power], they're too big." (Succumbing to Doris's persuasion, the man did give a ten dollar donation.) However, later, when a letter challenging part of the U.S. Forest Service environmental impact assessment was being circulated, "only two residents who could be reached declined to sign the letter. They no longer live in Clover Hollow" (152).

BRIDGING SOCIAL CAPITAL

Bridging social capital connects "people who have less in common, but may have overlapping interests, such as neighbors, colleagues, or different groups in a community" (Furbey et al. 2006:7). Bridges were built among three circles of people. First, the Giles County community members were not solely old-timers. As in other Appalachian communities, the number of "brought-ins" (new residents not native to the area) has expanded substantially in recent years. The power line protest brought people from these groups together as one constituency. For example, Doris Lucas Link, Nancy Kate Givens, and David Brady—who have different connections to the area—are all members of the Greater Newport Rural Historic Society, all are members of the organizations that were founded to protest the power line, and all contributed in different ways to the effort. Doris, the sixth-generation resident, belongs to the Loosely Woven Quilt Group in the county. The quilters provided quilts for raffles to raise funds for Citizens Organized to Protect the Environment. Nancy Kate Givens, retired from teaching in another locale and settled back into the place of her ancestors, is a local historian. She concentrated her efforts on "gathering the facts to prove that most of our lands were still in the hands of the descendants of the original settlers" (Link, Brady, and Givens 2002:148). Her voluminous work on the history of landholdings in the area was used to gain Rural Historic District status in the Virginia and National Register of Historic Places. David Brady was a newcomer to the area—a retired military officer turned Christmas tree farmer. As an engineer, his knowledge was instrumental to understanding and questioning the purported need and purpose of the power line.

Second, the Giles County group benefited from its relationship with other county-level organizations who were protesting other potential routes of the same power line, such as Craig County, who had come under scrutiny earlier. In turn, the Craig County group was connected with a West Virginia group. It is in the West Virginia group that cultural attachment to land was first raised, was made a "significant issue" in the environmental impact assessment, and was extrapolated to the nearby Virginia counties. Eventually citizens of five different counties lay under proposed routes and mounted protest efforts.

This particular set of bridges, however, became strained as several potential routes were identified and then each studied by the SCC in competition with the others. The procedures of the courtlike system separate need from route and hear these as separate issues. Then each proposed route has separate hearings in turn, which promulgates NIMBYism (Not in My Back Yard). An attorney for one opposing county said he could not be the attorney for another without fear of conflict of interest. This one-at-a-time competitive process hammered away at early coalitions until some dissolved into individual groups with "just don't put it here" philosophies.

Third, the protest organizations called upon the members of an organization that had protested an earlier 765,000 volt power line in Floyd County, Virginia, built a decade before. The organization had disbanded after the power line was no longer an issue, but its leaders lent their insights to the fledgling protest groups.

Linking Social Capital

Linking social capital forms relationships "between people or organizations beyond peer boundaries, cutting across status, and similarity, and enabling people to exert influence and reach resources outside their normal circles" (Furbey et al. 2006:7). This type of linkage was made to people with specialized knowledge and methodologies in an attempt to level the playing field between a national power company—with funds to pay a cadre of lawyers and experts—and rural communities. For example, an expert on electromagnetic fields was hired, and a university geology professor was asked to provide information about the effect of herbicides (to maintain the power line corridor) on water used for people and animals. To further the Giles County communities' "proactive strategy" of seeking state and national designation as a Rural Historic District, "a historic preservation specialist retained by the Virginia Department of Historic Resources" provided aid (Link, Brady, and Givens 2000:145).

My own link to the project is in this category. Residents were pleased that a cultural intangible—cultural attachment to land—was being studied as part of the environmental impact assessment. However, the findings of the original subcontractors for this part of the assessment (reported in the Draft Environmental Impact Statement [DEIS]) left the residents puzzled and troubled by the methodology employed. I, in turn, connected them to anthropologist Benita Howell, who, from her vantage point as an applied ethnographer and Appalachian studies scholar, "became a *pro bono* consultant to the community . . . working with them to obtain information about the contract firm's research procedures and answering questions that arose as they prepared their written comments on the DEIS" (Link, Brady, and Givens 2002).

Citizens from Craig County who knew me and my students because of the Appalachian studies seminar project about protest in Appalachia asked us to also do a study of cultural attachment to land in their county. They trusted that we would use proper ethnographic methods and ethics. The study we completed served as a supplement to the environmental impact assessment. Then, we linked with the communities from Giles County to do the same type of research for another proposed route, and finally with Bland and Wythe counties for yet another route.

Definitions of social capital include trust as a bellwether of the connected relationship. However, this trust and feeling of reciprocity are not born fully formed in linked relationships. I was not fully aware of the distrust the local residents had for the colleges and universities in the area until I received this letter of thanks from Craig County resident Charles Spraker: "We're all proud of you and your students for helping us open our eyes and see that what we know, feel, and are can be of value and is not useless. . . . You know, Melinda, when we first started getting involved in this process . . . we were actually scared of our own colleges, as some of us thought they were looking down on us."

As in traditional anthropological ethnographic fieldwork, the role that we played was not always interpreted the same way by the anthropologists, on the one hand, and by our informants, on the other hand. For example, I had told our major informant in a phone conversation that this kind of work was called cultural conservation. When my students and I drove to his house to make entrée and to become oriented to the county, he observed, "I know you think you have a culture to conserve here, but we have a power line to stop." Nevertheless, the rapport gained between residents and university faculty and students who interviewed them yielded a nearly fictive kin relationship, and certainly a symbiotic one. Charles Spraker wrote: "We gained a lot from our involvement with you and your students and you all made us feel good about our station and way of life. So you, dear Melinda, learned from us and we learned from you, so in the end we're all winners."

The third phase of the project took us into new territory and gave us new roles. Our two earlier research reports on cultural attachment to land had been given to citizens' groups, to do with as they liked in their efforts to conserve their culture and preserve their environment. This time I was asked by representatives of two adjoining counties, Bland and Wythe, to present our report directly to the state regulatory body for utilities, and to testify in a hearing before this body. This brought us face-to-face with the legal arena and carried with it the new role of expert witness.

The very short time allowed for this study demanded other changes. It would not be possible for a cadre of trained students to compile extensive participant observation field notes and to conduct and transcribe interviews, undertake analyses of these texts, and write the report, as we had done in the past. Citizens suggested that they themselves could conduct and transcribe the interviews.

This was a new level of citizen science. Previously, residents with whom we worked had provided orientations for me and the student researchers and smoothed our entrée into their communities; this time residents would be collecting data themselves in participatory research. To help resident interviewers with data collecting, a comprehensive project manual compiled with my colleague Mary LaLone—which included open-ended questions that had been tested in my previous research—was developed, and a workshop on ethnographic interviewing was conducted.

If our experiment worked, perhaps it could serve as a model for allowing citizen input in the legal arena, especially for communities with little money or in situations with little time allowed. My colored glasses became even rosier, and I wrote, "The objective of this project is to create ways in which citizens' environmental concerns—such as cultural attachment to land—are rendered audible in a legal venue by being articulated through scientific means" (see Wagner 1999, 2002; Wagner and Hedrick 2001).

Is Social Capital Empowering?

County residents' social capital contributed in a number of ways to the state-level process of decision making on the power line. Linking with a university professor and students was empowering with regard to demonstrating to the culture-bearers that others valued and were interested in their cultures. It chipped away at the accretions built up by years of stereotyping of rural Appalachian people. When students presented a play that they had created to the Craig County Historical Society, impersonating Craig County residents with words from the students' interviews with them, an audience member commented that she had never before felt proud of her heritage. Local historian Nancy Kate Givens says that letting families know about the results of her research on genealogy and land records was pleasurable. "They knew they had been here forever, but no one had presented that as something to brag about" (Link, Brady, and Givens 2002:150).

Citizen involvement in the research—enhanced by various forms of social capital—was critical to empowerment. Let the words of Doris Lucas Link illustrate: "When I became involved in the AEP fight in 1993, I never imagined it would take me to college [to teach my classes about her community], make an amateur architect of me, send me to the state capitol to speak before the [SCC], . . . [and cause me to speak] at an Appalachian Studies Conference" (Link, Brady, and Givens 2002).

The project was of course empowering for the student researchers as well. After the presentation of the Craig County play, one of the students sent the research team a message that she could not sleep at night because she was overwhelmed by the positive reception their work had received.

Residents realized the value of both citizen research and linking social capital. About citizen research, David Brady wrote: "Clover Hollow and Plow Screw's experiences demonstrate the value of citizen participation in environmental assessments. Active participation by communities at risk, especially proactive strategies, will be necessary in the future to ensure that consideration of cultural intangibles such as attachment to land can produce tangible protection for communities" (Link, Brady, and Givens 2002:147).

Linking social capital was also recognized as helpful to the communities. Nancy Kate Givens relates the story of her father, who in the 1950s, during another struggle against utility lines, had not had this support. He and his neighbors "had been helpless in finding resources to fight the utilities giant" (Link, Brady, and Givens 2002:148). But this time around, she felt, things were different.

The residents made contact with those on the other side of the table whenever they were allowed to. The U.S. Forest Service was the lead agency coordinating the environmental impact assessment, since several of the proposed power line routes would cross Forest Service land. The residents attended public meetings with the U.S. Forest Supervisor of the affected region and wrote letters. They provided testimony to the SCC.

Anthropologist Benita Howell (1999:7; see also Howell 2002) identified this power line situation as a "path-breaking and potentially precedent-setting case" because cultural attachment to land was designated a significant issue in the environmental impact assessment process. Resident David Brady wrote, "These studies helped the community identify and assess key intangible dimensions of attachment to land in Clover Hollow and Plow Screw and articulate the issue of attachment to decision-makers at the state and federal level" (Link, Brady, and Givens 2002:145).

Originally the ethnographic research that utilized citizen researchers as interviewers was criticized at one of the SCC hearings and ultimately rehabilitated by the three-judge panel. Its critic was one of the attorneys employed by AEP, who, for example, noted with disdain that interviewers had interviewed their relatives (Wagner and Hedrick 2001). The lawyer's criticisms were repeated in the hearing examiner's report to the three-judge panel that ultimately would make the final decision—a forty-three-page summary of some three thousand pages of testimony from public hearings. The criticisms were ably refuted in the Exceptions to the Report of the Hearing Examiner, written by the attorney hired by the county. In their order laying down their decision, the SCC disagreed with its own hearing examiner and rehabilitated the ethnographic research. (This was the only instance of disagreement with their hearing examiner in their sixty-two-page order.)

Although we can say that the community-university collaboration had an impact on the decision-making process, it had limited effect on the decision itself. The SCC separates the decisions regarding the need for a power line and its placement. Thus, once need is established in this court, the only decision remaining is where the power line will be built. The SCC's order showed that they had attended to the research. In the ultimate order granting authority to construct the transmission facility, the SCC wrote:

> With respect to the testimony of public witnesses and certain parties, it is readily apparent that residents along the possible routes have a strong attachment to the land that would be affected by the Project. In their testimony before the Hearing Examiner, many spoke of generations of a family living and working on particular farms. Their words by themselves conveyed the strong attachments the witnesses have. In addition to individuals' testimony, the study [of local history and genealogy] sponsored by Protestant witnesses John Dodson and Denise Smith documented the particular attachments to the land of the residents of the Dry Fork community in Bland County. Further, Protestant witness Melinda Bollar Wagner collected additional expressions of attachment to particular farms and communities and of continuous habitation in her study of cultural attachment of residents of Bland and Wythe Counties.
>
> The Commission disagrees with the Hearing Examiner's conclusions on bias in Ms. Wagner's study. We give weight to the study's conclusions that residents of the two counties, especially the Dry Fork and Walker's Creek communities, have individual and communal ties to particular pieces of land. We accept her conclusion that these residents have "emotional, economic, and social connections to their surrounding landscapes."
>
> In addition to their attachment to the land, those living along the proposed routes expressed deep concern over the intrusion of the towers and conductors into the rural landscape. They were joined in these expressions of concern by those who might have views of the line or might encounter the line as they travel through the affected communities.
>
> The Commission has considered carefully these and other expressions of concern about the line. As noted earlier, members of the Commission personally inspected much of the route on the ground, and one Commissioner viewed the routes from the air. Reading statements made at the hearing, reviewing the statements and interviews collected in the Wagner and Dodson and Smith studies, and our viewing of the route give us some insight into the concerns of these people. We have been mindful of these concerns as we have discharged our responsibility to consider the impact of the line on the environment, and to approve the route that, on balance, minimizes adverse environmental impact.
>
> Unfortunately, any of the alternatives we have considered would have undesirable impacts that may, in some individual instances, be significant. Nevertheless, the record demonstrates clearly the potential negative consequences of failing to take appropriate action. We must make a decision that inevitably and regrettably will have some negative impact. . . .

We have considered the residents of all areas that would be impacted by this line and the alternatives. . . . Members of the Commission visited these communities, among others. We saw first hand the potential impacts where the proposed line would cross the mountain's face. While [one of the protest groups] suggested in its Comments that participation in the process was in vain, the Commission values all expressions of views and efforts to provide information. (SCC 2001)

However, news articles at the time the power line was completed quoted Representative Joe Barton, Republican-Texas, chairman of the Federal Energy Regulatory Commission, as saying, "'Never again will it take 15 or 16 years to build a project like this, if it's a necessity,' thanks to 2005 congressional legislation easing restrictions," implying a potential rollback in the decision-making process, to the detriment of citizen involvement in environmental impact assessment (Dellinger 2006).[2]

Whose Values Should Inform the Choices?

We provided linked social capital to citizens along three routes. Two of the areas avoided power line construction. In 2006 the power line was built in the third area we studied, the corridor that passed through Bland and Wythe counties. The last line splice took place at a ceremony pictured in the *Roanoke Times,* with reception tents in the background and the governors of Virginia and West Virginia looking on (Dellinger 2006).

Research enhanced by linked social capital can bring into focus the concerns and values of local people. It is worthwhile to continue the links between anthropological ethnographic research and local communities, because "as soon as our attention turns from a community as a body of houses and tools and institutions to the states of mind of particular people, we are turning to the exploration of something immensely complex and difficult to know" (Redfield 1960:59). The stories of the human community—in all their fullness and all their complexity—have to be told.

But can social capital ever propel those values into head-to-head equality with the values of the decision makers? When the power of place struggled with the place of progress, who won? In the long run, were the ultimate values upon which decisions are made affected?

Early in the study, I expressed concern to our main contact in Craig County that research on cultural attachment to land—whatever its ultimate findings— might have no impact on the final decision. He said that we should forge on with the study, because "sometimes decision-makers want to do the right thing, and they just need a reason to do it." Nevertheless, once the decision to build the power line was made, one community of longtime residents/power line protestors was going to lose, no matter how much social capital was invoked.

At the beginning of this chapter, we asked, "Who ought to sit at the table when the big decisions get made? . . . Whose values should inform the choices?" (Liebow 1998/99:18). We have made a case that social capital helps to make a place at the table for local communities. However, the Energy Policy Act of 2005 demands that more environmental decisions be made at the federal level. As a result of this legislation headlines cry, "Opponents of a proposed transmission line along the [New York] Upper Delaware River have found state officials to be sympathetic, but a new law may give the federal government the final say" and "Energy policy threatens Florida's coasts" (DePalma 2006; Davis and Miller 2005). These concerns show that the values that come to bear in the balancing act between the power of place and the place of progress—values that overwhelmingly privilege economic concerns—have not changed. In the meantime, local communities can only watch as the decision-making table moves out of sight.

Notes

1. I must register a bit of discomfort when using terms such as "stakeholders" and "social capital." In writings in progress, I have decried the overwhelming place economy has in our society when set beside concerns for environment and sense of place. Yet now we in social science are using economically derived terms to describe ways to help communities voice their concerns and to balance economic needs with other cultural values. Nevertheless, the vocabulary of social capital may help to describe ways participatory development unfolds. So, with some trepidation, I will proceed to use the term.

2. American Electric Power chairman, president, and chief executive officer Michael Morris said, "that will help AEP's next proposed project, a 765-kilovolt line covering some 550 miles from West Virginia to New Jersey. AEP is seeking commission approval to build most of the line outside its service territory" (Dellinger 2006).

References

Allen, Barbara. 1990. "The Genealogical Landscape and the Southern Sense of Place." In *Sense of Place,* Barbara Allen and Thomas J. Schlereth (Eds.). Lexington: Univ. Press of Kentucky. Pp.152–63.

Anderson, Howard P., Jr. 2000. Report. Case No. PUE970766, Oct. 2. Richmond, VA.

APST 460. 1993. Appalachian Studies Seminar. Radford Univ., Radford, VA. Spring Semester.

Basso, Keith H., and Henry A. Selby. 1976. *Meaning in Anthropology.* Albuquerque: Univ. of New Mexico Press.

Davis, Jim, and Jeff Miller. 2005. "Energy Policy Threatens Florida's Coasts." *St. Petersburg (FL) Times,* Apr. 25.

Dellinger, Paul. 2006. "End of the Line." *Roanoke Times,* May 9.

DePalma, Anthony. 2006. "Chafing at a Plan to Add Power Lines to the Landscape." *New York Times,* July 10.

Downs, Roger M., and David Stea. 1977. *Maps in Minds: Reflections on Cognitive Mapping.* New York: Harper and Row.

Furbey, Robert, Adam Dinham, Richard Farnell, Doreen Finneron, and Guy Wilkinson. 2006. *Faith as Social Capital: Connecting or Dividing?* Bristol, UK: Policy Press.

Gilchrist, A. 2004. *The Well-Connected Community: A Networking Approach to Community Development.* Bristol, UK: Policy Press.

Halmo, David B., Richard W. Stoffle, and Michael J. Evans. 1993. "Paitu Nana Suagaindu Pahonupi (Three Sacred Valleys): Cultural Significance of Gosiute, Paiute, and Ute Plants." *Human Organization* 52(2):142–50.

Howell, Benita J. 1999. "Contesting Bureaucratic Impact Assessment: The Need for Community-Based Research." Paper presented at the annual meeting of the Appalachian Studies Conference, Mar. 19. Abingdon, VA.

———. 2002. "Appalachian Culture and Environmental Planning: Expanding the Role of the Cultural Sciences." In *Culture, Environment, and Conservation in the Appalachian South,* Benita J. Howell (Ed.). Urbana: Univ. of Illinois Press. Pp. 1–16.

Hufford, Mary T. 1998. "Tending the Commons: Ramp Suppers, Biodiversity, and the Integrity of 'The Mountains.'" *Folklife Center News* 20 (4):3–11.

Liebow, Edward B. 1998/99. "The Heart of the Problem: The Local Burden of National Policies." *Common Ground: Archaeology and Ethnography in the Public Interest.* Double issue, *Stewards of the Human Landscape* (Winter 1998/Spring 1999).

Link, Doris Lucas, David Brady, and Nancy Kate Givens. 2002. "Defending the Community: Citizen Involvement in Impact Assessment and Cultural Heritage Conservation." In *Culture, Environment, and Conservation in the Appalachian South,* Benita J. Howell (Ed.). Urbana: Univ. of Illinois Press. Pp. 137–52.

Low, Setha. 1994. "Cultural Conservation of Place." In *Conserving Culture,* Mary Hufford (Ed.). Urbana: Univ. of Illinois Press. Pp. 66–77.

Ortner, Sherry B. 1973. "On Key Symbols." *American Anthropologist* 75(5):1338–46.

Pritt, Charlotte. 1995. "Drawing the Lines in West Virginia." *Southern Exposure* (Summer):19–24.

Redfield, Robert. 1960. *The Little Community: Peasant Society and Culture.* Chicago: Univ. of Chicago Press.

Relph, Edward C. 1976. *Place and Placelessness.* London: Pion.

Ryden, Kent C. 1993. *Mapping the Invisible Landscape: Folklore, Writing, and the Sense of Place.* Iowa City: Univ. of Iowa Press.

Simonson, Harold P. 1989. *Beyond the Frontier: Writers, Eastern Regionalism, and a Sense of Place.* Fort Worth: Texas Christian Univ. Press.

State Corporation Commission, Commonwealth of Virginia. 2001. Order Granting Authority to Construct Transmission Facilities, Case No. Pue970766, May 31, Richmond, VA.

Wagner, Melinda Bollar. 1999. "Measuring Cultural Attachment to Place in a Proposed Power Line Corridor." *Journal of Appalachian Studies* 5(2):241–46.

———. 2002. "Space and Place, Land and Legacy." In *Culture, Environment, and Conservation in the Appalachian South,* Benita J. Howell (Ed.). Urbana: Univ. of Illinois Press. Pp. 121–32.

Wagner, Melinda Bollar, and Kristen L. Hedrick. 2001. "University/Community Study of Cultural Attachment to Place in Proposed Power Line Corridors." *Practicing Anthropology* 23(2):10–14.

Wagner, Melinda Bollar, Shannon Scott, and Danny Wolfe. 1997. "Drawing the Line between People and Power: Taking the Classroom to the Community." In *Practicing Anthropology in the South,* James M. Wallace (E.). Athens: Univ. of Georgia Press. Pp. 110–18.

Woolcock, M. 2001. "The Place of Social Capital in Understanding Social and Economic Outcomes." *Isuma: Canadian Journal of Policy Research* 2(1):1–17.

Better Connecting Schools with Urban Appalachian Communities

Kathryn M. Borman and Patricia Z. Timm

*Nurturing youth and fostering human capital formation are crucial for com-
munity development. In order to reduce the high dropout rates that characterize
many Appalachian communities, we must know their cause. Borman and Timm
conclude that explanations offered by experts differ fundamentally from community residents in an Appalachian neighborhood in Cincinnati. The experts
assume structural changes in the larger society are necessary to reduce the poverty
and bureaucracy that ultimately limits students' educational achievement. The
authors point out that community residents are more concerned with changing
school policies and practices, such as assignment to schools outside the neighborhood, that conflict with their value of family solidarity and the formation of
bonding social capital that is kin-based. The authors conclude with recommendations for school organization, programs, and governance that would contribute
to Appalachian family-friendly schools.*

Appalachian descendents in Midwestern cities experience disproportionately high rates of leaving school early. Nearly 70 percent of white Appalachians in Cincinnati lack a high school education according to 1990 census data (Maloney 1991). In many central cities Appalachian students leave school before graduation at higher rates than do African Americans and other non-Appalachian whites. Like African Americans, Midwestern urban Appalachians live in poorer neighborhoods. These Appalachian enclaves are characterized by high levels of social cohesion evidenced by families remaining three or four generations, even when economic means exist for them to move on (Borman, Mueninghoff, and Piazza 1988). In this chapter we examine the central role individual agency exerts in decisions to leave school, the perspectives taken on such decisions by a group of local leaders and Appalachian advocates, and the possibility that participatory development might successfully combine bonding and bridging social capital to improve school outcomes.

Theory

Leaving school prior to high school graduation is viewed by social scientists as "dropping out" (see, e.g., McNeal 1997). Over the life course, individuals who do not obtain a high school diploma are handicapped in the labor market with respect to wages and other outcomes (U.S. Department of Commerce 1990). Indeed, the transition to adulthood, including the decision to remain in school, is arguably the most complex in the student's career. The pathway chosen by the individual has consequences that rebound throughout the remainder of the life course.

By the end of the twentieth century the nation had achieved a historically low dropout rate of 25 percent. However, dropout rates are unevenly distributed across communities, and many urban school systems report 30 to 50 percent of students leave school before graduation. This uneven distribution points to the impact social structure has to limit students' success in school. Constraints such as deteriorating neighborhood conditions, decreased opportunity associated with race, ethnicity, gender, and socioeconomic status, and an unstable labor market interact with individual, family, and school characteristics to shape young people's educational achievement, out-of-school activities, and attitudes toward self and society.

Several forces have worsened the problems of poverty for schools in recent years: (1) the 1980s generated a massive redistribution of income and wealth in the United States so that the rich became a lot richer and the poor tragically poorer; (2) the changing labor market altered conditions for the worse for many with the disappearance of well-paid blue-collar jobs and weakening of union power reducing incomes for many working-class and lower-middle-class families; (3) between 1980 and 1992, the White House was occupied by two presidents who represented the economic interests of the rich by sharply reducing social services and promoting tax reforms that transferred more income upward. In 1991, the median American family earned $35,035 and paid federal taxes of $6,116, a tax rate of 17.6 percent. That same year the Bushes reported an adjusted gross income of $1,324,456 and paid federal taxes of $209,964 (their tax rate was 15.9), and as residents of the White House, their housing and transportation costs were paid largely by the American taxpayers (Berliner and Biddle 1995).

Wheelock (1992) studied factors that contribute to a dropout rate approaching 50 percent in Boston public schools. She found policies and practices concerning attendance, nonpromotion, failure, and suspension all contribute to students' perception that school is no longer an option. Truancy was tolerated in some schools where 20 percent of middle-school students were absent more than 15 percent of the school year. These virtual dropouts were still carried on enrollment rosters, and poor academic performance was no doubt an outcome of this sporadic attendance.

Official school policy in the Boston district encourages retention in grade under the assumption that social promotion is even more harmful. As a result, however, one of six students was not promoted to the next grade during the 1985–86 school year, leaving large numbers of overage students to clog the middle schools. By 1985, one in nine students had been held back two or more years.

The policy of suspension is another contributory factor to the eventual push out of students. About one in ten students were suspended from middle schools in each of the last several years in Boston. Black and Hispanic students are suspended at higher rates than whites. Seven of twenty-two middle schools in Boston were responsible for half of all students suspended, with five schools suspending fewer than 5 percent of their students.

This study of Boston middle-school policies and practices involving attendance, retention in grade, and suspension provides an indicator of the system's health. The data reveal how schools as institutions respond to students. Attendance, and particularly truancy, tells us something about the ability of schools to engage students. An inability to attract and hold middle-school students on a day-to-day basis portends a much weakened holding power in terms of high school graduation, as the nearly 50 percent dropout rate in Boston attests.

Many ninth graders in schools nationally end their first year in high school with credit deficiencies as the prospect of graduation begins to dim. In the Milwaukee Public School system, another conventional school system unable to function effectively, three-quarters of the total school enrollment were suspended during the 1984–85 school year. The suspension rate at four high schools exceeded 100 percent of their populations. The challenge to schools is to extend the benefits of a high quality education to the group of students leaving school without a diploma in the face of their personal, family, and social characteristics.

Finally, two national studies illustrate the importance of social structure in affecting human lives in urban, suburban, and rural places. In the first case, using the percentage of workers in a neighborhood that held professional and managerial jobs as an index of neighborhood quality, Crane (1991) determined in a sample of 92,512 adolescents that the neighborhood effect is extremely large for both blacks and whites in urban ghettos. In all cases the jump in adolescent pregnancy and school leaving occurred at the same point in the distribution—that is, neighborhoods where only 4 percent of the workers held high-status jobs.

The second example is drawn from an analysis of "High School and Beyond," a national longitudinal survey initiated in 1980 with high school sophomores. Researchers followed this cohort through a subsequent series of studies. The students who eventually left school before completing twelfth grade differed in a number of ways from those who remained. The dropouts had lower test scores, did less homework, came from homes with weaker educational support, had poorer school performance, exhibited more behavior problems in school, were more alienated from school life, and had more friends who were themselves alienated from school (Ekstrom, Goertz, Pollack and Rock 1986). While these findings may not be surprising, they do illustrate factors beyond individual characteristics, such as intelligence and personality, strongly influence success in school.

In 1980, 16.6 percent of Americans lived in poor families. This is roughly three times the percentage of people living in poor families in Norway, Sweden, or West Germany. More than a fifth of U.S. children live in poor families, or four times the number in the countries mentioned previously. Poverty directly impacts the lives of those who experience it and indirectly impacts the social system in which those families live. As a result of poverty, the local social system lacks taxes to pay for school, parents do not have the option of sending their children to private schools, and, finally, poor families lack the resources to provide home support for education and proper health and nutrition. In general, it is true that the larger the proportion of citizens who live in poverty, the greater the challenge for public schools. As such, "school is a political institution that contributes to the perpetuation of the existing class structure" (Villegas 1988:260).

Social structures in which human lives are embedded, including neighborhoods, families, and peer groups, are relentless in their impact on school completion. Nonetheless, individual lives can display great strength and resilience in the face of alienation, structural constraints, and family hardships. Leaving high school before graduation can be, and frequently is, an appropriate action, particularly for members of racial and ethnic groups who value family solidarity above individual accomplishment exemplified by inner-city African Americans (Stack 1974) and urban Appalachians in Cincinnati (Timm and Borman 1997).

Early school leaving may well be a constructive survival mechanism for urban Appalachian young men and women who live with a push-pull set of value constructs. Appalachian neighborhoods clearly represent gemeinschaft communities, in which bonding social capital is hypothesized to outstrip bridging social capital. Because of this, linkages to social institutions are weak and high school graduation rates suffer. Thus, school leaving may be thought of as an adaptive strategy in which bonding social capital is strengthened while bridging social capital is weakened (see Keefe, this volume).

Study Background

Riverbend is an insulated Appalachian community in Cincinnati.[1] Geographically, socially, and economically, it is similar to other Appalachian neighborhoods in the city and in other cities such as Dayton, Cleveland, and Detroit. Riverbend's natural geographic formations contribute to the isolation of the community. It is bounded by a long, narrow strip of land on the floodplain of the Ohio River, a steep hillside to the north, and the river to the south. The residents of Riverbend are descendants of farmers and miners who migrated from the Appalachian Region between 1940 and 1960 in search of employment in Cincinnati's machine shops and large manufacturing firms, including General Electric and Cincinnati Milacron.[2] Currently, the neighborhood is a site for urban development as housing for the upper middle class is constructed and existing structures are renovated. The median annual income of Riverbend residents in 1990 was $5,000 (which is below that of other neighborhoods in the city). Although per capita income is extremely low, Riverbend's location provides residents with rather generous lots, access to several parks and playgrounds, and proximity to a handful of shops and stores, including a gas station, bar, and restaurant managed (but not owned) by community residents.

The majority of Riverbend households is headed by two parents and includes children and extended family members. Seventy-two percent of the fifty families we interviewed reported having relatives in the neighborhood. These social networks provide stability in the midst of declining social institutions. An illustration of the deterioration of social institutions is the demise of the public school system. Neighborhood schools in Riverbend have been closed, so students are bussed to distant elementary, middle, and secondary schools. The rate of high school completion for neighborhood residents is far below other county residents and the goals set by national leaders. In 1990, only 35 percent of Riverbend's residents were high school graduates. Study participants left school early independent of parental educational attainment.

Long-term residency in the neighborhood indicates that living in the Riverbend community can reduce one's chances of completing school. In the study population there was a high incidence of moves between district and rural schools. However, no evidence indicated the multiple moves explained students' failure to attain higher levels of education. While Riverbend residents and Appalachian leaders expected school leaving to be associated with transitions from elementary to middle school and middle school to high school, this pattern was not characteristic of study participants. Analysis of taped interviews of community residents shows that racial conflict, early entry and participation in the labor market, peer influence, pregnancy, responsibilities at home, and uncaring teachers and administrators best explain school leaving decisions.

Urban Appalachian women's self-esteem, considerable energy, and competence were evident in their narratives about their own schooling and that of their children. They have persisted despite constraints of poverty and the ruthless arm of public policy even as the social infrastructure of their neighborhood is disrupted. Their emotional strength and their capacity to keep control of their families, including their refusal to give control to a distant school, remain the underpinning of the community life.

Women report exerting extraordinary effort to intervene at the schools on behalf of their children. On many occasions when the women went to school seeking to understand their children's academic and behavioral difficulties, they endured long waits to gain admittance to an administrator's office. Most of the women reported the negative effect of teacher attitudes toward them, their neighborhood, and cultural origins. Virtually everyone made references to their belief that the school's attitude "made you so that you don't care."

Advocates for Appalachians who have moved to inner-city neighborhoods hold the view that dissonance between such values as loyalty to kin and others including neighborliness, and identification with place and person rather than goal orientation, are fundamentally in conflict with school values and practices. The skills, strengths, and values of minority and poor children are maladaptive in schools operated by representatives of the middle class. The school is blamed for policies and practices that "push out" the culturally different.

Parents in Riverbend and other similar Appalachian neighborhoods often present a mixed message to their children about school performance and school attendance. Urban Appalachian girls and young women receive from their families the values of both their cultural heritage, such as independence and individuality, and values of the working class, such as respect for authority and a desire to maintain respectability. Caught between these two spheres, families expressed the desire "to stand tall, and bow only if the personal cost is not too great" (Borman et al. 1988:237). The grandmothers believed it was essential that their children graduate from high school, although none of them had graduated themselves.

In addition to the conflict between what they do and what they say, the messages from mothers reflect the conflict between their aspirations for their children and their cultural values. On the one hand, they wish their children to graduate, but they also value active engagement with life over studiousness; they wish for their children to complete college and enter professions, but they feel that these aspirations are unrealistic and expect their children to work in trades or industry; they want their children to get along at school, but they expect them to stand up for themselves when challenged by schoolyard bullies. In the end, individual achievement is not as important as what is best for the family. Attachment (or lack of it) to school is an issue for both students and their parents. Women are particularly attached to their family, to extended kin, and neighborhood. Their views and their experiences should be understood from this orientation. As stated earlier, the pull of family, kin, and neighbors always prevails.

When participants were assigned to schools outside the neighborhood, the importance of kin was magnified through a dramatic decline in attendance. The issues are multiple. Children experience discomfort being away from home and family; they may feel insecure in competition with youth from other neighborhoods; their parents may experience difficulty monitoring school attendance; and, finally, parents may have a lack of opportunity to engage in their children's education.

Compared to residents of Lower Price Hill, an urban Appalachian neighborhood on Cincinnati's west side, Riverbend's inhabitants have been at least equally if not more engaged in community-based political action. For example, Riverbend's community council, under the leadership of two of the community's most powerful women, actively opposed the construction of high-rise condominiums priced outside the range of housing affordable to the large majority of community members. The incident was widely discussed by the city's two major daily newspapers in stories that often portrayed community activism as both justifiable and admirable. Similarly, Lower Price Hill's battle with the city's health department and with the manufacturing firm whose toxic processes the city refused to regulate was also taken up by the media. In the latter instance, Lower Price Hill's case was actively supported by the Urban Appalachian Council, a neighborhood-based advocacy and social services agency.

In addition, a highly detailed report documenting effects of the manufacturer's processes on the toxicity of soil and air as well as the action steps to correct the situation was authored by experts at the University of Cincinnati's College of Medicine. Contributors to this report also included a somewhat marginal political hopeful, Roxanne Qualls, who headed a small but influential environmental organization. Qualls would be elected to city council the year the report was published (1989) and became mayor of Cincinnati in 1993. It seemed that urban Appalachian communities in Cincinnati were particularly well positioned politically to have their concerns taken up by a mayor in office sympathetic to their concerns, with the strong advocacy of the United Way–funded Urban Appalachian Council and the commitment of a number of University of Cincinnati–based (and other) professionals, in addition to politically adept talent pools at the neighborhood level. However, as Halperin (2006) reveals in her recent study of the East End (i.e., Riverbend) this has not been the case.

Why Students Leave School Early in Riverbend

A four-member focus group led by Pat Timm, who was raised in Riverbend, was assembled in the spring of 1996 to discuss changes at the local school level to benefit urban Appalachian girls and young women. Participants included Dick Westheimer, a former elementary school teacher in the Cincinnati Public Schools; Ginger Rhodes, an assistant principal and former Cincinnati School Board member and high school social studies teacher originally from the flatlands at the base of the southern Appalachian Mountains; Zane Miller, a professor of history at the University of Cincinnati with lengthy experience researching the city's historically Appalachian neighborhoods; and, finally, Paula Paul, a member of the Urban Appalachian Council and GED instructor of urban Appalachian students who have left school before completing their high school studies.

The focus group was organized as a means to generate policy discussion focused on decisions to leave school before completion by Appalachian young men and women. The major topics for discussion included both core issues facing the urban Appalachian community and tenacious structural and systemic problems besetting public schools. Both sets of issues were seen by focus group members as intractable. While focus group members readily agreed the most difficult systemic issue at the community level was persistent unemployment and attendant poverty, racism eventually emerged as an equally influential force. Within the sphere of education, the bureaucratic nature of school system policies and practices at the local level was perceived to be most difficult.

Focus group members insist the educational system must be placed within a larger social context. Former teacher Westheimer asserts, "There's something about the entire system, the broader system, . . . the context in which our schools exist . . . [that] leads me to believe that discussions of the schools independent of the demise of literacy . . . [and] the economic, social, and spiritual conditions of the neighborhood, somehow are inadequate." This larger social context for urban Appalachian families is profoundly influenced by poverty secondary to the suburban/urban split, unemployment, and destabilizing race relations. Professor Miller clarifies the two problems with the poor: "[For one thing], the trouble with the poor is they're poor. . . . in a capitalist society that part isn't gonna get you very far because nobody's really seriously interested about changing that. [The second factor is that] . . . there's no hope . . . for some kind of upwardly social and or physical mobility." The federal government itself is to blame for an inadequate educational system secondary to its structural organization on a national level. Assistant principal Rhodes advises, "I have to think that is . . . a huge historical blunder that we've all made as a country . . . to lump education in with the things that we associate with victimization and poverty and inability and everything else that we did in [the Department of] Housing, Education, and Welfare."

While the larger social system, poverty, and conceptualization of education by the federal government were all topics readily broached by focus group members, the influence of racism on early school leaving was only reluctantly addressed. However, the topic led to a detailed analysis of its influence. Focus group members had difficulty finding words to express the influence of racism on early school leaving. Paul, an urban white Appalachian herself, relates her observations: "[In the] white Appalachian neighborhoods, and I still am seeing and have been seeing, these Appalachian people drop out of school because the, of the intimidation of blacks. And I know that's not a nice thing to say and probably we wouldn't want to think about that."

Paul estimates nine-tenths of the urban Appalachian dropouts are due to intimidation by blacks. Assistant principal Rhodes believes lack of contact with

African American children and their families contributes to the development of negative stereotypes of black people among some Appalachians. She illustrates this position by relating an event at her school. A boy sneaked up on a girl in the schoolyard and squirted her with a water gun. The girl was very upset and went to the assistant principal crying, sweating, and shaking. The assistant principal realized the girl was responding more emotionally than necessary and asked the student to describe the child who squirted her so she could call security and have him removed from the school premises. Upon questioning the girl as to the appearance of the boy, the girl responded, "I don't know. He was black. You know Miss, he was just black. I mean, what do they look like?" Rhodes continued probing "Well, they might be tall, they might be short, they might have long hair or short hair. You know."

The child remembered no details of the child with the squirt gun. Finally, the assistant principal determined the assailant was probably a third grader: "He was a little kid. I thought there'd have been, you know, some huge hulking teenager that really scared her to death or something. And it was really, you know, just a kid incident. But she was ready to drop out of summer school because of it. . . . She did not see this little kid with a water gun. She said, 'People just don't do this to other people in my neighborhood.' . . . [In her mind the incident was elevated to the little boy being a] large black man and God knows what he was going to do. . . . All that stuff came very explicitly from mom."

Negative stereotypes contribute to the interpretation of any behavior by a black person as intimidation. Because of the fearfulness of the urban Appalachian children, Rhodes concludes they are likely to be victimized. She insists, "To a great extent, problems between blacks and Appalachians are not based on real differences or conflicts, but result from perceived differences voiced by parents who are likely to be highly protective of their children." Miller agrees with Rhodes by asserting difficulties in mixed-race schools is not simply "a problem between poor whites and poor blacks, but mutual misunderstanding, fear, and apprehension between the races that cuts across class lines, gender lines, throughout the society."

Like focus group participants, community members recognize race relations as an important component of early school leaving. While white residents of Riverbend talked of friendships and work relationships with blacks, they spoke with fear about blacks from other neighborhoods.[3] One study participant reflected on the reasons her two close friends left school after the eighth grade: "They just didn't want to go to Withrow High School. Probably because of the blacks. Because then, they had just had that big riot and all that big uproar over there . . . [referring to the race riots in the early 1970s]. It was a bad place to them. To people who hadn't gone there, it was a bad place."

Community members observed problems between black and white students often began with the bus ride to the new school location. The school bus harbored battle zones where there is no protection from bullies. Many urban Appalachian families were concerned and frustrated when their children were suspended from school for being involved in fights on school buses. School policy often punishes the victim as well as the offenders, a practice bewildering to Riverbend residents, who take pride in teaching their children not to provoke others but to protect themselves.

Focus group members and community members alike agree the large size of schools, their lack of connection to community resources and work opportunities, inability to prepare students for adult roles, and the organizational structure of schools all contribute to early school leaving. Westheimer concludes, "We've had years and years and years of stark evidence that the institution that we've set up to serve people is clearly not."

Unlike community members, all focus group participants credited the absence of hope as a core problem with Appalachian students succeeding in school. Paul argues schools do not fail because they have inadequate resources; rather, they accede to what she argues are public institutions' expectations for conformity among students to a single agenda. Because parents are not involved enough with school activities, they are unable to exert leadership and influence and to moderate unreasonable school expectations and practices, as is commonly done by parents whose children attend parochial school or schools in upper-middle-class suburbs.

While Miller concludes, "there is no great mystery about the problem of public schools; they're terrific when they have resources," Paul does not accede. Paul proffers the example of the Catholic school system, which succeeds in retaining a high proportion of their at-risk students. Paul instead adjures, "The problem is not a lack of funds, but lack of consistent dedication of teachers and administrators to the schools and educational process."

Solutions to Early School Leaving

Riverbend community members outline dimensions of participatory development as they formulate solutions to the problem of school leaving. They encourage reopening neighborhood schools to retain and protect Appalachian cultural heritage; collaboration between administrators, teachers, and parents in designing school protocols and educating children; visualizing schools as creating economic and social capital for children, allowing them to successfully move into adulthood; and, finally, developing inherent capacities of community members through their systematic and meaningful participation in schools.

Community members argue for neighborhood schools rather than school bussing. In addition to the requisite traditional school infrastructure of appropriate space and technology, these local school facilities should house social services needed to ensure students get appropriate health care, vocational counseling, child care services, and nutrition. The intergenerational ties of Riverbend residents should be a foundation of school organization. Likewise, traditional qualities of student engagement and quality instruction must be present for students to achieve.

Intergenerational educational programs should exist at all levels. Adults from the community, including parents and grandparents, should be considered participants in the educational program both as learners and tutors. Classrooms should be multiaged. One current example, present in public schools in many cities, is a continuous progress model. In this model activities promote cross-age mentoring and tutoring arrangements with the participation of both older children and parent volunteers. As students matriculate through the school program from the early elementary grades onward, they acquire basic and more sophisticated academic skills. Newly developed skills are then shared with less advanced students.

A successful school program will develop student interests and enthusiasms, providing a pathway to acquiring skills and knowledge that lead the student to expanded interests. The educational program should use the talents and skills of the community whenever possible. All students need to be counseled in developing vocational skills and exploring career opportunities. Apprenticeships as well as work opportunities can be provided. School programs should be designed in concert by professional educations, parents, and community members.

Finally, policies governing school versus parental authority should be defined in a contract agreed to by the parents and staff. Both can be responsible for assisting the student toward school success and for intervening when student behaviors are self-destructive or endanger the safety of others. A parent-staff governing council should be responsible for developing and implementing school policies and procedures, including appropriate behavior modification practices. In addition to supporting school professionals, the council must also be accountable to all students and parents.

Like community members, focus group participants believe urban Appalachian youth success in school is dependent upon reconceptualization of the whole system. This new paradigm includes a role for the community in school. Westheimer comments schools must be seen as "real life businesses. Community centered . . . an economically, socially integrated facility, with lots of things going on, including, but not limited to, instruction of young people in essential skills." Rhodes imagines Schools for Humanity, a program similar to Habitat for Humanity. The school she envisions is a "place where we can do things that are a base for learning activities, many of which wouldn't take place there at all.... I would hire the parents to do [the building of the physical structure]. And use that money to develop children's capacities rather than sort them into so-called ability tracks, which is what we're so good at in the public system." Finally, Paul concurs with the importance of parental involvement and notes the ideal school would have staff consisting of "co-moms," who were supportive of parents' needs, and parents who carry out responsibilities as co-teachers. She concludes, "Sure there would be a building, but most of the learning would take place outdoors . . . integrating it with something they saw as fun."

Many of the provisions for involving the community directly in the operation of the school that we have outlined here were also included in the original design of the East End Community Heritage School (Halperin 2006). While the school has changed its location from the Riverbend neighborhood to one some distance away, a strong social justice agenda is still present in the school. In addition, the school's academic success has been sustained.

Participatory Development and School Change

While focus group participants point to the educational system and resources as the core reasons for school dropouts, community members identify the nature of the interface between the home community and the school community as the problem. On the other hand, both focus group members and community members look to the participatory development model when they describe their preference for the family to be the foundation of the educational system, the importance of linking schools with community, and the ideal of creating an institution that will act as a bridge to adulthood. Participatory development has been shown to be an effective strategy to institute social change in Appalachian communities and in other school settings. This approach works well for Appalachian communities because it is founded on enlisting bonding social capital, which characterizes Appalachian enclaves, to create or enhance bridging social capital. Successful examples of the use of participatory development in school settings include the Chicago Public School System and the Catholic school model. The former institutionalized parent-dominated school advisory councils with responsibility for major hiring and resource allocation decisions (Hess 1992), while the latter practices participatory development by creating a functionally effective community through value consistency, face-to-face interaction, and social relationships that extend beyond the school setting (Coleman and Hoffer 1987). Both examples of participatory development reduce alienation between students, parents, and the school system and produce higher proportions of graduates.

Notes

Caroline Peterson assisted in the preparation of this document.

1. Riverbend is the name we have given the neighborhood in which this study took place.

2. The Appalachian Region, as designated by Congress, comprises 397 mountainous counties from rural Maine to Alabama.

3. Riverbend is a segmented neighborhood with differentiated upper and lower segments. Our study took place primarily in the upper, predominantly white Appalachian neighborhood. Rhoda Halperin's work focused on the lower East End, which has historically been an integrated neighborhood. According to Halperin (personal communication, 2008), the racism described here would be highly unusual in the lower East End.

References

Berliner, D. C., and B. J. Biddle. 1995. *The Manufactured Crisis.* Reading, MA: Addison-Wesley.

Borman, K., E. Mueninghoff, and S. Piazza. 1988. "Urban Appalachian Girls and Young Women: Bowing to No One." In *Class, Race and Gender in U.S. Schools,* L. Weis (Ed.). Albany: SUNY Press. Pp. 230–47.

Coleman, James Samuel, and Thomas Hoffer. 1987. *Public and Private High Schools: The Impact of Communities.* New York: Basic Books.

Crane, J. 1991. "Effects of Neighborhoods on Dropping Out of School and Teenage Childbearing." In *The Urban Underclass,* C. Jencks and P. E. Peterson (Eds.). Washington, DC: Brookings Institution. Pp. 199–320.

Ekstrom, R. B., M. E. Goertz, J. M. Pollack, and D. A. Rock. 1986. "Who Drops Out of High School and Why? Findings from a National Study." *Teachers College Record* 87(3):356–73.

Halperin, Rhoda. 2006. *Whose School Is It? Women, Children, Memory and Practice in the City.* Austin: Univ. of Texas Press.

Hess, G. Alfred. 1992. "Anthropology and School Reform: To Catalogue or Critique." *Anthropology and Education Quarterly* 23:175–84.

Maloney, Michael. 1991. *The East End Community Report.* Cincinnati: Legal Aid Society and Urban Appalachian Council.

McNeal, Ralph B., Jr. 1997. "Are Students Being Pulled Out of High School? The Effect of Adolescent Employment on Dropping Out." *Sociology of Education* 70(July):206–20.

Meier, Deborah. 1995. *The Power of Their Ideas: Lessons for America from a Small School in Harlem.* Boston: Beacon Press.

Newmann, F. Forthcoming. "How Secondary Schools Contribute to Academic Success." In *Adolescent Experiences and Development: Social Influences and Educational Challenges,* K. Borman and B. Schneider (Eds.). Chicago: National Society for the Study of Education.

Stack, Carol. 1974. *All Our Kin.* New York: Harper and Row.

Timm, Patricia, and Kathryn Borman. 1997. "'The Soup Pot Don't Stretch That Far No More:' Intergenerational Patterns of School Leaving in an Urban Appalachian Neighborhood." In *Beyond Black and White: New Faces and Voices in U.S. Schools,* Maxine Seller and Lois Weis (Eds.). Albany: State Univ. of New York Press. Pp. 257–83.

U.S. Dept. of Commerce, Bureau of the Census. 1990. "Statistical Abstract of the United States: 1990 (110th ed.)." Washington, DC: U.S. Government Printing Office.

Villegas, Anna Maria. 1988. "School Failure and Cultural Mismatch: Another View." *Urban Review* 20(4):253–65.

Wheelock, Anne. 1992. *Crossing the Tracks: How "Untracking" Can Save America's Schools.* New York: New Press.

Urban Development, Imagined Community, and Class Indigeneity in the East End Community Heritage School

Rhoda H. Halperin

The focus of this chapter is a grassroots charter school in a diverse urban Appalachian neighborhood in Cincinnati. The school is planned and executed by a participatory development team consisting of members of the largely working-class community and outside experts. This multidisciplinary team battles urban developers and the Cincinnati public school power structure for the right to create urban education that fosters local knowledge and a local moral economy based on indigenous working-class practices of "gifting the children" (that is, contributions and donations to the school from the staff and community members). This alternative economy is based on the social and cultural capital of the East End—in other words, the social networks, trust, and reciprocity built by community members with generational depth in the neighborhood. Civic leaders from the neighborhood, who strongly identify with the community and the goals of the school, are crucial to the success of the charter school.

The central questions addressed in this chapter are the following: Can a grass-roots, community-based, development/heritage project in a diverse urban Appalachian neighborhood of Cincinnati survive after being wrenched from its community of origin and transplanted to another urban Appalachian community? The project is a small, public community charter school called the East End Community Heritage School (EECHS). What kinds of transformations will the school undergo before it becomes stable? Will the costs of moving to another urban Appalachian community destroy the school? The argument is that indigenous cosmopolitanism manifested by creative (indeed ingenious) forms of class indigeneity is preserving the school in the face of enormous political, economic, and cultural challenges. The concept of class indigeneity is new; it simultaneously builds on and departs from ethnic forms. Theoretically, the school should be able to retain its indigenous cultural/class roots even as it changes location.

In October of 2006, I left a phone message for KB, our school grant writer, expressing my worry about the financial situation in the school after its relocation outside of Cincinnati's East End—in particular, the apparent need to let go of the school nurse. She and I had a long history as two of the "founding mothers" of EECHS. She responded as follows:

Oct 17, 2006

The situation is much worse than saving the nurse. We are $200,000 in the hole and have fallen to 154 (from 200) students. Evylyn, Jenel, and some board members have been pouring personal cash into meeting pressing obligations. If we cannot bring the numbers up we will have to close. We have let teachers go and cut everything we can and still stay true to our charter. We are assigning Robbie and Mr. F to recruiting for the next 2 weeks. Any help would be appreciated but you may want to call S. to get a financial picture. Our liability insurance, without which we cannot operate, is due at $9,000.

The young and caring school nurse did in fact leave EECHS in the fall of 2006 and is now working at Cincinnati's Children's Hospital. Basic nursing services for the school have been arranged by a longtime friend of the community and advocate from the University of Cincinnati, College of Nursing. The nurse's exit proved to be only one of numerous cuts for the academic year 2006–7. In late January 2007, I spoke to Kara, an instructional assistant, who had been part of the school staff since it opened in the fall of 2000. In response to my question, "How are things going?" she replied, "Not good. We only got half a paycheck today. It's a struggle, but we're doin' it."

By mid-February 2007, the principal was spending part of her time in the classroom and voicing her commitment, along with East End school leaders and residents, that EECHS would go on, perhaps not in its current location, but that it would go on.

This chapter grows out of a long-term research/advocacy project embedded in an ongoing urban economic development planning process and a strong grassroots social movement in Cincinnati, Ohio. Here I focus on the relocation and subsequent reorganization of a public community charter school now in its seventh year of operation. The relocation represents the third phase of an ongoing urban economic development process. In all phases of planning, grass-roots leaders and residents are active, engaged, and forceful in their efforts to work for community revitalization and change. Local knowledge, authenticity, and sheer grit have kept the newly relocated school going—even in the face of seemingly insurmountable financial, cultural, and psychological obstacles. Identity issues for school staff, families, and children are paramount. How can a person be an authentic East Ender (read: working-class person) and be successful at work and school and become part of the modern urban global world (Appadurai 1996, 2001; Foucault 1980; García Canclini 1995, 1997)?

Theorizing Development and Engaging Indigenous Cosmopolitanism

One theoretical frame grows out of the work of Arturo Escobar, who, in his book, *Encountering Development* (1995), develops a critique of conventional economic views of the power of late capitalism in the global economy that builds on the work of Marx, Polanyi, and others who understood and theorized alternative economic formations in complex global economies. Elsewhere I have called these alternative economies "cultural economies" (Halperin 1994). The East End and East Enders have always operated, indeed survived, using a robust alternative economy with strong informal sectors, legal, extralegal, and illegal. Even a very brief visit reveals the sights, sounds, and smells of a quasi–third world village (Halperin 1999). Small demographically (population 3,000 in 1990) and tightly knit, ten generations of diverse and large extended families have lived along the banks of the Ohio River across from the northern side of the Kentucky border and east of downtown Cincinnati. East Enders have a long history of using the river for transportation, trade, and commerce. Many people worked on barges that are still seen today. Fifty-year-olds tell stories of swimming in the swiftly moving river to find relief from the hot, humid summers that are legion in the Ohio River Valley. Their fathers remember taking small boats from East End to workplaces in adjacent downtown Cincinnati.

In *Encountering Development*, Arturo Escobar puzzles over the fact that industrialized Euro American nations were touted as models of progress and modernity for third world countries, so that eventually third world countries would catch up and "even become like them." The use of Euro American models of progress puzzled Escobar, and we can appreciate the obvious ethnocentrism. Using thinking parallel to Escobar's, although independent of it, my 1999 article, "Third World at Home," drew on Eric Hobsbawm's discussion of *Bandits* (1959) to talk about grassroots leaders as Robin Hood–like women who rob from the rich and give to the poor. They do so in order that working-class people, especially children and youth, can be heard, educated, provided health care, and remain proud of their history and heritage.

Schools, especially schools such as EECHS that are defined hegemonically as development projects, leave me with an intensified sense of Escobar's same puzzlement. Development means gentrification, and the children who succeed in achieving school success (as measured by proficiency tests mandated by the recent policy of No Child Left Behind) must shed their heritage, working-class identity, and authenticity and become like them: models of upper-class achievement ready for college, preferably Harvard.

If Escobar contributes to a "cultural critique of economics as a foundational structure of modernity, including the formulation of a culture-based political economy," the analysis of the EECHS project contributes to a cultural critique of schooling and school economic practices as they are conventionally conceived. It argues for working-class creativity, ingenuity, and generosity in the tradition of "doing whatever it takes" to carry out a moral, social justice driven agenda now in the greater Cincinnati community. This agenda and its execution is the essence of working-class indigeneity.

The second and related theoretical frame engages the literature on indigenous cosmopolitanism and identities (Appiah 1996, 2005; Ferguson 1999; Goodale 2006; Knauft 2002) and addresses the issue of how indigenous (often marginalized and, in this case, working class) populations maintain authenticity while becoming modern and urban in the largest global sense. While most of the discussion of indigenous cosmopolitanism focuses on rural people in the Third World, the identity issues for working class urban "indigenismo" (indigenousness) are parallel to those in the third world.

In the EECHS context, what I will call "working-class indigeneity" is a complicated and multilayered concept. Outsiders, especially educated people and people in power, do not acknowledge the East End as a long-lived residential place, nor are East Enders regarded as equal or even legitimate citizens of the city. Derogatory terms such as "hillbillies," "river rats," and "ridge runners" are consistently applied to East Enders in both blatant and subtle forms. As

East Enders put it: when something good happens in our neighborhood, it is referred to as Columbia Tusculum (a historically recognized and recently upscaled segment of the East End), and when something bad happens, the press reports it as happening simply in the East End. It is ironic and unjust that East Enders are considered to be rural and rough (even primitive) by other Cincinnatians and yet have, along with other working-class folks for decades, maybe centuries, provided the infrastructure for the city: garage attendants, car mechanics, hotel housekeepers, doormen, waitresses, etc. The power structure and the press (often one and the same) feel free to attribute powers of pollution to East End women by referring by name, not too long ago, to a very respectable African American East End elder and pillar of the Mt. Carmel Baptist Church as "flushing raw sewage directly into the Ohio River." The story was supposed to be about the fact that there were no sewers, until recently, but it became personalized and embarrassing in ways that people in power never experience. Stories related to pollution abound in the community and involve both poor whites and people of color.

Working-class indigeneity grows out of attachment to place and to almost ten generations of working-class jobs in the city. Driving trucks, waiting tables, landscaping, bartending, working construction or on river barges, odd jobs, and flea marketing are only some of many intersecting and, for some, overlapping formal and informal occupations of East Enders. These occupations grow out of longstanding rural traditions (Halperin 1990).

The East End version of indigenous cosmopolitanism also has moral dimensions centered in large extended families and in seeing the family as the metaphor for the community in general and the community school in particular. Working-class authenticity requires seeing the world from the same vantage points as fellow East Enders (the term "real East Ender" is code for working-class authenticity) and is an important part of working-class indigeneity.

The colonizers of the East End are, of course, outsiders with power. Developers, landbankers, and other upper-class Cincinnatians, along with the educational power structure (including school board members and city officials), disrupt, displace, and dislocate East Enders and East End institutions; in this case, the East End Community Heritage School. Like many other powerless/impoverished populations, East Enders live in a high-tech, global, transnational world of terrorist cells, security alerts, Starbucks, and fair trade coffee. Graduating from high school and attending college is a major goal. Doing better than your parents translates as "working in air-conditioning and sitting at a desk." Going to college and becoming a teacher can also be included here.

The East End Community

East End is a small-scale (population 15,000 in 1950; 3,000 in 1990), face-to-face, diverse, multicultural, working-class community in Cincinnati, named after the East End of London. Historically, East Enders are part of the rural-urban migration streams from the rural south (Alabama, Georgia, and Kentucky) and from Europe (especially Germany) to cities such as Cincinnati, Chicago, and Detroit. African Americans and people of Scotch-Irish, English, and German descent migrated seeking work in industrializing northern U.S. cities. East End is unique in Cincinnati, however, because historically it has welcomed all ethnicities and races and remained a diverse neighborhood. East Enders, especially grandparents, say repeatedly: "It is not about being black or white; it is about being poor."

When our also diverse research/advocacy university-based team first began working in the East End in 1990, I immediately noticed third world qualities to the East End. People live close to the elements, especially the Ohio River, which is its southern border. One community advocate claimed that East Enders engage with the river, and by that he meant using the river for multiple purposes, while yuppies only look at it (river views). Indeed, many people used the river in the last century as a source of livelihood and spirituality. "We are river rats" is a commonly heard expression that an outsider dare not utter.

One should not romanticize the community, however. The marginality of the East End is evident in many ways. Housing stock has deteriorated and disappeared markedly in the past half century. Sewers have only recently been installed with the accelerating gentrification. With the construction of more market-rate housing units than affordable ones, many Cincinnatians, especially those of high social class, had heard of the East End but had no idea where it was (even though East End is adjacent to downtown Cincinnati between the suburbs to the east and the city to the west). The ambiguous perception of East End's location can be attributed to the fact that professionals have driven through it on their way to work downtown for at least the last several generations but did not recognize it as a place where people lived.

Phases of Urban Economic Development in Cincinnati's East End

Phase I: The Urban Development Plan (1990–1994)

Urban economic development planning focuses on infrastructure and modernization (Escobar 1995). In 1990 our diverse University of Cincinnati–based interdisciplinary team of researcher/activists was invited to work in this narrow, eight-mile community along the Ohio riverfront. To strengthen the community's voice in a city-generated economic development planning process was our first mission. Our team's work followed a survey-driven deficit-based report known as "The East End Report," published by the Legal Aid Society and the Urban Appalachian Council. Only low socioeconomic status numbers were contained in the report: high rates of school dropout, unemployment, alcoholism, low rates of literacy, and the like. While there was never any doubt that the community is poor and marginalized by all echelons of the power structure, our qualitative, ethnographic methodology (which included elaborate genealogies and associated life histories; audio recordings and transcriptions of all meetings; continual conversations with grassroots leaders, residents, and family members; and many late-night phone conversations) immediately yielded strong positives: charismatic grassroots leadership, an elaborate and growing legal informal economy that is essential for making ends meet, and strong community networks and identities going back almost a dozen generations (Halperin 1998). East End leaders took great delight in declaring repeatedly: "We didn't know we were illiterate until we read it in the East End Report." What followed after our team arrived was a plethora of writing: poems, short essays, and now a novel written by a high school student.

PHASE II: PLAN IMPLEMENTATION (1994–2005)

Neighborhood leaders did succeed in maintaining the character of the neighborhood in the plan, including provisions to restrict the heights and densities of buildings and to retain historic structures, such as an old trolley car barn (now a Heritage Center) and the Highlands School building, where generations of East Enders attended school. In the course of our work in the East End, which continues into the present, our team worked collaboratively with community leaders and residents to build the Heritage Center, a new health center, affordable housing, and other community institutions, including a neighborhood development corporation. It is important to realize that, especially in a global neoliberal economic climate (Harvey 1990; Sassen 1998, 2000, 2001), restricting the heights and densities of buildings and creating community projects in historic buildings coveted by developers for restaurants and upscale condos, is regarded by the hegemonic system as antidevelopment and supportive of subaltern (read: off-the-books, illegal) economic practices. "Some communities should not survive," stated a prominent self-described liberal dean at the university after reading an early draft of my previous book, *Practicing Community* (Halperin 1998).

East Enders succeeded in implementing several projects, including a new health center and affordable rental housing (almost twenty units in 1994) before the East End Community Heritage School was born. In fact, the school's charter was written in a whitewashed brick room in the new Heritage Center, which opened in 1998. For the first time, community owned and controlled space became available for meetings. Prior to that, meetings were held in public parks, around hoods of cars, and in city-owned recreation facilities.

The vision and mission of the school grew in response to astronomical dropout rates and high rates of school failure. In the ten years prior to the opening of EECHS in 2000, no one in the East End graduated from high school, and kids were dropping out of school in the sixth and seventh grades. To East Enders, the school represents a repository of working-class indigeneity growing out of a grassroots social movement, really a kind of crusade to save the children by bringing back the kind of education their parents and grandparents received in the old Highlands School building, where many generations of East Enders had attended school. Located in the center of the community's plan area, the school was envisioned by its founding mothers (who spoke regularly to community children about what they would like to see in a new community school) as a kind of historic cultural center, a place where many heritages could be explored, expressed, nurtured, and taught.

The school opened in 2000 and spent six years in the old Highlands School building as a public community charter school chartered under Cincinnati Public Schools. The school served East End children and drew many students from the entire Greater Cincinnati area. In the spring of 2006 the achievement scores jumped two steps up in the state No Child Left Behind report card: from academic emergency to continuous improvement (Halperin 2006a).

The pathways to continuous improvement were extremely rough and included several phases: First, a very conservative principal attempted to deterritorialize the school by turning it into a conventional Cincinnati public school, and there were attempts to discredit and fire East End grassroots leaders from their school-based jobs. Next, the school endured a period of retrenchment, which was equally rough, only in different ways. The conservative principle and numerous teachers were replaced, and the staff started from scratch to implement the school's mission. A period of reorganization and reterritorialization followed before the exit of the school from the East End. These crises are documented extensively in my book, *Whose School Is It? Women, Children, Memory, and Practice in the City* (Halperin 2006a). Throughout all of the stressful events, a core of East End leaders and residents remained employed in and loyal to the school's historic mission and represent to this day the pillars of continuity and the agents of indigenous cosmopolitanism. In most instances, the school became stronger after each crisis.

In spring 2006, in a rather violent anti–charter school effort, the Cincinnati Public School District sold the Highlands School building to a developer and gave up the public charter (Pandey 2006). The developer, who would have allowed the EECHS to remain in the building for a few years as a tenant, was forced to sign a codicil prohibiting the lease of the building to a school of any sort for twenty-five years. In the fall of 2006, EECHS relocated to another, primarily African American, working-class community in Cincinnati called Bond Hill. A large sign saying "East End Community Heritage School: Bond Hill Campus" sat prominently in front of the building. When Cincinnati Public Schools, under which the school was originally chartered, abandoned EECHS as its sponsor, they also removed funding in the hundreds of thousands of dollars from the school.

PHASE III: DETERRITORIALIZATION AND RELOCATION (2006–PRESENT)

As soon as it became apparent that the school would have to move, new locations were investigated by the school's two accountants along with several staff members. Buying a building was an attractive but expensive option. Many buildings were considered, including ones in marginal urban spaces where high rates of prostitution and drug addiction scared school staff for the children's' safety. "How can we keep our babies in lockdown?" asked one school staff member as she viewed the needles and condoms in a building's parking lot. Finally, after months of searching, the Bond Hill location was identified as a suitable home for EECHS. It is on a large property, in a building connected to a large, beautifully kept Catholic church. There's a sense of spirituality to the place, even though it is juxtaposed to the gang violence of the old schoolyard and tennis courts. I was amazed the first time I saw the courts (three in a row), since they seemed simultaneously extravagant and too vacant with their high fences. Sure enough, they were often the staging grounds for fights involving kids with too much time on their hands. I thought of Frankie, a longtime East End neighborhood leader and chair of the East End Health Center Board who always talked about (and acted on) the need to keep kids busy to keep them out of jail. Where was he now?

The School Economy

In fall 2006, EECHS opened at the Bond Hill site. School relocation transformed the school economy (but not the school culture): the uncoupling of EECHS from Cincinnati Public Schools meant both the loss of a public charter and the loss of over $200,000 in district monies. Other costs included moving, infrastructure (wiring and networking computers), and the loss of eighteen staff members, including three East Enders, one a founding mother of the school. The two accountants on the board argued that, looking at the bottom line, they had to make hard financial decisions—catering in lunches from outside could eliminate the need for cafeteria workers, and chartering the school under a nonprofit corporation in Dayton, Ohio, about an hour north of Cincinnati, could eliminate the need for a human resources director.

In the 2006–7 school year, there is one person teaching each subject to grades nine through twelve: social studies, language arts, math, and science. The social studies teacher, for example, teaches American History, World History, Economics, and a few other subjects. In the lower school, classes are paired in one room and the principal spends at least half of her time teaching.

In mid September 2006, Principal J.G. gave me her update with the following words: "We are in survival mode, and I mean survival." Because bills have not yet been paid to vendors of cafeteria supplies such as plastic and Styrofoam plates, cups, and bowls, school staff members must purchase these from Sam's club, Wal-Mart, and other venues. The principal herself has spent considerable time and money on these purchases. The outside catering service does not provide them. "Gifting the children" (Halperin 2006b, 2006c) becomes more and more elaborate and extended by school staff. In addition to the extra hours spent working with children and families, staff members engage in many extracurricular activities that provision the school in small but important ways.

Gifting the children is part of a deeply embedded community economy that has both moral and spiritual dimensions. Early in the school's life staff members assiduously watched the sales on school supplies at the local grocery, Wal-Mart, Target, Staples, and other large stores, often purchasing large amounts of notebooks, pencils, and other supplies in the summer and stockpiling them in garages in the community. On the first day of school, the supplies would be given, free of charge, to the children as they entered the building. And during the holiday season, goods were purchased for the "Christmas store" for children to give to their family members. Often staff members would informally adopt children in a manner similar to ritual co-parenthood, or *compadrazgo* in Latin America, so that when parents were unable to provide, the fictive (practical) mom or dad could take on responsibilities for food and cloth-ing, as well as housing in some instances (Halperin 2006b, 2006c).

Indigenous cosmopolitanism includes gifting, which itself is part of the larger picture of taking hold of situations and finding ways to improve them for the greater good of working-class children of all heritages. In a conversation with Evylyn, the school coordinator, on October 26, 2006, she spoke positively about reconstituting the management team, a coalition of grassroots leaders, teachers, and administrators to determine how and where the budget cuts would be made. The team consisted of one primary teacher, the main special education teacher, the high school English teacher, a founding mother, the school coordinator, and the principal. They worked under the premise that "we are the people who have to live with the decisions." The cuts were rather drastic, but they succeeded in cutting almost twenty thousand dollars out of the budget. Several full-time teachers went to part-time. Several others were cut entirely. Evylyn confessed to me that at least part of the accountant's salary needed to be cut, but that she did not think it was the place of this team to suggest that. "We don't know what she is doing and there is no accountability. She holds office hours in the other four charter schools, but not in ours." The sense of agency taken on by the school staff situates them as local actors in a local set-ting of working-class culture. The ability of the local team to pull out of a crisis has been successful repeatedly in the past, and there is every reason to believe that the school will be sustained once again.

Shaping Moral Working-Class Citizens in an Imagined Community

Can EECHS survive as a working-class community school (an imagined com-munity of sorts) that draws from the entire region surrounding the City of Cincinnati (Anderson 1983)? A public school is being built right across the street, threatening the very existence of EECHS. But public schools are strict about who they reject and who they expel—working-class children who speak the wrong dialect of English, wear the wrong clothes, and carry the stigma of the meal card. It is possible that "Heritage" as EECHS is often called, will receive refugees from this conventional public school and from other schools in the city and region. At EECHS, everyone receives a free breakfast and a free lunch and the principles of tolerance and respect for difference provide comfort levels for kids rarely experienced elsewhere.

Moral citizens (Ong 1999, 2003) model their behaviors after the now ritual-ized ones of the founding mothers and staff (Bloch and Parry 1989). That is, staff work tirelessly and generously to meet the needs (educational, economic, psychological) of kids and their families. School supplies are provided without cost to the children, even if they must be purchased by staff and board members out of pocket. Indigenous cosmopolitanism does require reinventing traditions and transforming them as well (Hobsbawm and Ranger 1983). Traditions such as "gifting the children" are extremely important; in fact, they are sustaining the school for the foreseeable future (Halperin 2006b, 2006c).

It appears that EECHS has become sufficiently institutionalized and established, through the sheer grit and cleverness of its staff, that it can survive anywhere in the city, maybe even the region. A working-class-imagined community may indeed be taking hold. The fact that youth are central to the school's mission and that word of mouth is the best recruitment and retention tool in the educational world, lends additional hope to the project. The role of youth in the future of the school is a topic for another discussion, but there is no doubt that rebuilding, reinventing, and transforming traditional forms of class indigeneity will be in the hands of the next generation.

Everyday (Certeau 1984), practical (Bourdieu 1977) sophistication and cleverness, tempered by feelings of powerlessness and dependency, characterize the mood of EECHS staff. East Enders refer to this complex set of practices, ideas, and feelings as "common sense" (in contrast to book learning). As Geertz (1983) goes to great lengths to point out, common sense is a cultural system. In this case the ethos of "doing whatever it takes" has prevailed beyond all reasonable expectations. The word on the street (which I trust more than many other sources of information) is that the school will go on even if it has to move to yet another location. To repeat Kara's words: "It's a struggle, but we're doin' it."

Class indigeneity is more than doing whatever it takes because it relies on the moral economy (the social networks, the trust, and the binding intergenerational reciprocity). The moral economy of the school community and the greater working-class, East End–based community is the basis for class indigeneity.

Class indigeneity is, no doubt, practiced in many parts of Appalachia, albeit in different ways, formal and informal. Historically, for example, the well-known Foxfire movement, which produced several schools, can also be said to exhibit forms of class indigeneity that are similar to the ones narrated here. Many of the recommendations of the focus groups noted in Borman and Timm's piece (this volume) were, in fact, written into the EECHS charter, including multiage classrooms, intergenerational learning, and strong community involvement, to name a few. Most of these practices still work in the third iteration of the school at its third site in North Fairmount on the west side of Cincinnati. EECHS still serves working-class students from the greater

Cincinnati area, and it functions as an oasis in a public school system that has increasingly alienated urban youth.

References

Anderson, Benedict. 1983. *Imagined Communities: Reflections on the Origin and Spread of Nationalism.* London: Verso Books.

Appadurai, Arjun. 1996. *Modernity at Large: Cultural Dimensions of Globalization.* Minneapolis: Univ. of Minnesota Press.

———. 2001. *Globalization.* Chapel Hill: Univ. of North Carolina Press. Appiah, Kwame Anthony. 1996. "Cosmopolitan Patriots." In *For Love of Country,* Joshua Cohen (Ed.). Boston: Beacon Press. Pp. 21–31.

———. 2005. *The Ethics of Identity.* Princeton: Princeton Univ. Press.

Bloch, Maurice, and Jonathan Parry. 1989. *Money and the Morality of Exchange.* Cambridge: Cambridge Univ. Press.

Bourdieu, Pierre. 1977. *Outline of a Theory of Practice.* Cambridge, UK: Cambridge Univ. Press.

Certeau, Michel de. 1984. *The Practice of Everyday Life.* Berkeley: Univ. of California Press.

Escobar, Arturo. 1995. *Encountering Development: The Making and Unmaking of the Third World.* Princeton: Princeton Univ. Press.

Ferguson, James. 1999. *Expectations of Modernity: Myths and meanings of Urban Life on the Zambian Copperbelt.* Berkeley: Univ. of California Press.

Foucault, Michel. 1980. *Power/Knowledge: Selected Interviews and Other Writings, 1972–1977.* New York: Pantheon Books.

García Canclini, Néstor. 1995. *Hybrid Cultures: Strategies for Entering and Leaving Modernity.* Minneapolis and London: Univ. of Minnesota Press.

———. 1997. "Urban Cultures at the End of the Century: The Anthropological Perspective." *International Social Science Journal* 153:345–56.

Geertz, Clifford. 1983. "Common Sense as Cultural System." In *Local Knowledge,* Clifford Geertz (Ed.). New York: Basic Books. Pp. 73–93.

Goodale, Mark. 2006. "Reclaiming Modernity: Indigenous Cosmopolitanism and the Coming of the Second Revolution in Bolivia." *American Ethnologist* 33(4):634–49.

Halperin, Rhoda H. 1990. *The Livelihood of Kin: Making Ends Meet "The Kentucky Way."* Austin: Univ. of Texas Press.

———. 1994. *Cultural Economies Past and Present.* Austin: Univ. of Texas Press.

———. 1998. *Practicing Community: Class, Culture, and Power in an Urban Neighborhood.* Austin: Univ. of Texas Press.

———. 1999. "Third World at Home: Social Banditry as Metaphor for Urban Grassroots Leaders in a Midwestern City." *City and Society* (American Anthropological Association) 11(1–2): 49–57.

———. 2006a. *Whose School Is It? Women, Children, Memory and Practice in the City.* Austin: Univ. of Texas Press.

———. 2006b. "Gifting the Children II: The Moral Economy of a Community School." Paper presented at the Society for Economic Anthropology meeting on the Moral Economy. Ventura, CA.

———. 2006c. "Gifting the Children I: The Ritual Economy of a Community School." Advanced Seminar, Mar. 2–3, 2006, Cotsen Institute of Archaeology, Univ. of California, Los Angeles. E. Christian Wells and Patricia A. McAnany, co-organizers.

Harvey, David. 1990. *The Condition of Postmodernity.* London: Blackwell.

Hobsbawm, Eric. 1959. *Bandits.* London: Weidenfeld and Nicholson.

Hobsbawm, Eric, and Terence Ranger (Eds.). 1983. *The Invention of Tradition.* Cambridge, UK: Cambridge Univ. Press.

Knauft, Bruce (Ed.). 2002. *Critically Modern: Alternatives, Alterities, Anthropologies.* Bloomington: Indiana Univ. Press.

Ong, Aiwa. 1999. *Flexible Citizenship: The Cultural Logics of Transnationality.* Durham: Duke Univ. Press.

———. 2003. *Buddha Is Hiding.* Berkeley: Univ. of California Press.

Pandey, Gyanendra. 2006. *Routine Violence: Nations, Fragments, Histories.* Stanford: Stanford Univ. Press.

Sassen, Saskia. 1998. *Globalization and Its Discontents.* New York: New Press.

———. 2000. "Whose City Is It? Globalization and the Formation of New Claims." In *The Globalization Reader,* Frank J. Lechner and John Boli (Eds.). Malden, MA: Blackwell Publishers. Pp. 70–76.

———. 2001. *The Global City.* Princeton: Princeton Univ. Press.

SmartMoney Community Services

A WORKING MODEL FOR ECONOMIC DEVELOPMENT IN APPALACHIAN COMMUNITIES

Phillip J. Obermiller and Jennifer Jervis Tighe

Often located in marginal urban and rural areas, Appalachian communities can lack banking institutions with standard financial services, such as interest-bearing savings accounts, check cashing, and competitive loans, which are crucial to economic development. Obermiller and Tighe describe a community-based economic development organization that partnered with a credit union to provide affordable financial services, guaranteed credit, brokering, and financial education for residents in the Over-the-Rhine neighborhood in Cincinnati.[1] Trust, symbolized by a handshake, was the basis for initial cooperation between the financial cooperative and the credit union, and social criteria are considered in making loans to those who fail to qualify by traditional criteria. The participatory governance structure and locally based administration contribute to the success of the organization that serves the economic development of the neighborhood.

Would you tolerate a charge of fifty cents for each check you write, a fee of 5 percent of the amount of each check you cash, or a 60 percent annual percentage rate on a collateralized loan? Probably not, but these charges are typical in low-income areas where banking services are often expensive or unavailable.

The residents of underserved communities have always been creative in finding alternatives to traditional financial services. For instance, numbers games and lottery gambling provide a way of "saving" money because the cash bet on a number is safe from the demands of daily needs; "interest" is paid if the number hits. Unfortunately, operators of pawnshops, check-cashing stores, and buy-on-the-lot and rent-to-own schemes have also been creative in finding low-income communities to exploit.

Residents and businesses in underserved neighborhoods still need the standard financial services that their more affluent counterparts take for granted—writing and cashing checks for reasonable fees; keeping their money in a safe, accessible place; paying bills; obtaining loans and credit; and getting good financial information. This chapter explores the alternative economy typically found in low-income areas, reviews some of the standard responses to these conditions, and describes SmartMoney Community Services (SMCS), a community-based economic development organization that can be used as a model in both the urban and rural areas of Appalachia.[2]

The Alternative Economy

Even the poorest area often has a cash flow of hundreds of thousands of dollars. Checks come into the community for salaries and wages, pensions, social security benefits, veterans' benefits, unemployment compensation, child support, general relief, and supplemental security income for the disabled. With a dearth of banking choices, residents of low-income and working-class neighborhoods who receive these checks often fall victim to fiscal exploitation (cf. Caskey 1994; Obermiller 1988).

With the deregulation of the banking industry in the 1980s and its further consolidation in the 1990s, many low-income areas lost their local bank branches. The automation of the banking system and the imposition of fees for unprofitable accounts continue to erode the financial services available in these communities. More recently, tariffs on nearly every banking transaction have become common as banks increasingly rely on fee income to boost profits. Just as black markets flourish in areas of economic chaos, a gray market economy usually springs up when standard financial services are withdrawn (cf. Caskey 1997).

Small grocery stores or local bars will cash checks for patrons, but the tariff is the purchase of merchandise at inflated prices or, more frequently, a sizable percentage of the check's value. Although providing financial services in such neighborhoods can be lucrative, it is hazardous as well. When "check day" arrives each month, small businesses are swamped; they also become likely targets for robbery because of the extra cash they must have available to meet the demand.

Instead of writing checks, neighborhood residents can purchase money orders for forty to sixty cents each in local stores. This seemingly nominal fee, however, is often a substantial percentage of the face value of the money order. The vacuum left by deregulated retail banks has also been filled by unregulated and frequently unscrupulous profiteers. In lieu of formal banking services, check-cashing companies open offices that charge fees ranging from 2 to 10 percent of the face value of each check redeemed. Although some states regulate the fees charged by these businesses, many do not.

As the end of the month approaches, some residents run short of cash. Loans are available from local pawn shops, provided the customer has collateral and is willing to pay an effective annual rate of 60 percent plus storage charges. Another strategy for bridging end-of-the-month cash shortages is to sell next month's check at a discount before it arrives, in effect borrowing against anticipated income. This type of loan puts the borrower in even greater economic jeopardy, while assuring a low-risk profit to the individual providing the advance.

Unable to pay cash, and lacking access to the competitive rates on consumer loans offered by banks and similar financial institutions, residents of low-income communities must do without major purchases or make them at the highest interest rates allowed under state law. Many of these neighborhoods attract used-car dealers specializing in "pay on the lot" financing, as well as appliance and furniture outlets offering "in store" or "rent-to-own" financing. These businesses derive much of their profit from the high carrying charges they impose on loans to their customers. In order to keep the monthly payments affordable to a low-income clientele while maintaining high interest rates, they minimize principal costs by combining inferior merchandise with extended repayment periods.

Those who are able to travel from the area may be able to obtain banking services in nearby communities. In many cases, however, low-income people lack the financial wherewithal to make frequent trips to a bank, or they cannot meet the minimum requirements or afford the fees for maintaining an account. As a result, they are forced to keep a month's income in cash on their person or in their residence. The possession of cash makes many people, especially women and the elderly, susceptible to assault, burglary, and fraud.

Just as some people in the mainstream use bank trust departments to oversee their assets, many low-functioning residents of neighborhoods without banking services require custodial care for their monthly incomes. Agencies such as the Social Security Administration respond to this need with a payee system: a responsible person is designated "payee" on behalf of the agency's clients and is expected to channel the money to the client in a prudent manner. Although guidelines exist for selecting and auditing payees, constraints on agency time and personnel leave this system open to abuse by unscrupulous persons.

Some residents seek to break the cycle of poverty by investing in a modest home or starting a small business. These potential homeowners and local entrepreneurs need both a means for planning their financial futures (economic education) and capital to support the costs of their plans (mortgage and small business loans). Either of these are hard to come by when banks are no longer present or doing business in a community.

Financial Service Needs in Rural Appalachian Counties

Although many Appalachian counties are becoming increasingly metropolitan in population size and density, other counties still have small, widely dispersed populations. Low-income residents of these rural counties have essentially the same financial service needs as those in more densely populated areas of the region: a means to write and cash checks, maintain savings accounts, establish credit, and obtain useful financial information.

In rural Appalachian counties checks are often cashed at grocery stores or pharmacies, which may require minimum purchases of up to twenty dollars. Bills are frequently paid by means of costly money orders purchased at convenience stores or the post office. "Savings" are usually accumulated through the purchase of lottery tickets or by buying retail items on layaway plans. Consumer credit is provided through pawn shops, but more frequently from finance companies charging up to 35 percent interest, pay-on-the-lot auto dealers, or rent-to-own furniture and appliance outlets.

The bank branches remaining in rural communities offer little in the way of alternatives. Savings and checking accounts that do not maintain minimum balances (often of $500 or more) are eroded by relatively high monthly fees, although the banks will sometimes waive these fees for customers over a specified age. Regular bank hours do not accommodate blue-collar workers who must work past bank closing time on weekdays. Traditional banking hours also work to the detriment of low-income people who need to convert their checks to cash as soon as possible due to a lack of cash reserves; government checks received on Saturday may have to go uncashed until Monday, resulting in missed meals on the weekends for some families. Moreover, banks located in population centers such as county seats are of minimal utility to individuals located in distant hamlets and hollows.

Credit is provided by rural bankers on a highly selective basis. Some loans are provided to members of "good" families with relative ease and minimal paperwork, while others find that the reputation of their kin networks is a hindrance to their creditworthiness. In many cases, family members are required to cosign on loans, even when the borrowers are adults holding full-time jobs. As family collateral becomes fully pledged over time, potential cosigners become fewer and fewer. Credit dries up until earlier loans are repaid and the cycle starts again. Because of the paucity of alternatives, even minimal banking services in many rural Appalachian areas are offered on a take-it-or-leave-it basis.

Some Standard Alternatives

Communities have responded to the problems caused by lack of banking opportunities with a variety of solutions. These include instituting systems for screening and assigning competent, ethical payees for residents who need custodial care for their finances; installing automated teller machines (ATMs) at central locations in bankless neighborhoods; establishing community development credit unions as a means of bringing low-cost financial services to neighborhoods; founding a community bank owned and operated by minority entrepreneurs; monitoring the loan activities of local banks under the Home Mortgage Disclosure Act and the Community Reinvestment Act; and lobbying for legislation to provide "lifeline banking" to the poor and to cap fees for check cashing and pawn brokering.

While each of these strategies has its advantages, none provides a comprehensive, community-based response to the financial service and economic development needs of low-income areas. Moreover, each has its own drawbacks. For example, ATMs cannot provide the coins needed by small businesses; "lifeline banking" is useless in an area without a bank branch; and it is extremely difficult to start and maintain minority banks and community credit unions under today's stringent regulatory conditions.

The SMCS Model

SmartMoney Community Services is a community-based response to the financial service and economic development needs of the Over-the-Rhine neighborhood in Cincinnati, Ohio. Over-the-Rhine, a former port-of-entry neighborhood for Appalachian migrants to the city, has a population of 7,600 and is home to many low-income African American and urban Appalachian households (Obermiller 1996).

SMCS's founding board, consisting of representatives drawn equally from among neighborhood residents, agencies, businesses, churches, and the surrounding community established four goals: providing affordable financial services to the residents and businesses of one of the city's poorest neighborhoods; guaranteeing credit to individuals and entrepreneurs who have been denied loans through normal channels; brokering cash and credit into the neighborhood from outside sources; and helping residents to become educated consumers of financial services. Since its founding in 1988, SMCS has implemented each of these participatory development goals with a specific action plan.

Affordable Financial Services

SMCS contracts with a well-established local credit union to operate a branch in the neighborhood. The credit union would not serve the neighborhood without SMCS's willingness to subsidize any operating deficit the local branch may generate, and SMCS would have a hard time complying with the regulatory burden and operational responsibilities inherent in running the equivalent of a full-service bank branch. This mutual support forms the basis for a working relationship between the two organizations. In 1996, after renting a small storefront office, SMCS bought and rehabilitated an abandoned bank building in Over-the-Rhine, which is now used by the credit union branch. The purchase confirmed the community identity and stability of both the branch and SmartMoney.

In its first fifteen years of operation, the credit union branch has enrolled nearly four thousand members, has taken in deposits of $4.5 million, and has a loan portfolio that currently totals over $2.4 million. The branch now conducts more than twenty thousand transactions a month in an office located in the heart of the neighborhood. Members write and cash checks with modest or no service charges, build interest-bearing savings accounts with a minimum deposit of five dollars, and obtain loans at competitive rates.

Through the SmartStep Savings and the SmartConsumer Savings programs, SMCS provides a 2:1 match ($100 for every $50 dollars saved) for individuals who open savings accounts at the credit union branch for mortgage down payments, small-business startups, or continuing education.

GUARANTEED CREDIT

SMCS operates a loan guarantee fund called SmartLoan (SLF) to make loans available to individuals turned down by the credit union on the basis of standard underwriting criteria. Applicants to the fund fill out a simple two-page form. A subcommittee of the SMCS board judges each application according to both financial standards and social criteria, such as whether the loan will contribute to the applicant's dignity and independence, or to the economic capacity building of the neighborhood. Those who obtain SmartLoan backing from SMCS receive their guaranteed loans through the credit union branch. Each recipient of a SLF-backed loan agrees to work with a volunteer financial advisor and to join the pool of advisors after the loan is repaid, thereby increasing both the financial and social capital of the community.

The original funds for the SLF were contributed by an individual donor interested in working with SMCS to expand its programs. SMCS found that even though the credit union was able to make loans available to neighborhood people, there were still people in need of very small loans who were falling through the cracks. With its SmartLoan program, SMCS focuses on meeting the needs of those neighborhood residents who have to borrow small amounts of money for a short period of time. SMCS's goal is to help this group establish a good credit history so that they can eventually qualify for regular credit union loans.

Over time the pool of money in the SLF has grown from $10,000 to $30,000. In a recent five-year period the fund guaranteed fifty-four loans with a total value over $70,000. These loans financed car purchases for people who need transportation to work, assisted with debt consolidation at lower interest rates, apartment deposits, small business ventures, and other needs identified by SMCS's SmartLoan committee. Each loan is reviewed and considered as a unique case; because guaranteeing loans is a high-risk venture, the decision is based on the relationship with the person, their past and present experience with credit, and their personal commitment to repay the loan.

There are instances when a third party other than the SmartLoan fund will volunteer to secure a loan for someone. In these cases SMCS's SLF is used as a medium to hold the third party's collateral funds. This has been particularly successful with religious organizations that do not want to be directly involved in lending money but want to assist in the capacity-building of the neighborhood. By utilizing the SLF, a secured loan can be made to an individual without involving the church. The church provides the collateral via the SLF and SMCS works with the borrower to ensure repayment.

Brokering

Because of its interest in community-based development in Over-the-Rhine, SMCS also acts as a financial broker for investments in the neighborhood. SmartMoney Friends is a program that collaborates with local banks and insurance companies to make special-rate mortgage and commercial loans readily available to neighborhood residents and businesses. For instance, SMCS obtained an ATM as a donation from a local bank and installed it in an area that has many family-run businesses selling fresh produce, meat, and cheeses. Although the ATM mainly serves customers who come from outside of the neighborhood, it bolsters the small businesses necessary for the economic vitality of the local community.

Financial Education

Another dimension of SMCS's development work in Over-the-Rhine is culturally competent financial education. Its SmartDollars & Sense economic education program begins early: staff members show local youths in summer job programs how to cash their paychecks and open savings accounts. SMCS staff and board members make presentations at community meetings, schools, social welfare agencies, nonprofit organizations, and local businesses. These training opportunities lay the groundwork for teaching people what financial services SMCS has available and how to use them wisely. Individual counseling is provided through the SmartChange Financial Counseling program, in which participants review their spending patterns, set savings goals, and learn credit-building techniques.

Tellers in the credit union branch are constantly engaged in informal tutoring as well. For example, if a member does not have a checking account, the teller will explain how having one can save them money as opposed to purchasing money orders to pay bills. The tellers also provide assistance in balancing checkbooks for people who need the help. Most important, tellers work conscientiously with many neighborhood residents who are physically challenged, illiterate, or mentally ill to ensure that service is provided in an honest and respectful manner. Financial education is an ongoing process that happens continuously throughout all programs as SMCS staff and credit union employees teach basic fiscal skills to people so they can remain fiscally responsible and as independent as possible.

Other SMCS programs provide a service with an educational component built in. SmartTax assists residents with tax forms while informing them of the most recent tax credits available to taxpayers with low to moderate incomes.

The SmartBusiness and SmartHome Ownership Workshops help neighborhood entrepreneurs develop and fund a business plan, and first-time home buyers establish a budget and save for a down payment on a mortgage.

Elements of a Successful Community-Based Financial Services Organization

SMCS is a comprehensive response to neighborhood financial service and economic development needs. Key factors, such as the governance of SMCS, its relationship with the credit union, its administrative philosophies and practices, and its funding, play an important role in making it a successful organization.

GOVERNANCE STRUCTURE

A primary component to the success of SMCS is the commitment of individual board members to the mission of the organization. Board members representing different constituencies may not always see eye to eye on other community issues, but when it comes to restoring financial services in Over-the-Rhine, all come to the table willing to work together to ensure that SMCS meets its goals.

Balance in the membership of the board is critical to ensure that all facets of the neighborhood are represented. This type of equilibrium provides information on issues that are important to the community, such as location of the branch, the services it offers, and special SMCS programs like the SmartLoan fund. For example, a butcher from the open air market can explain the problems that local merchants have in getting change and making daily deposits. Representing another sector of the community, a nonprofit administrator can communicate the needs of a large population of payees in the Social Security program who need access to small amounts of cash daily. Obtaining information directly from neighborhoods through this kind of participatory research allows SMCS to make decisions on which financial services are most needed, and develop programs to meet those needs.

Another important part of SMCS's success has also come from board members who are knowledgeable about how to run a nonprofit organization and how to raise operating funds. This expertise has come primarily from board members in the "at-large" category who provide business skills, legal expertise, access to philanthropic resources, and experience with financial institutions. While this group constitutes only a fraction the board, its contribution is critical in a community-based organization of this type.

In sum, the composition of the SMCS board invites participation from all sectors of the community, tapping a deep well of social capital on its behalf. The SMCS staff and that of the credit union branch are hired in part for their cultural competence and their ability to participate knowledgeably in neighborhood capacity building.

ADMINISTRATIVE STRUCTURE

One of the philosophical goals of SMCS is to fill staff positions with neighborhood residents. While this is not a hard and fast rule, SMCS employees and credit union branch employees are often neighborhood residents. This has the effect of creating good jobs in the neighborhood, as well as building the knowledge base of the community through credit union training programs and branch operating experience.

There are other important outcomes of hiring locally. At the outset, having local people staff SMCS and the branch helped to create a strong rapport with the community. Hiring neighborhood residents also ensures that the program will not be unduly harmed by bad checks and other scams; local tellers demand respect, honesty, and accountability from their peers. The premise of hiring locally has been crucial in the case of SMCS's financial counseling position and the credit union branch staff. "Inside" knowledge of the community is critical to the early success of operating a financial organization because it allows the organization to get to know their customers and gain their confidence rather quickly. Another benefit of hiring people from the neighborhood is their personal commitment to the vision of the organization. The services provided by SMCS meet neighborhood employees' needs as well because they live in the neighborhood and thus have an added incentive to see the organization succeed.

The staff of the credit union branch includes a manager and two tellers. The efficiency of SMCS's staff of five is maintained by training its employees to use technology effectively. SMCS staff members have access to state-of-the-art computers, used for everything from searching the Internet for program funding opportunities to checking credit reports. The effective use of technology allows the staff to work at full capacity, and is even more compelling at a time when funding agencies are more disposed to commit money for improved equipment than for increased operating costs.

RELATIONSHIP WITH THE CREDIT UNION

Perhaps most integral to the success of SMCS is its relationship with its partner, the Cincinnati Central Credit Union. By contracting for a credit union branch,

SMCS quickly restored retail financial services to the neighborhood without the administrative and regulatory difficulties of founding a whole new financial organization.

The partnership began as a "handshake" agreement between SMCS and the credit union. The handshake concept is important because it signifies a willingness to work together in uncharted territory. Normally, financial institutions do not look for low-income communities in which to open new branches, and nonprofit organizations do not typically raise funds to operate credit union branches. Knowing that this endeavor is unique, both parties keep in close communication to ensure that the partnership is successful. Over time the handshake has developed into a set of quarterly reports used to determine how much it costs to run the branch and what kind of services are being provided to the neighborhood. This relationship benefits both organizations—SMCS accomplishes its goal of bringing financial services to the neighborhood, while the credit union operates its branch under the protection of SMCS's guaranteed subsidy.

FINANCES

How does SMCS pay for the services it provides? Funding comes from private foundations, corporations, government agencies, churches, banks, and individuals. Each year SMCS estimates the cost of running the credit union branch by calculating the ratio of loans to deposits. Based on the amount of income produced by the credit union branch, SMCS can determine the additional funds needed to subsidize the branch. This cost has varied each year, but the amount of subsidy has generally decreased as the branch continues to increase its deposit base and loan portfolio to break-even levels. At times the SMCS board will increase the amount of the subsidy in order to obtain additional services at the credit union branch—for example, adding extra tellers on "check day" at the beginning of the month.

While it has not always been easy to raise funds, SMCS continues to draw support from funders interested in a variety of issues such as economic development, human services, community reinvestment, and education. Banks and other financial institutions are particularly eager to use SMCS as their proxy in the neighborhood. To meet their obligations under the federal Community Reinvestment Act, local financials would rather contribute to SMCS's operating budget than attempt to reopen a branch in the neighborhood.

In another fund-raising strategy, SMCS solicits depositors who waive the right to receive dividends on an account at the credit union branch. This type of deposit, often ranging in the tens of thousands of dollars, typically comes from churches and nonprofits with endowments or building funds, as well as from large foundations and corporations. This type of socially responsible deposit helped to build initial trust in SMCS as a stable organization by providing large infusions of capital to get the branch started and also reduces branch operating costs. This strategy is particularly successful because it allows funders to keep their principle intact while donating the interest income from their deposit.

Using the SMCS Model in a Rural Setting

Many elements of the SMCS model are directly applicable to meeting the financial service needs in rural Appalachia. Check cashing, low minimum deposit savings accounts, a loan guarantee program, and financial education are service needs common to both urban and rural low-income populations. These services, however, have to be delivered in a geographically appropriate manner. Where ATMs and fixed-branch banking may work well in densely populated urban neighborhoods, another approach is needed in rural areas.

Transportation is key to accessing services in rural areas. Meals on Wheels programs deliver food, passenger vans bring patients to physicians and clinics, and bookmobiles extend library services into the countryside. Similarly, traveling credit union branches would be highly effective means of providing financial services in rural areas through a regular schedule of visits to churches, community centers, schools, flea markets, and other local gathering places. Combined with a small permanent office, a mobile branch incorporated into a van would provide additional teller windows to the "main office" on high traffic days such as the first of the month. Mobile bank branches are already in use in some metropolitan areas in the United States. They are also common in the rural areas of Europe, where they bring ATMs, teller services, and financial advising to areas underserved by traditional banking venues.[3] Mobile branches could provide an effective rural alternative to fixed branches, particularly when used in multicounty service areas within the Appalachian region.

Although SMCS is situated in an urban setting outside of the region, many of its features are directly applicable to rural Appalachia as well. Partnering a community-based nonprofit with a credit union has many advantages, not the least of which is the fact that credit union members vote for their own leadership and policies. The SMCS model gives consumers a say in the governance not only of SMCS, but of the credit union as well.

The power of the SMCS model comes from the fact that it develops a natural constituency by meeting the everyday financial service needs of people in the community. In doing so, however, a pool of capital is created for the development needs of the whole community. Individuals, small businesses, community groups, and organizations are all served equally well by the SMCS's format and philosophy. With the modifications suggested in this chapter, it can serve as a very effective economic development model for Appalachian planners, organizers, and community-based activists.

Notes

1. Phillip J. Obermiller holds appointments at the University of Kentucky's Appalachian Center and at the University of Cincinnati's School of Planning. He is a founding member and past president of the SMCS board of trustees. Jennifer Jervis Tighe, SMCS's first executive director and now an instructor in communication at Xavier University in Cincinnati, is a former resident of Over-the-Rhine. The authors gratefully acknowledge the insights provided by community organizer Terry Kessinger and by the financial service consumers in Appalachian Ohio she arranged for the authors to interview. Those wanting more information about SmartMoney Community Services can write or visit its office at 19 Elder Street, Cincinnati, OH 45202, call (513) 241-7266, or go to http://www.smart-money.org/.

2. Initially named Co-operative Fiscal Services and known as "the CO-OP," the organization changed its name to SmartMoney Community Services in 1998.

3. For an example of current European applications, see "NatWest to Launch Mobile Banking Service in South Wales" at http://www.natwest.com/global_options.asp?id=GLOBAL/MEDIA/136; for photographs and more information about mobile branch vans available in the United States, see "Mobile Branch Facilities" at http://www.mobileatm.com/index2.html.

References

Caskey, John P. 1994. *Fringe Banking: Check-Cashing Outlets, Pawnshops, and the Poor.* New York: Russell Sage Foundation.

———. 1997. *Lower Income Americans, Higher Cost Financial Services.* Madison, WI: Filene Research Institute.

Obermiller, Phillip J. 1988. "Banking on the Brink: The Effects of Banking Deregulation on Low-Income Neighborhoods." *Business and Society* 27:7–14.

———. 1996. "A Capital Idea: A Financial Services Model for Neighborhood Economic Development." *Social Insight* 1:26–30.

Guidelines for a Partnership Approach to Appalachian Community and Heritage Preservation Work

Mary B. LaLone

LaLone begins her chapter with an example of nonparticipatory development she observed doing fieldwork. It is a stark contrast to her partnership approach to development and planning, what she calls "anthro-planning," developed over the last couple of decades in southwest Virginia. LaLone identifies terms used commonly by mountain people that serve as a guide for practice: "porch setting" for rapport building and "calling in favors" for mobilizing reciprocal aid. She concentrates on the assets based on social and cultural capital present in mountain communities and the potential for assembling resources in even small, rural communities. Finally, she provides extensive examples of partnership projects that she and her students have completed in heritage preservation and community planning, all of which have relied on intentional cooperation with local communities.

Many will be familiar with an item that has appeared for years in Sunday newspaper comic sections—the single-frame picture of a scene with a caption that asks the reader to locate the faces or objects concealed within the picture. This chapter starts by posing a similar task for the reader—to picture the scenes described in a case study, and then see how many problems and sources of misunderstanding you can identify. The case study is based on my observations during a day of participant observation in an Appalachian town, preceded and followed by numerous conversations with community members over a two-year period.[1]

The chapter then offers some guidelines for working in Appalachian communities, emphasizing the advantages of adopting a partnership approach and anthro-planning for community-based work. Anthro-planning is a strategy that blends anthropological perspectives and methods with a participatory planning style (see LaLone 2005a). The guidelines focus on techniques for operating in culturally appropriate ways in order to build and maintain strong working relationships with communities. They include carrying out rapport building activities in the initial stages of a project; working with the community pace of life rather than against it; learning about the cultural history of the community; identifying and making use of community assets; incorporating abundant opportunities for community input and participation into a project; and other recommendations. Then, some case study examples are provided to demonstrate how a partnership approach and anthro-planning has served as a strong, effective foundation for organizing my own research and planning projects in Appalachia.

A Case Study Offered for Thought and Analysis

This case took place in an Appalachian town that was largely dependent on coal mining for supporting the town's economy. Around 1990, the town discovered that the coal mines in the region were planning to shut down operations in the near future. Concerned about their economy, citizens formed a grassroots effort to develop alternative forms of income and decided to explore the possibilities for developing heritage tourism around the region's mining and railroad history. As part of their effort, they enlisted and received assistance from the nearby universities, which resulted in the development of a preliminary set of designs for heritage tourism. Based on that design report, the town applied for and won a grant for more than $30,000 to conduct a feasibility study. Armed with its grant money, the town bid out the job and signed a contract with a professional development firm to do the feasibility study.

Although I had assisted with developing the original design report, once the contract was bid out to a professional firm I shifted my research focus away from the tourism project to engage in an oral history study of the coal mining culture of the region. I was in town quite frequently and, having developed rapport and good friendships with community members, I was included in many discussions in which they expressed positive anticipation and eagerness for the professional firm to begin its work. I was told such things as, "They're supposed to be a good firm. They looked good on paper, and they did an impressive interview to get the bid." A period of time elapsed between when the firm received the contract and when it actually sent a team to town, but anticipation remained high. Then I received a call from the town telling me that the firm's team was coming for a two-day visit and asking if I could be available to be interviewed by the team. I organized my activities so that I would be in town with a group of students to work on my oral history project and would also be available to be interviewed by the firm on the first day of their visit. Since both activities were taking place at the Town Hall, it provided me with an excellent opportunity to do participant observation during the day's events.

An atmosphere of chaos pervaded the Town Hall when I arrived early that morning, a feeling that had been building for a number of days. Apparently wanting to efficiently pack in as much work as possible during its two-day visit, the firm had communicated by telephone that the town should make the arrangements for them to have a full two-day schedule of nonstop interviews lined up, most scheduled to take place at fifteen-minute intervals. In conversations with the people in charge of scheduling, I perceived that these individuals were by now quite frustrated after days of trying to make these arrangements. They said things like, "They wanted me to set up all these appointments for them to pack into two days," and "How do you think they're going to get everything done in just two days?" They were having difficulty getting individuals to commit to fill the interview slots, and they seemed to be getting worn down after days of trying to pin down people and having to constantly reschedule. Frequently they said things like, "They may be surprised if so-and-so isn't here when they expect to begin the interview" or "I have no idea if so-and-so is going to show up." At one point during the morning, an individual told me with a flabbergasted tone of voice, "Do you know, they called back and even wanted me to hire a helicopter to fly them over the area this afternoon."

Finally the team arrived in town, coming directly to the Town Hall, just at the time the interviews were scheduled to begin. The three individuals were dressed in cosmopolitan-style clothing and carried themselves with a businesslike manner. The men wore suits and ties and the woman was wearing a trench coat. As I observed from a distance, I was struck by verbal and nonverbal mannerisms that conveyed the sense that they were entering as a visiting team of experts, carrying an air of authority and expecting to get right down to business with the interviews. The team's clothing clearly made an impression with members of the community. From my vantage point sitting in the front office of the Town Hall, I began to hear comments such as, "They aren't dressed like they knew where they were coming to." As the day progressed into the afternoon, the bystanders became quite perplexed by the female team member's behavior and kept saying to one another, "Why doesn't she take off her trench coat?"

The team's interviews took place in the back offices of the Town Hall, often with two separate interviews running simultaneously. The team attempted to keep to the brisk rate of the interview schedule that generally allotted fifteen minutes per interview. In the outer office, town organizers still were uncertain who would show up and so readjustments and replacements had to be organized on the spot. My vantage point placed me where I could clearly see and hear people as they came and went from their interviews. I noticed that the individuals returning from the first interviews often came out wearing nonverbal expressions of puzzlement and shock. When asked how their interviews went, many said they had not had time to talk about much of anything, and certainly not all the things they felt the team should know. Some were clearly distressed at the rush. Then my turn came. Having worked on the original design report, I too had been allotted a fifteen-minute spot. I walked out of my interview with the feeling of being patronized by the interviewer, as well as rushed. In spite of my attempt to cram all the information I could into the allotted period, I personally felt that there was much more that I needed to convey to the team about cultural patterns and resources in the region. I wondered to myself, if I—someone used to operating in a fast-paced academic world—felt distressed by the rush of the interview process and felt treated like a child, how were the community members likely to be feeling and thinking? But I returned to my professional stance of objectivity and, in the role of anthropologist, continued my participant observation in the outer office of the Town Hall as members of the community came and went.

Over the day, I witnessed people's attitudes change from the early positive anticipation to confusion and concern about the operating mode of the firm's team by midmorning, and then in the afternoon to escalate into thoroughly upset feelings. This was a textbooklike example of the potential hazards of miscommunication and misunderstanding taking place before my very eyes. By the end of the afternoon, shortly before I was leaving, a new wave of discussion began in the outer office. A whisper started going around that the consulting team had already said that the town's ideas for a living history museum, laid out as a coal mining camp, were unfeasible. Instead, it was said that the team wanted the town to put an RV (recreational vehicle) park on the site planned for the coal camp museum. Reactions started as shock and disbelief and then developed into anger. Typical comments followed the line of, "I hope they don't plan to do that, or I'm going to have something to say about it." As I drove home that evening with my students, I could tell by their questions that they too were affected by the scene they had witnessed and that their observations had been similar to mine.

From follow-up conversations with community members, I learned that at the end of the two-day visit the team did, in fact, tell the town's tourism committee that it felt the coal camp museum was not very feasible and that the site could be better put to a more commercial use like an RV park. The team then left the region, not to return again for nearly six months. The recommendations given at the end of their two-day visit angered many townspeople who had great pride in their mining heritage. It set in motion the beginnings of a factional split that formed in the tourism committee and among concerned citizens. One side was strongly opposed to the firm's work and felt that their grant money was being wasted; the other side was more supportive of the firm and argued for the town to take a wait-and-see approach. The following six-month period, with little communication between the firm and the town, did not help the matter. Nor did it help when, after finally making two additional one-day visits toward the end of the contract period, the firm asked the town for an extension beyond the due date to file their report. After the report was submitted, I heard many people express dissatisfaction with the results and lament that the grant money, now gone, could have been better spent in other ways. In addition, the factional split within the community lingered on long after the firm had terminated its work, causing stressful relationships and bringing a halt to what had been a strong grassroots heritage tourism movement. Fortunately, after time, those relationships were mended and the community began to work together, applying for new grants to go ahead with selected aspects of their tourism plan and receiving relatively good success. Asked if they used the firm's report when applying for the grants, I was told, "No," that they generally try to minimize references to it.

So what happened here? The town was originally impressed by the firm and awarded it the contract. How did these favorable and confident feelings disintegrate in a two-day period into feelings of frustration, puzzlement, perplexity, concern, and in some cases anger? Was it avoidable? Could actions following the first visit have been taken to rectify, rather than enlarge, the problems?

Admittedly, my observations and discussions reflect primarily one side in the interaction between an Appalachian community and a development firm— they reflect the community response. This case is presented solely to point out the potential for unintended misunderstandings to arise and escalate, and the need for researcher-practitioners to be aware of the advantages of adopting culturally appropriate behavior and the spirit of team-based partnership when organizing and conducting community projects. The point of this chapter is to provide guidance to researcher-practitioners on ways to work successfully *with* Appalachian communities. As this case indicates, one cannot work effectively *with* a community without understanding and anticipating how the community is likely to react and interact with the practitioner. A project's success depends to a large extent on the individual or firm's ability to study and learn from the community, and in their ability to interact in a culturally attuned manner with that community. This involves gaining a sense of the cultural-historical place, trying to anticipate culturally appropriate ways of interacting, keeping a sensitive awareness of cues coming from the community, and providing the community a sense of partnership in the project. While the following guidelines are offered especially for applied practitioners, they are also of value to researchers, teachers, and other individuals who will be working closely with Appalachian communities.

Getting to Know One Another

Jimmie L. Price (1995), pastor of an Appalachian community church, shared some advice with me at the time I was beginning a new research project in his community. He said, if you want to work in the community, and get people to work with you, you need to come sit on people's porches and spend some time letting them get to know you. As I have found on many occasions before and after having this conversation, this is perhaps the most important piece of advice for any practitioner planning to work in Appalachian communities. What he was talking about is what anthropologists call "rapport building." It involves finding culturally appropriate ways to build trust and understanding among the people with whom you will be working.

This one piece of advice actually conveys multiple aspects of the culturally appropriate manner of entering into an Appalachian community to work. First, it means that one must plan into a project a period at the beginning for getting to know people in order to establish people's trust. Rapport building takes time. One does not barge onto the scene and immediately find people trusting and willing to work with you and help you out on your project. Why should they be willing? Even if you think your project is worthy of their participation, you need to convince them of this by building their confidence and knowledge of who you are. Even if the community has been "informed" through prior arrangements or contracts, a feeling of tentativeness still exists—a hurdle that the practitioner-fieldworker needs to take down through conversations and time invested in getting to know one another. In Appalachia, a good project is not one that gets down to business right away.

How is rapport building done? As Jimmie Price suggested, by sitting on people's porches—in other words, visiting in their home or in other contexts that are part of the person's familiar surroundings. This allows people the chance to see how you interact with them while being safely on their own ground. Most initial meetings go much smoother when this advice is taken to heart. Meetings set up in office buildings or other formal surroundings tend to start off and remain stiff. It is often wise to allow people to choose home or community settings in which they feel most comfortable for carrying out first meetings.

Rapport building also is aided if the researcher-practitioner attempts to come across in a friendly manner as a social equal, someone who is there to learn from the community, rather than someone entering the community (especially at the beginning) conveying an authoritative or otherwise socially elevated manner. Since a person's style of dress conveys instant messages to the viewer, ranging from casual friendliness to formal authority, taking time to choose a culturally appropriate style of dress can pay off. When I do fieldwork in Appalachia, I do not wear the same style of clothing that I wear for my job in a university setting. My students often ask what to wear when doing interviews with Appalachian families, and I advise them to choose casual clothing that will not stick out as too different from clothing worn by the people they plan to interview. In the case study described above, one wonders why the consulting team chose to enter a small Appalachian community in apparel more appropriate to a metropolitan setting. The trench coat, especially, was conspicuously inappropriate for work in an Appalachian town, and the messages conveyed by continuing to wear the coat throughout most of the day were of formality and business, rather than friendliness and visiting.

Gaining the necessary rapport may even require you to think about further types of involvement in the community. While setting up my research project in 1995, I received another piece of advice about rapport building from someone else: if you want to get people to know and trust you, you might seriously consider going to church a couple times in the community. Why church on Sunday morning? It is because this is another culturally appropriate place in which people typically come together to get to know one another. Getting to be seen and getting to be known: these are essential features of gaining the trust that will ease a project along. While one usually does not find it necessary to go so far as living in the community and going to church, taking the general spirit of the advice to heart is very important. Not making the effort to build rapport can ensure that your project will not get past the starting gate or will be rocky. In assessing the case presented above, one might ask how much easier the project could have gone if the practitioners had taken some time at the beginning to spend visiting—not working—with people in order to build up a solid level of familiarity and trust.

Time May Cost Money, But Taking Time Can Buy Success

Rapport building takes time, but it is an essential beginning to any project that you may wish to carry out successfully. Other activities undertaken throughout your project—for example, interviewing or community discussions—might also benefit from adjustments that allow those activities to correspond to the timing and pace of life of the community. Some might argue that taking time to sit around and chat would cost too much money, that it is not cost effective. Those concerned with time management and keeping costs to a minimum also need to weigh the detriments of having a project fail because the community did not trust you, was offended by your actions, or quietly refused to cooperate. These are among the range of reactions that can occur when the Appalachian sense of how one operates is violated either intentionally, to streamline a project, or simply from a lack of understanding of the Appalachian pace of life.

Our own assumptions about timing and the correct pace of activities are deeply ingrained within our thinking and behavior. This can easily foster the idea that everyone else must surely operate in much the same manner. However, assumptions about timing and pace of life often vary significantly from place to place. Edward Hall (1959, 1966), through his many enjoyable writings, first shed light on the potential misunderstandings and detrimental consequences that can occur when people do not operate on the same sense of timing. Many unfortunate misunderstandings can arise when practitioners, researchers, and other outsiders fail to understand the cultural significance of time and pace within the community where they plan to work. One needs to be acutely aware of the pace of life within the community—and the ways in which it differs from your own pace—and one needs to adjust project activities accordingly. This can save you from having disgruntled feelings toward the community when your plans cannot be carried out at the pace you had expected. Additionally, it often safeguards your project from possible misinterpretations of your behavior.

The practitioner needs to expect that the sense of timing and pace of social interaction will flow at a more relaxed rate in Appalachia than it does in the workaday world of an urban American setting. When someone coming from a fast-paced environment enters into an Appalachian community, that person needs to slow down and operate on the timing coming from within the community's cultural system. To not do so can cause the practitioner to become frustrated with her/his job, and that frustration, in turn, can affect the practitioner's attitude when carrying out the project's work. In the case study described above, one can imagine that some frustration must have occurred within the consulting firm, first when its efficiently envisioned schedule of interviews did not always go according to plan during the two-day visit, and later when it realized that at least part of the community was no longer positively anticipating the firm's final report.

In addition to practitioner frustration, there is the problem of miscommunication. To not operate in accordance with cultural rules is likely to result in having your actions misinterpreted by community members in ways that can escalate and negatively impact on your project. Violating the rules of time and pace of life can cause individuals or the community at large to feel perplexed by your behavior; or possibly to interpret your behavior as being unfriendly or rude according to the social standards of the community; or even to interpret your behavior as displaying a lack of care and concern for them and their well-being. Whether or not these interpretations accurately reflect your intentions is beside the point. In community work, it does not matter if you had good intentions; what does matter is if you can communicate and work with the community successfully to reach a goal satisfactory to all. If your actions cause misunderstandings that deteriorate that vital link of communication and result in negatively affecting the way the community responds to your behavior, miscommunications will surely arise that will negatively impact on the progress of your project.

Referring once again to the case study described at the beginning of this chapter, one realizes that the major source of difficulty that the development firm encountered came from their own actions in staging a whirlwind two-day visit to the community, in which they violated many of the culturally appropriate rules discussed here, followed by a long period of absence from the community in which they might have rectified some of the damage done. One wonders if they took the time to gain an understanding of the Appalachian community culture they planned to work in. A rigidly scheduled two-day visit, perhaps considered normal and efficient in the more fast-paced work world of urban America, was not appropriate as a form of entry into a small Appalachian community. For one thing, where was the time for rapport building? For another thing, the brisk pace and rigid structure of the interview schedule was most inappropriate and caused a series of escalating problems. They expected people to arrive precisely on time and say everything of consequence in fifteen minutes—that is simply not the Appalachian way. In the Appalachian pace of life, fifteen minutes is barely enough time to carry out introductory conversation, let alone anything else. The frustration level of town organizers was elevated, even before the team arrived, by trying to accommodate to the firm's request to set up such a schedule, yet running up against cultural barriers to such scheduling. Essentially, they got caught in the middle, between the firm and their friends and neighbors. The mood of the interviewees at being briskly shuffled along ranged from perplexity to distress, and this mood spread as they returned to the outer office and relayed their frustrations to others. This style of entry into the community acted in setting up a barrier of frustration and distrust that led to misunderstandings and sore feelings. Certainly this was not the intent of the firm, but good intentions were not what counted in successfully interacting with the community. One wonders what alternative responses the firm might have received if it had planned into its program of action a few more relaxed visits to the community—time for getting to know the people and gaining rapport, time to hear people express their goals and discuss the available resources at their own pace, and time to receive input about the ideas the firm proposed.

The challenge for practitioners in Appalachia is knowing that a slower pace exists, and then putting that knowledge to work to ensure the success of your project. Practitioners should try to anticipate the differences in normal modes of operation, especially in assumptions about timing and pace of activities, and should factor these into project designs. Practitioners and researchers will find that adequate time and flexible scheduling are essential attributes of a successful project.

Learning the Cultural-Historical System

Another key aspect of a successful applied project involves studying the cultural system and history of development in the region where you are working. How can one recommend and/or undertake a course of action if one does not understand how those actions are likely to affect the community in the short run and the long run? A good understanding of the structure and interlinkages of components in the cultural system is necessary in order to make educated predictions about how potential changes introduced into the system will affect it in either positive or detrimental ways. To study the cultural system requires time spent examining the literature on Appalachian community structure, and also time spent on-site talking to people informally, interviewing, and observing.

Again, the wisdom in taking time to understand the functioning of the community cultural system cannot be stressed enough. The literature on culture change provides instructive case studies in which development projects failed because the introduced changes set in motion a series of unforeseen negative repercussions throughout the target societies' cultural systems.[2] The key here is that the potential repercussions were unforeseen. This occurred largely because the development projects had not taken care to incorporate sufficient studies of the existing cultural structures into the planning stages of their projects. While still in the planning stages, after research of the cultural system had been done, they needed to more carefully consider the potential affects that the planned actions could produce both in the short run and over a longer period of time.

One needs to ask, what should be the motivation and goal of the project? Is it simply to gain a contract and drop the service or item on the community, or is it to ensure that the project has the most beneficial effects on the community with the least disruptions possible? The practitioner, firm, or agency's reputation will ultimately rest on the long-term results and degree of satisfaction within the communities they affect—a reputation that lasts far longer than the dollars they receive in the short run, and a reputation that may haunt them when making bids for future contracts. Not only is it wise, but it is necessary, to incorporate two tasks into the planning stages of any development project: first, to undertake a period of study of the cultural system of the community; and, second, to try to anticipate the course of change as it moves through the cultural system, working this through on paper so that appropriate planning can take place prior to introducing any change into the system. This can help ensure positive results and head off potentially detrimental ones.

Learning about the community's cultural system also helps the researcher-practitioner make knowledgeable decisions about how to operate on-site so that work will go more smoothly. One thing that commonly occurs to practitioners, researchers, and other outsiders, is that they find their project becoming the source of escalating controversy or even brought to a crashing standstill because they have unknowingly stepped on someone's feet and/or wound up on one side of a community factional split. Recognizing that this frequently tends to happen when working in small face-to-face communities, such as those in Appalachia, practitioners would be wisely advised to do some investigation of the lines of power and social organization within the community in which they plan to work. This would include study of (1) the organization of local politics; (2) potential factions within the community; (3) who to be sure to talk to if you want to get things done; and (4) who to include in your discussions if you do not want anyone to feel slighted. Often the social structure of family connections and community stratification intersects with the local political structure in ways that affect the flow of power and decision making in the community. It is worth the time to investigate the sociopolitical structure so that you strategically plan your actions to take advantage of the traditional channels of action, rather than unknowingly trying to operate outside the appropriate channels or at odds with them. It is also wise to investigate potential rivalries within the community so that you can organize your activities knowingly, doing your best not to become associated with only one group within the community. This type of study requires some time actually spent observing and talking to people within the community. Relying on information obtained from a few sources over the telephone in order to set up a project is often asking for trouble.

In addition to studying community life at the present time, one also needs a solid understanding of the region's history. Practitioners in Appalachia need to take the time to learn about the historical forces that shaped the community, influenced people's thinking and behavior, and created potentials and limitations for development today. Communities do not develop in isolation of wider economic-political contexts. In the coal field region of Appalachia, for example, the practitioner would be wise to do some reading on a number of issues including (1) the dynamics of power that were shaped as externally based mining corporations gained control within the local economy and political structure; (2) the degree of dependency on coal mining and the effects of this process on shaping the local economy; and (3) and process of resource depletion (environmental and tax-based) in the region that usually accompanies mining by externally owned corporations.[3] These and other historical processes place their marks upon the present economy and social structure. One may find that people's responses to your ideas and plans may come as much from the way they feel about their history and heritage identity as from their personal response to you. More important, these historical issues need to be addressed in planning for such things as tourism and economic development.[4] While the practitioner or firm cannot correct long-standing historical problems, awareness of the forces that have caused detrimental economic effects in the region can guide the practitioner so as not to make recommendations that repeat mistakes and perpetuate regional problems. This assumes that the practitioner or firm accepts some obligation for socially responsible as well as profitable work.

Additionally, Appalachians are proud of their heritage. While change and economic development for a viable future may be forefront in their minds, they often wish to bring their heritage along with them into the future and will react quite strongly when those desires are challenged. This is seen in our case study, with the community's outraged response to the firm's recommendation that the site for the desired coal camp living history museum be used instead for an RV park. Having accepted a contract to study heritage tourism, one wonders at the wisdom in this action. What response did they expect to generate? Were there other, subtler ways to introduce these matters into discussion with the community after taking more time on site to understand the community's reasoning and desires, and thoroughly investigate community resources for the museum project?

Identifying and Making Use of Community Assets and Resources

A good feasibility study for a development project should do more than focus on the potential for external investment and demand—it also should identify and give credibility to potential contributions from within the community. In Appalachia, this means investigating the traditional ways in which people's labor and resources have been, and still are, utilized within the community. This is not something that one can learn from reading economic reports at a distance—it requires time spent on site, getting to know the ways of the community and its social capital, the support networks based on trust and reciprocity (see also Susan Keefe's discussion on social capital in the introduction to this book).

Appalachian communities have a long history of developing strong internal systems for economic assistance and community action. Within a community there are usually numerous channels for getting work done. Foremost among these are the deep-seated relationships of reciprocal obligations between kin and neighbors. These are particularly strong in the coal mining and farming communities of Appalachia, where neighbors and kin relied on one another for support. People helped each other out in cases of birth, death, sickness, and tragedy. They came together to provide mutual assistance by pooling labor for economic activities such as hog killing, building houses, and laying plumbing.

While the particular tasks have changed over time, the strength of the structure of mutual obligation has stayed intact (see LaLone 1995, 1996, 1997; LaLone, Wimmer, and Spence 2003). Throughout Appalachia, people have come together as communities to organize grassroots political action to fight coal companies and advocate for environmental and labor reform (see, e.g., Fisher 1993). Appalachia is a region in which there is a long tradition of helping each other and pooling local labor to get things done. If something needs to be done for the benefit of the community, strong and effective action can be mobilized along the existing connections between families and neighbors, which in turn penetrate into local business and politics, forming the internal structure of each community. The existence and reliability of these types of resources might be surprising and not outwardly apparent to the outside practitioner, unless that practitioner takes the initiative to ask and study the community.[5]

One of the problems in our case study, in my opinion, is that the firm underestimated the contributions of local community resources when making assessments of feasibility. The building of a coal camp museum was ruled out in favor of an RV park because of dollars-and-cents bottom-line determinations of what would cost less and bring in the most money. Perhaps the feasibility of including the coal camp museum as part of the tourism plan would have received a more favorable assessment if the firm had spent more time in the community investigating traditional resources and had given greater credibility to the community channels for getting things done. Specifically, I am referring to the potential for assembling people's labor, dollars, and assistance with donated supplies/services from local businesses in order to build and maintain the coal camp. Perhaps these community resources seemed like peanuts to a development firm, but they might have been taken more seriously as a way in which to retain the coal camp museum within the overall plan, along with the features deemed more profitable. On many occasions I heard a leading community member say that he could readily assemble the supplies and labor to build the camp utilizing local channels of support available to him. I, for one, am confident that efforts of these types could indeed be carried out in the community under study. One wonders why these local resources were not more thoroughly investigated and incorporated into the plan.

By way of demonstrating the potential for mobilizing resources at the community level, let us consider what another Appalachian region did in its grassroots effort to preserve its coal mining heritage. Concerned that Virginia's New River Valley mining heritage should be preserved, a group of local citizens came together in 1994 to form a Coal Mining Heritage Association. They had a dual-focused dream: to construct a monument honoring miners who had lost their lives in the mines and to have an annual coal mining heritage day established by the county government. In a truly inspiring effort, they mobilized the resources and had the monument built in two months' time. They did this entirely by using community resources, including funds received through five- and ten-dollar donations and local volunteer labor from people who felt a deep commitment to the mining heritage. Taking their people to county supervisor's meetings, they were able to lobby successfully for an official Coal Miner's Day. Now, each year the association repeats its resource mobilization effort for Coal Miner's Day (Kelley 1994; Price 1995). Following a dream, this Appalachian region was able to mobilize labor, cash, and business support to get the job done. If an outside firm had been asked to do a feasibility study, and if the firm had not recognized and taken into account these typical Appalachian channels for getting things done, quite possibly the recommendation might have deemed the project as economically unfeasible. Try telling that to the residents of the New River Valley, however.

The system of "owing one a favor" is one of the common ways in which re- sources can be mobilized within a community. When working with the case study community, I often heard community members describe how the town's efforts at promoting its tourism endeavor advanced by leaps and bounds by using the system of calling in favors. Many times I had the opportunity to witness the effectiveness of "owing one a favor" to get something done. For example, during a discussion of ways to get newspaper and radio publicity for the town's tourism efforts, I remember a town member saying, "Oh, no problem. I'll call up so-and-so—he owes me a favor." And, indeed, with no problem, the promotional publicity was arranged and it required no cash outlay from the town. Or on another occasion, when the town wanted to gain access to some coal mining equipment, I heard someone say "No problem, I know someone at the mining company who owes me a favor," and shortly thereafter an arrange- ment was made to gain access to the desired materials. This potential access to services and supplies through long-standing channels of reciprocal obligation is contained within the community structure of most Appalachian towns.

People and their sheer determination to attain their goals need to be con- sidered when assessing the potential for getting a project done. Channels of reciprocal obligation that can be called upon to mobilize labor, money, and other forms of support need to be considered as available resources. These are basic foundations of Appalachian communities, available to be tapped for proj- ects of all types, rather than written off as insubstantial. While these resources alone might not carry a project—as they did in the case of the New River Valley—they certainly need to be examined, given credibility, and incorporated into feasibility and design studies.

Community Participation

Another well-known guideline from applied anthropology is that development projects of all types have a much higher rate of success and have fewer detrimental effects on the cultural system when the community itself is directly involved in the planning and implementation processes.[6] The culture change literature is filled with cases from the past to the present in which change projects were done to populations without their consent or without enlisting their participation, usually resulting in demoralized feelings and severe disruption to the cultural systems of the target populations. As elsewhere in the world, Appalachian people do not appreciate having an outside practitioner, firm, or agency do something "to" them without their participation and input. Why should they, especially when they feel they have had little opportunity to offer input or to have their input actually incorporated into the plan, design, or report? They also will respond negatively when they feel that they are being patronized by an outsider who, in their opinion, has little knowledge about how things work within the community. When people feel that they are left out of the planning and implementation processes, they can react in a variety of ways, including passively ignoring the project (i.e., giving no support to it); talking against the project in ways that can snowball into enlarging negative community sentiments; and actually taking action to mobilize resistance to the project. The key point here is that a project approach that excludes the community will cause forms of reaction against the project rather than cooperation with it.

A partnership approach is one in which the researcher-practitioner carries out a project *with* the community. This is a different approach than would be taken by designers, planners, and other practitioners who assume that they know, by virtue of their training, what is "best" for the community. While practitioners may indeed have more formal training, it is a very patronizing and unrealistic approach to assume that community members have little of value to contribute. In fact, the local population has had years of on-site training in the workings of their communities. To apply a model or design to a particular situation successfully, it must be fine-tuned by adjustments that incorporate information provided by cultural insiders. The approach of working with a community to some extent requires that the practitioner give up some degree of control over being in charge—a feature which may be somewhat threatening at first—and give community members the sense of empowerment by being real partners in the planning and implementation processes. This partnership approach usually produces more successful results at all stages of the project, enhances (rather than strips) people's sense of dignity, and gives community members credit for their knowledge and contributions.[7]

One of the ways that community input and participation can be fostered is by holding a series of community discussion sessions at various stages of the project. Certainly at the beginning of a project, before much time has elapsed, project members need to come into the community and visit for a while. Since this is the time for rapport building and getting to know the people, resources, and community structure, much of this time on-site would be wisely left unscheduled. But to foster the sense of participatory involvement, some organized community discussions might also be arranged to take place in this initial period. These could either be done on a large scale, as in a town meeting, or as smaller group discussions that bring together a broad range of key members of the community. The appropriate choice needs to come from study of the particular community. Judging from the response displayed in our case study, the agenda for initial group sessions should not be rigidly arranged but instead should allow plenty of time for people to get to know you and give input on the project at their own familiar pace. Additionally, the practitioner would be wise to avoid saying, "This is what I think should be done," until much later in the project, after demonstrating that time was taken to weigh community input from these early group meetings. This early stage is an important time to listen to what community members have to say about their reasons for wanting a project, the goals they wish to attain, and the resources they can identify. Planning with the community can then proceed, designing the project to incorporate community goals as well as the practitioner's goals. Additional community discussions should occur in the intermediate stages of the project to give the community opportunities to examine the preliminary plans/recommendations and give more input, with adequate time still remaining to incorporate those ideas and make alterations in the design or plan.

Throughout the project, various things can be done to heighten the sense of working in partnership with the community. Some of the techniques that I frequently use include structuring the project design so that local groups and/ or institutions are linked with the research team in an actively collaborative framework; emphasizing in publicity for events/meetings that these are collaborative cosponsored activities; asking community members to play active roles as event/discussion leaders; and making a point of giving the community its share of the credit by publicly emphasizing the ways in which community-generated ideas have been incorporated into the project. The idea, in other words, is to find ways to allow community members to have real forms of collaboration, and to see and claim the contributions of their own involvement in the planning process. Finally, toward the end of the project, sharing the project results in tangible ways with the community at large may help promote the sense that the project was done for the whole community rather than for a selected few. For example, a project might end with the widespread distribution of a report and an associated celebratory community event, with publicity for both.

These are only a few general recommendations that, of course, need modification and fine-tuning when applied to specific projects. The primary idea is to operate from a partnership approach that fosters, rather than excludes, significant community input and participation in the project.

Putting a Partnership Approach and Anthro-planning to Work

Witnessing the events described in the opening case study had a profound impact on my own research style. It influenced me to develop and hone a collaborative partnership style as the foundation for my research and planning projects with Appalachian communities and to advocate the use of a partnership approach to community work for both academics and applied service professionals (e.g., LaLone 1999, 2001, 2005a, 2005b). I started in 1993 by developing what I called a "partnership approach," a simple model for community-based work that used the guidelines described above as guiding principles for project design. As a university professor, the model has served dual functions: as the design framework for my own community-based work in applied anthropology projects focused on regional heritage preservation and community development, and simultaneously as a vehicle for student service learning. My research teams, composed of Radford University students, experientially learn the craft of applied anthropology while working on actual community-based projects that I design and direct using the collaborative partnership framework. As I refined the model for applied planning projects, I began to interchangeably label it as "anthro-planning" (e.g., LaLone 2005a), to emphasize that the project design involves a community planning style highly infused and enhanced with anthropological perspectives and methods, using community partnership and participation as the core features.

While my research has largely focused around heritage preservation projects, the basic project design guidelines should be transferable to applied community-based projects of all types. The major guiding principles of the partnership model I use are the following:

Building and emphasizing a spirit of partnership and collaboration as the structural framework of the project;

Taking a nonhierarchical approach that makes all partners and participants feel equally valued;

Spelling out clear benefits for all partners (that are reinforced and not lost over time);

Taking ample time for rapport building before starting the work of interviews, focus groups, and community meetings or events;

Studying culturally appropriate behavior for timing, pace of life, dress, etc. and adjusting project activities to synchronize with those community customs;

Learning the cultural history of the region and using that knowledge to better guide project planning, especially for development and change projects (for reasons described earlier);

Providing abundant opportunities for community input and citizen involvement in all stages of the project design and implementation;

Identifying and making use of community assets, including community-based labor, materials, and knowledgeable citizens who serve as key resource people;

Employing anthropological data-gathering methods to learn about individual and community behavior relevant to the project (not only interviewing but also observation, participant observation, and rapid ethnographic assessment techniques) and using the behavioral data to inform and guide planning/development project plans and recommendations;

Viewing the practitioner's job as multifaceted, requiring flexibility to shift between various roles to act as a researcher, coordinator, synthesizer of the ideas from all project participants, liaison between different interest groups, and even a negotiator at times; and

Producing tangible results at the end of the project (something concrete that has benefits for the community partners).

The key theme in the model, whether one calls it a "partnership approach" or an "anthro-planning approach," is a design based on establishing a collaborative working relationship and a sense of partnership as the structural foundation of projects that link a research or development team and their community client groups. Although every project differs in specifics, the overall method I follow in undertaking a project is to use the guiding principles offered above and to incorporate as many forms of collaboration as possible. Part of a collaborative approach is a matter of attitude and part is a matter of project design. In terms of attitude, my experience has been that a nonhierarchical stance is a key to working in Appalachian communities. Too often academics and practitioners enter communities with the attitude that they are the trained professional experts who know best how to proceed. As discussed earlier, this stance may lead them to devalue local knowledge or resources and to alienate community members unintentionally. An alternative stance, which I try to foster in all aspects of each project, is to operate from the perspective that the research team is "joining forces with the community" to solve a problem and that every participant, professional and community member alike, brings differing contributions of value to the project (a collaborative nonhierarchical stance and team-based approach). As part of the structural framework for any new project, I attempt to seek out and establish partnership linkages with community groups, institutions, and resource people within the community, and then design the project so that the community partners have real roles working with the research team. Community partners share in designing project orientation sessions for the research team, participate in focus groups and community meetings, share information and perspectives as key resource people for the team, and see concrete results in the form of some tangible product that the research team produces to aid the community's efforts (such as a consulting report or other tangible item).

The partnership model formed a very effective basis for a 1995–98 heritage preservation project in the New River Valley in Appalachian Virginia. There, coal mining had ceased by midcentury and knowledge of the mining way of life was in danger of disappearing as the remaining mining population grew older, so a rapid oral history documentation effort was needed to collect and preserve the oral history knowledge for heritage education. As the foundation for the oral history project, my Radford University research team joined in a partnership with the newly formed grassroots Coal Mining Heritage Association (CMHA) to tackle the problem. Neither the academic research team nor the community heritage group could have carried out the project as effectively working alone: the academic team contributed the skills and labor for the interviewing and transcription activities while the community group aided with the rapport building and contact arrangements needed to conduct the interviews. The partnership was seen as mutually beneficial, furthering the heritage group's goals to preserve their elders' knowledge while simultaneously providing a training field for my student interviewers. Both the academic and community partners recognized that their joint efforts were needed to capture the heritage knowledge rapidly before more of the elders passed away. Community group leaders worked with me to design and carry out project orientation sessions, helped to arrange contacts for the interviews, and served as key resource people to provide needed information and assistance throughout the project. The research team undertook the work of interviewing and transcription, in total conducting sixty-one interviews with forty-three men and thirty women who described their coal mining lives. Rather than leave the project outcome in the rather inaccessible form of oral histories placed in a library archive, the research team ended the project by compiling the project results into the more tangible format of two oral history books, *Appalachian Coal Mining Memories* (LaLone 1997) and *Coal Mining Lives* (LaLone 1998), which the community heritage group has put to use in its efforts to promote heritage education in the region.[8]

The partnership model was applied in an even more expansive manner as the structural foundation for a Coal Mining Heritage Park planning project that I organized in 1999–2000, again in the New River Valley. Merrimac, once the site of a booming coal mine and mining community, had closed down in the 1930s and had become a near-forgotten archaeological ruin. In the late 1990s, the old Huckleberry Railroad line that passed through the Merrimac site was converted into a modern paved walking and biking trail. The problem, however, was that the public passing through Merrimac, now thoroughly over-grown with brambles and weeds, had no idea of the site's historical significance. The challenge for my applied anthropology research team was to join the com-munity together in an effort to retrieve the heritage site and to develop a set of plans for converting it into a Coal Mining Heritage Park that combined com-munity recreation with heritage education. The first step was to establish the framework for a four-way partnership linking my Radford University research team with the community mining heritage group, the county-level planning office, and the state-level archaeologist. The partners joined with me in setting the project scope and in designing and conducting orientation sessions for the research team. Former miners, county planners, and the state archaeologist worked collaboratively with the academic team as it gathered data on the Mer-rimac site and began to formulate ideas for a heritage park design. The team also visited other regional heritage parks to examine potential models for park design and heritage interpretation.

In addition to working with our project partners, multiple forms of com-munity collaboration were built into the research stage of the project. To this end, two evening community meetings were held in order to involve the public directly in the planning process. The meetings were organized under collabora-tive sponsorship with the community-based heritage association and great care was taken to stage the meetings in a culturally appropriate style. In this case, we started with food, local music, and ample opportunity for visiting with friends as a way of breaking the ice before introducing the night's business. Later, the crowd was broken down into smaller focus groups that discussed issues and generated an extensive set of ideas for heritage interpretation, recreation, educational activities, and needed park amenities. In addition, a survey was mailed to residents asking for input on activities and amenities for the park. The research team recorded all of the public-generated ideas and made sure that those ideas were incorporated into the park design. To our delight, the project became a magnet for community participation. Numerous individuals served as key resource people, helping the team develop special aspects of the park. For example, former miners helped develop a plan for an interpretive walking tour of the mine site, while local school teachers helped develop ideas for park nature education. Soon the sense of partnership extended to include the Merrimac church, senior citizen groups, recreational user groups, railroad buffs, residents living near the proposed park, teachers, and many others. In the final stage of the project, the team synthesized all of the research and community input and developed a consulting report for the park (LaLone 2000). On the strength of the project report and community effort, the county board of supervisors brought a successful conclusion to the planning project by voting to pursue development of the Coal Mining Heritage Park. The park had its dedication ceremony in September 2000.[9]

Ten years later, the Radford University–CMHA partnership still forms the basis for collaborative work on heritage-based projects. The mining association had begun to collect artifacts for a mining museum (one feature of the heritage park), but recognized that its members lacked training in museum procedures—so in 2005 it partnered with my Radford University anthropology research team to develop initial planning for a mining museum collection. Again, I applied the elements of the partnership model to guide the project design. CMHA leaders helped plan orientation sessions and engaged in ongoing interactive collaboration with the team throughout the four-month project period. The research team took standardized museum procedures and, with much input and participation from the CMHA, developed a set of museum policy and record-keeping procedures closely tailored to the needs and abilities of this small community nonprofit organization. As a tangible product, the research team prepared a consulting report (LaLone 2005c) detailing a cataloging system, collection policy, and exhibit recommendations that the CMHA can use as it continues to develop its museum collection. The research team then conducted a video documentary project in collaboration with the CMHA in 2005–6. The tangible product from that collaborative partnership is a forty-five-minute documentary, *Memories from the Mines* (LaLone, Beheler, and Juarin 2006), a permanent record of mining men and women describing their work, household life, and community activities. The documentary now provides a visual tool for the CMHA to use in its heritage education efforts in the region.

Since the partnership approach had been so effective for working on projects with the mining population, I decided to apply the same basic collaborative model in a set of heritage preservation and park planning projects with the farming segment of the region's population. The first project, conducted in 2002–3, was designed to document Appalachian family farming memories and perspectives starting with the 1930s and continuing to the present. As the structural framework for the project, I developed a collaborative partnership linking my university research team with the Virginia Farm Bureau through its New River Valley branch in Montgomery County. As before, this partnership worked well because it was based on clear mutual benefits, collaborative activities, and tangible results. Through the project, the Farm Bureau addressed its concern that the local knowledge of agricultural life be documented for use in school heritage education, and Radford University student interviewers gained enhanced field training while working on the documentation effort. Farm Bureau members joined in conducting orientation sessions for the team, facilitated rapport building, and arranged and participated in interviews. The research team, for its part, carried out thirty interviews in which thirty-three men and twenty women described farming life, prepared the transcriptions, and compiled the project results into a book of oral histories, *Appalachian Farming Life* (LaLone, Wimmer, and Spence 2003). The book provided our Farm Bureau partners with a tangible product that they were able to distribute to local schools for use in heritage education studies.

The rapport built through the farm oral history project paved the way for a second, applied anthropology project to follow in 2003. This time the research team was engaged in developing a conceptual plan for a regional Farm Heritage Park that could serve as a focal point for a farmer's market, agriculture-based community events, and farm heritage conservation.

The first step was to establish cooperative linkages between my university team, the county parks and recreation office, and the Farm Bureau. Again, as in the previous cases, all of the partners collaborated to conduct orientation sessions for the research team. Collaborative partnership in conducting the orientation sessions is an essential part of the project design since it serves a vital rapport-building function and it enables the project partners to have critical input in the planning process from the very start, orienting the research team to relevant history, issues, needs, and concerns from a variety of perspectives. In this case, besides gaining an orientation to the academic park planning literature, the team learned of needs, issues, and feelings from the perspective of the farming community (which ranged from heritage and business topics to citizen taxpayer issues), and the planning and municipal issues from the perspective of local government (including legalities and funding issues). Since a specific park site had not yet been identified, the team's task this time was to develop a conceptual set of recommendations to submit for county consideration. Thus, our techniques were tailored more toward identifying and working with key community resource people in collaborative small-group brainstorming sessions rather than holding the large-group meetings that had been employed in developing the Coal Mining Heritage Park plan. Farmers, schoolteachers, and agricultural extension agents helped us identify local needs and generate educational and design ideas for a potential farm park. Again, the project ended by synthesizing the collected ideas and research into tangible form as a consulting report (LaLone 2003b), an initial plan that received a positive review from the county's Recreation Commission and is now being considered for possible future development.[10]

Using a similar participatory development model and community outreach techniques, I also directed a university research team in developing a set of plans and recommendations for the Farm at Selu, a 1930s-period farm heritage museum at the Selu Conservancy owned by the Radford University Foundation. The project design extended the sense of partnership beyond the university into the community by seeking assistance and input from civic groups and local resource people as a key part of the planning process (e.g., the local chapter of the American Legion, local retiree organizations, and interested citizens). Synthesizing data gained through oral history interviews with the farm's former residents, focus group interviews, a community questionnaire, knowledgeable citizens' guidance on targeted topics, documentary research, and participant observation on site and at similar heritage facilities, the team developed plans to turn the historic farmstead into a heritage education site with a reconstructed farmhouse museum as the central focus. The final report provided an initial set of recommendations for facilities and amenities, site layout, and interpretive exhibits and activities (see LaLone 2001b). That farm heritage facility is now under construction.[11]

These cases have demonstrated the feasibility of using a partnership approach and anthro-planning in a variety of community-based projects, ranging from oral history projects to applied planning projects at the conceptual and more advanced stages. They show the potential for achieving success when researcher-practitioners use a participatory, collaborative, and nonhierarchical framework strengthened with the anthro-planning guidelines presented in this chapter. These examples stand in striking contrast to the opening case study, which illustrates the pitfalls that can occur when a participatory and culturally sensitive style is missing and causes a potentially good project to flounder because the development firm failed to "connect" with the client community it was serving.

Now, let's see how well you did in identifying the problems and sources of misunderstanding posed in the opening case study. Referring back to the case study and using the guidelines discussed in this chapter, how would one categorize the development firm's approach to the community? Did the firm's actions foster the feeling of community participation and a partnership approach? Prior to the two days of interviews, the firm apparently did not take time to place people in the community for on-site rapport building or on-site study of the cultural system. Prior to coming on the scene, telephone calls were made asking the community to organize a two-day visit densely packed with back-to-back interviews at fixed fifteen-minute intervals, in a manner that left some town organizers feeling that they were being ordered to make a set of near-impossible arrangements. The team arrived on time to start the interviewing and tried to keep community members on schedule, expecting them to arrive for appointments punctually and limit discussion to fifteen minutes. At the end of the two days, before appearing to take time to weigh people's input and do an investigation of the potential assets and resources at the community level, the firm announced (or let leak) its opinion that one of the key components of the town's tourism plan was unfeasible, proposing an alternative that it appeared to have decided upon before discussion with the community. Then the team left the community, which they must have realized was startled and confused by their behavior, with few forms of communication over the succeeding months, further aggravating damaged feelings. How many of the guidelines discussed above have been unheeded? You may also have identified additional issues of concern, such as the inappropriateness of team members' dress for the cultural situation and the social messages conveyed to the community by the clothing coupled with their abrupt arrival and take-charge behavior. Applying anthro-planning guidelines and cultural sensitivity, readers probably will detect other aspects of concern not selected for discussion here. The result of these events was a series of unfortunate escalating misinterpretations and miscommunications that soured both parties to the project, a situation which perhaps could have been avoided using a participatory development model with a more carefully planned partnership approach and anthro-planning strategies.

As in all good applied sciences, we hone our craft by learning from past mistakes. The opening case study in this chapter is offered as an educational tool. The hope is that researchers and applied practitioners working in Appalachia, and other parts of the world, can learn valuable lessons by analyzing past cases that have gone awry, such as this one, and then will apply the lessons about the value of participatory research and development toward designing ever more effective projects in the future.

Notes

1. This case study is offered strictly in the spirit of providing an educational tool to help practitioners assess the potentials for culturally based misunderstandings and miscommunications, with no intention of offending anyone. The town and all parties involved in this case study intentionally remain anonymous. The case study is a composite reconstruction based on the investigator's observations and conversations held while using the fieldwork technique of participant observation during the first day of a two-day visit by a consulting firm to the town, plus the investigator's personal feelings while being interviewed. The dialogue is not attributed to any specific person(s), but is reconstructed based on statements heard by the investigator in the course of investigation. Discussion of preceding and following events is based on information and feelings conveyed to the investigator during conversations with community members.

2. One of my favorite classic cases, which I use in my course on culture change to illustrate the effects of introduced change on cultural systems, involves the introduction of steel axes into a small-scale Australian society (Sharp 1952). Although the case involves a tribal group in Australia, the lesson it conveys about the effects of change on a small-scale group or community can be applied throughout the world, including Appalachian communities. The principle lesson of the article is that even seemingly helpful and insignificant changes, such as the introduction of steel axes into a society already using stone axes, can set off serious disruptions within a small society or community. As I then emphasize to my students, taking time to learn the organization of the cultural system before simply dropping changes into a community/society is extremely important because it enables the applied practitioner to work through the likely consequences of change on paper in order to identify and anticipate the potentially negative impacts of introduced change. Then the practitioner has the ability to make adjustments that might head off some of the potential problems while still in the planning stages. During the 1950s and 1960s, as development anthropology was getting under way, some anthropologists specifically focused their efforts on compiling instructive casebooks of development projects that had gone awry. Some of these now-classic casebooks on culture change are Spicer (1952) and Niehoff (1966). More recent examples appear as instructive examples throughout current textbooks in applied anthropology (see, e.g., Gwynne 2003).

3. Much has been written on the historical forces that have shaped Appalachian regions. The reader is advised to examine the bibliographies on Appalachian studies prepared by Stephen Fisher as an excellent starting point (Fisher 1991, 2002), plus the "Annual Bibliographies" compiled by Jo. B. Brown for publication each year in the *Journal of Appalachian Studies.*

4. See LaLone (2003) for more discussion of the impacts and considerations of heritage identity on the practitioner's work in Appalachia.

5. For more discussion on developing cultural competency and identifying community assets, see Susan Keefe's introduction in this book, plus Keefe (2005); Kretzmann and McKnight (1993); and McKnight and Kretzmann (1996).

6. For example, in her 2003 *Applied Anthropology* textbook, Margaret A. Gwynne emphasizes that community participation is now considered one of the chief guiding principles in the field of applied anthropology. Similar emphasis on community participation and collaboration appears in other recent applied anthropology textbooks, notably by Chambers (1989), Van Willigen (2002), and Ervin (2004), and edited volumes such as Stull and Schensul (1987).

7. I also have emphasized the value of a partnership approach between educators and Appalachian communities (LaLone 1999, 2001, 2005a, 2005b). The idea is to establish mutually beneficial arrangements that create settings for experiential student learning while assisting a community group in its efforts to carry out desired activities. I call these "teaching partnerships" because the approach emphasizes the value of having Appalachian community members serve as real-life teachers and incorporates abundant opportunities for them to share their knowledge and experiences with students. I have used this approach as the foundation for numerous class projects. My teaching/research project model and descriptions of a wide range of my class projects can be viewed on my Web site at http://mlalone.asp.radford.edu/.

8. See LaLone (1999, 2001) for more discussion of the model used for the New River Valley Coal Mining Heritage Oral History Project.

9. See LaLone (2001, 2005a, 2005b) for more discussion of the Coal Mining Heritage Park planning project. The LaLone (2005a) article also provides more detail on the anthro-planning model. Readers can access the Coal Mining Heritage Park consulting report on the Web at http://www.montva.com/departments/plan/cmhp/rucmhp/rutoc.php.

10. See LaLone (2005b) for more discussion of the Farm Heritage Park planning project. Readers can access the Farm Heritage and Community Park consulting report on the Web at http://www.radford.edu/~mlalone/NRVFarmHeritageParkProj.htm.

11. See LaLone (2005a) for a more detailed description of the Farm at Selu project.

References

Chambers, Erve. 1989. *Applied Anthropology: A Practical Guide.* Prospect Heights, IL: Waveland Press. ·

Ervin, Alexander M. 2004. *Applied Anthropology: Tools and Perspectives for Contemporary Practice.* 2nd ed. New York: Allyn and Bacon.

Fisher, Stephen L. 1991. "Selective Bibliography for Appalachian Studies." In *Appalachia: Social Context Past and Present,* Bruce Ergood and Bruce E. Kuhre (Eds.). 3rd ed. Dubuque: Kendall/Hunt. Pp. 375–416.

―――. 1993. *Fighting Back in Appalachia: Traditions of Resistance and Change.* Philadelphia: Temple Univ. Press.

―――. 2002. "A Selected Bibliography of Books on Appalachia 1991–2001." In *Appalachia: Social Context Past and Present,* Phillip J. Obermiller and Michael E. Maloney (Eds.). 4th ed. Dubuque: Kendall/Hunt. Pp. 427–33.

Gwynne, Margaret A. 2003. *Applied Anthropology: A Career-Oriented Approach.* Boston: Allyn and Bacon.

Hall, Edward T. 1959. *The Silent Language.* Garden City, NY: Doubleday.

―――. 1966. *The Hidden Dimension.* Garden City, NY: Doubleday.

Keefe, Susan E. (Ed.). 2005. *Appalachian Cultural Competency: A Guide for Medical, Mental Health, and Social Service Professionals.* Knoxville: Univ. of Tennessee Press.

Kelley, Brian. 1994. "Coal Miners' Day to Honor Montgomery Heritage." *Roanoke Times and World-News,* Apr. 22.

Kretzmann, John P., and John L. McNight. 1993. *Building Communities from the Inside Out: A Path Toward Finding and Mobilizing a Community's Assets.* Evanston, IL: Institute for Policy Research, Northwestern Univ.

LaLone, Mary B. 1995. "Recollections about Life in Appalachia's Coal Camps: Positive or Negative?" *Journal of the Appalachian Studies Association* 7:91–100.

―――. 1996. "Economic Survival Strategies in Appalachia's Coal Camps." *Journal of Appalachian Studies* 2(1):53–68.

―――― (Ed.). 1997. *Appalachian Coal Mining Memories: Life in the Coal Fields of Virginia's New River Valley.* Blacksburg, VA: Pocahontas Press.

―――― (Ed.). 1998. *Coal Mining Lives: An Oral History Sequel to Appalachian Coal Mining Memories.* Radford, VA: Dept. of Sociology and Anthropology, Radford Univ.

―――. 1999. "Preserving Appalachian Heritage: A Model for Oral History Research and Teaching." *Journal of Appalachian Studies* 5(1):115–22.

―――― (Ed.). 2000. *Coal Mining Heritage Park, Montgomery County, Virginia: Study, Plan, and Recommendations.* Radford, VA: Dept. of Sociology and Anthropology, Radford Univ. Electronic document: http://www.montva.com/departments/plan/cmhp/rucmhp/rutoc.php.

―――. 2001. "Putting Anthropology to Work to Preserve Appalachian Heritage." *Practicing Anthropology* 23(2):5–9.

―――― (Ed.). 2001b. *The Selu Living History Museum: Recommendations for an Appalachian Heritage Education Center.* Radford, VA: Dept. of Sociology and Anthropology, Radford Univ.

―――. 2003. "Walking the Line between Alternative Interpretations in Heritage Education and Tourism: A Demonstration of the Complexities with an Appalachian Coal Mining Example." In *Signifying Serpents and Mardi Gras Runners: Representing Identity in Selected Souths,* Celeste Ray and Luke Eric Lassiter (Eds.). Athens: Univ. of Georgia Press. Pp. 72–92.

——— (Ed.). 2003b. *Farm Heritage and Community Park: Conceptual Plans and Ideas.* Radford, VA: Dept. of Sociology and Anthropology, Radford Univ. Electronic document: http://www.radford.edu/~mlalone/NRVFarm HeritageParkProj.htm.

———. 2005a. "An Anthro-Planning Approach to Local Heritage Tourism: Case Studies from Appalachia." *NAPA Bulletin* (National Association for the Practice of Anthropology) 23:135–50.

———. 2005b. "Building Heritage Partnerships: Working Together for Heritage Preservation and Local Tourism in Appalachia." *Practicing Anthropology* 27(4):10–13.

——— (Ed.). 2005c. *Coal Mining Heritage Museum and Video Documentary Project.* Radford, VA: Dept. of Sociology and Anthropology, Radford Univ.

LaLone, Mary B., Kenesha Moseley Beheler, and Nathan Juarin. 2006. *Memories from the Mines: Life in the Coal Mining Communities of the New River Valley.* Documentary. Radford, VA: Dept. of Sociology and Anthropology, Radford Univ.

LaLone, Mary B., Peg Wimmer, and Reva K. Spence (Eds.). 2003. *Appalachian Farming Life: Memories and Perspectives on Family Farming in Virginia's New River Valley.* Radford, VA: Brightside Press.

McKnight, John L., and John P. Kretzmann. 1996. *Mapping Community Capacity.* Evanston, IL: Institute for Policy Research, Northwestern Univ.

Niehoff, Arthur H. 1966. *A Casebook of Social Change.* Chicago: Aldine.

Price, Jimmie L. 1995. "Interview with Jimmie L. Price by Mary LaLone. July 31. Blacksburg, Virginia." New River Valley Coal Mining Heritage Oral History Project, Dept. of Sociology and Anthropology, Radford Univ., Radford, VA.

Sharp, Lauriston. 1952. "Steel Axes for Stone-Age Australians." *Human Organization* 11:17–22.

Spicer, Edward H. 1952. *Human Problems in Technological Change: A Casebook.* New York: Sage.

Stull, Donald D., and Jean J. Schensul (Eds.). 1987. *Collaborative Research and Social Change: Applied Anthropology in Action.* Boulder, CO: Westview Press.

Van Willigen, John. 2002. *Applied Anthropology: An Introduction.* 3rd ed. Westport, CT: Bergin and Garvey.

Community Coalition Building in the Madison County Health Project

Thomas Plaut, Suzanne Landis, and June Palmour Trevor

In this case study of a successful participatory project, Plaut, Landis, and Trevor describe the partnership that developed between citizens, community health professionals, and academic experts working on common goals. The Community Oriented Primary Care model used in this project has been used successfully in public health projects around the country. Illustrating the complex nature of mountain life, the project began by identifying more than seventy communities in rural Madison County, North Carolina. Techniques intended to involve community residents in the planning and implementation process included focus group research, establishment of a representative advisory board, promotion of community health fairs, and coalition-building action by citizens and professions working together to improve residents' health and quality of life. Productivity was high, with ten different interventions over a six-year period, including several funded by federal grants. The authors credit much of the success of the project to the time taken to understand the local context, to develop trust and mutual respect between local citizens and professionals, and to address needs conceptualized in the language of community members.

Studies in Appalachia most often approach Appalachian people as the "other" who are set apart from America (e.g., Looff 1971; Weller 1965) or are the victims of forces of modernization and globalization (e.g., Fisher 1993; Lewis, Kobak, and Johnson 1978; Whisnant 1980). A third approach has "reframed" the Appalachian people as citizens participating in the political process. Increasing numbers of researchers and other professionals are working in partnership with local people and organizations to articulate their own strengths and needs (Gaventa 1988; Hinsdale Lewis, and Waller 1995; Plaut, Landis, and Trevor 1992; Waller 1991; Waller et al. 1990). These partnerships are promising and productive, especially when combined with a postmodernist sensitivity to subregion complexities of class and culture (Banks, Billings, and Tice 1993). They can transform the "we and they" mentality of earlier research and change efforts into a context where researchers and local folk—people of different backgrounds, social locations, and values—work together to discover a common vision and direction. Those using research results are no longer just government agencies, corporations, providers, and academics, but also the citizen/research subjects themselves. This is a positive trend, promising a growing partnership between providers, researchers, and community members based on mutual respect, trust, and productivity.

The Setting

This chapter describes a community-based health project in Madison County, North Carolina, which has been rooted in the third approach. County residents defined their communities, strengths and needs. Supported by professionals—from physicians to sociologists—they designed and implemented projects they felt were appropriate.

Located along the state's mountainous border with Tennessee, Madison County consists of a 456-square-mile area with a population of 17,000 living in some 6,500 households. Historically, Madison has been a county of family farms where burley tobacco has been the major cash crop. But in the 1980s, major tobacco companies turned to cheaper overseas suppliers, while demand for tobacco also dropped. The number of farms in the county decreased 11.8 percent between 1982 and 1987. Of the remaining 1,305 farms, 1,142 (87.5 percent) had incomes less than $10,000, indicating that, for most people, farming has become a second source of revenue behind what county folk call "public work" in commerce, industry, and government (North Carolina State Center for Health Statistics 1989). The county's isolated and mountainous terrain has limited the development of manufacturing. The consequent lack of economic opportunity has led to the flight of the working-age population, leaving behind a significantly higher percentage of people (14.4 percent) over sixty-five than the state average (10.2 percent).

Forty percent of these elderly live below the poverty line. Some 15.5 percent (757) of the county's 4,881 families live in poverty, as do 22 percent of its children. Its 1992 per capita income was $13,799, well below the state average of $17,863. Its mean farm value in 1987 was $95,520, compared to a state average of $236,937. The average house value was $47,800 in 1990, about 17 percent less than the state's $57,881. In sum, resources in Madison County were, and are, limited.

The Project

The Madison Community Health Project (MCHP) began in August 1989 with funding from the W. K. Kellogg Foundation. The project's approach was based on the Community Oriented Primary Care model (COPC), which, although well known in public health, is unfamiliar to social scientists. COPC's goals and methods parallel those of participatory research in that the human subjects of a study and any action that might grow out of it must be intimately involved in the project's design and interventions. COPC is rooted in an often forgotten but vigorous side of medical epidemiology that focused on the *social* causes of disease. Modern epidemiology perhaps began with John Snow's tracking the source of a cholera epidemic to a single well in London in the 1850s. Its development continued through Adolphe Quetelet's moral statistics (*statistique morale*) gathering of quantitative data on nonphysical human characteristics, to researchers such as Friedrich Engels and Rudolf Virchow linking health to working and living (social or "moral") conditions. Virchow's report on an 1848 typhus epidemic in Upper Silesia prescribed education, freedom, and prosperity as the cure. One of his best-known assertions is that "medicine is a social science, and politics nothing but medicine on a grand scale." It is not surprising to learn that Virchow was well acquainted with anthropologist Franz Boas and the idea of the importance of cultural elements (both material and nonmaterial) in health maintenance (Trostle 1986a).

The medical team credited with developing Community Oriented Primary Care was also influenced by anthropologists and social research methods. Doctors Sidney and Emily Kark divided their time on a Nuffield fellowship at

Oxford between the Institute for Social Medicine and the Institute for Social Anthropology, where they worked with E. E. Evans-Pritchard, Meyer Fortes, and Max Gluckman. They came to Oxford after years of field experience in South Africa, where in 1934 they had established a Society for the Study of Medical Conditions among the Bantu. In 1939, Sidney Kark was asked to head a health center in Polela, a rural community in Natal. The program began with an extensive community assessment in which tribal chiefs and elders, women's groups, teachers, and area residents (in home visits) provided information about conditions, local health beliefs and practices, and people known locally for the dissemination of news and new ideas. In 1942, a house-to-house survey was conducted to assess the health status of the community. The Polela Health Center established a community gardening/nutrition program, providing people with seeds for new varieties of vegetables and information on how to prepare them in conformance to local preferences. It created a cooperative for buying seeds and a community market. The center's early medical initiatives included the establishment of a community clinic, a maternal and child health program, and examinations for schoolchildren. The Karks called this ongoing praxis of survey research mixed with social and medical interventions "community health diagnosis," which is at the core of their COPC method.

In the mid 1950s, politics intervened in the Karks' work. The application of the South African conservative government's policy of racial separation, Apartheid, to the medical profession led to a diaspora of COPC and its advocates. The Karks and a colleague, John Cassell, came to Chapel Hill in the late 1950s, bringing the idea of COPC with them (Trostle 1986b). By the time Suzanne Landis finished her master's of public health program in 1986 at Chapel Hill, she was well versed in COPC theory. Her experience as a National Health Corps physician in Appalachian eastern Tennessee had convinced her of the importance of community health diagnosis and community-based medicine. As project director for the Kellogg-funded Madison Community Health Program, she introduced COPC as having four essential elements:

1. Identifying the community—meaning the total population, not just users of the medical center. The entire community, its social institutions, structure, and patterns of relationships, traditional healing methods, diet, and economy are to be assessed.
2. Identifying community health problems.
3. Involving the community in determining priorities in health needs and designing and implementing consequent health interventions.
4. Constant monitoring of projects to evaluate their effectiveness and enable their ongoing modification.

The first goal of the Madison project's assessment process was to determine how residents defined and used the idea of "community." The county's three postmasters were asked to map communities within their zip code areas. Their maps were then validated and refined by key informants. We found that Madison County residents defined their communities as small neighborhoods, based on traditional kinship ties and landholdings. A total of seventy-two communities were identified, along with 350 "community helpers" (defined as people whom residents of a specific community would call if they needed advice or assistance).

The mapping exercise emphasized the MCHP should not plan for "community organization" because there were plenty of communities already well organized in frameworks comfortable for their residents. The task would be to network these numerous small groups for collaborative planning and action. As many groups as possible needed to be included in any assessment of county strengths, desires, and needs. When a country resident objected to the use of surveys for data gathering (saying, "These people are tired of being asked if they're poor"), we were forced to rely heavily on the qualitative data generated in group interviews. Forty focus groups were conducted: seven with teachers; eight with social services, mental health, and community support personnel (the sheriff's office, extension service, day care, and congregate meal site staff); eleven with medical providers; and fourteen with community groups such as churches and volunteer fire departments.

The interviews were conducted between August and December 1989, including 416 informants. The setting for each group was its own turf, be it a school, a fire department garage, church, or office. The size of each group was determined by interest and its membership; the median was seven participants. The community groups proved to be a source of data and also a means of involving people in the project's citizens' Community Advisory Board (CAB) and its interventions.

The focus group's questions were the following:

(1) What personal health problems or physical complaints appear to be most commonly mentioned by people in the community?
(2) What barriers to health care or medically related issues do people in the community talk about?
(3) What in this group's opinion are the serious health problems in the county?
(4) What are the causes of these serious health problems?
(5) What in this group's opinion are the serious barriers to health care?
(6) What needs to be done to alleviate these problems?

(7) Do you feel that there is any group of the population not receiving adequate medical care? Why not?

(8) Who do people call in this community when they need help or advice?

Qualitative Data: The Interview Responses

Health complaints most heard in the community related to pain, which was associated with arthritis/rheumatism and backache, allergies, and heart disease. When focus group members were asked for their own opinion of serious health problems in the county, diseases related to aging and the frail elderly topped the list (Alzheimer's disease, circulatory problems, cardiovascular disease, and "just getting old").

Alcohol abuse was the highest scored response to the question on a groups' own views of serious illness. Stress-related symptoms such as head and stomach aches were ranked second to alcohol. A number of informants talked about the stress felt by farmers, who must produce to make payments on farm equipment and land taxes before they can provide food, shelter, and medical care for their families. Depression was ranked within the top five health problems. Teachers said that family problems caused stress-related illnesses and depression among students. High school students are depressed by the choices they believe they will face after graduation: "They want to stay in the mountains, but have to leave if they are going to find jobs."

The causes of health problems cited were lack of preventive health care, lack of care of self in the early stages of an illness or injury, poor diet and poor parenting, poor hygiene, and abuse and neglect.

What should be done to alleviate the problems of poor health and inaccessible health care? Although there was general discussion about the need for a federal response to the health care crisis in the United States, the focus groups were encouraged by the facilitators to center their answers on what could be done locally. Consequently, preventive health education scored highest among needed solutions, followed by transportation for the elderly and for children, education on how to utilize existing health care services, preventive care, parenting, and nutrition; expanded home care services for the frail elderly; and development of support groups for parents.

Groups cited as not receiving adequate care included the elderly, people unable to qualify for publicly assisted care and unable to afford private insurance, people who *felt* they could not afford medical care, children, people without means of transportation, and people not educated to access health care.

The power of the small groups' testimony lay not just in the aggregated tallies listed above, but also in resident's descriptions of circumstances and conditions. Here are some examples taken from focus groups with teachers:

The [children's] stress comes from just trying to survive. Many [children] work in the tobacco fields and in tomatoes.

Kids don't sleep at night. They just come in here and put their heads down on the desk—and we let them sleep. They can't learn anything when they're that tired. We just let them sleep. Some of them stay up because they're working—in tobacco in the evening or digging night crawlers to sell to tourists.

[Due to the combination of the timing of factory shifts and single parenting] some children as young as the third grade are preparing their own meals. Some as young as the third grade have to dress and feed their younger brothers and sisters before school.

Kids are affected by alcohol abuse—both in terms of witnessing heavy drinking and by being victims or witnesses of physical abuse accompanied by drinking.

The kids get knocked around at home, so they do it to each other at school.

We can't teach as much now as we did ten years ago—we spend much more time now . . . trying to control their behavior.

In my first ten years, I never made a report to the Department of Social Services for suspected abuse. Now we have to report four or five cases every year in this one school alone.

Fifty percent of the kids at this school do not get taken to the doctor. Mothers work now. They send sick kids to school. Single parents can't afford to lose a day's work and stay home with a sick child.

Fifteen out of the twenty-five kids in my classroom have never seen a dentist.

Dental care is a big problem. How do I know? Just look in their mouths—you can see the cavities. One boy has a large cavity in a front tooth and he always tries to hide it by holding his lip down over his tooth.

Focus groups interviews allow a group synergy to develop, enabling feelings and insights to be expressed that are unlikely to be uncovered by individual interviews and surveys. In one-on-one interviews, the researcher often is perceived as the person with the status and power, making the respondent more reserved than she or he would be in talking with peers. Responses to surveys are limited by questions which can miss important data by not asking the right question or not asking a question in the right way. The great benefit of focus groups is they enable the researcher to observe a discussion amongst peers who are comfortable with their fellow respondents, who can reframe questions according to their own worldviews. The focus groups became the key to understanding the views and frustrations of county residents. For example, conditions causing resentment among volunteer firemen and "first-responder" emergency medical technicians vis-à-vis physicians could not be addressed until those feelings could be expressed. Focus groups held on a group's own turf, such as a fire department garage, provided the opportunity for expressions such as the following:

> The boy's body lay in a ditch for three hours before a medical examiner (a job rotated by local physicians) would let us move him. . . . We had to sit there and watch the "ooh-ah crowd" stand there and stare at the body.

> The doctors don't take any pride in helping the ambulance service in a wreck.

> The doctor charged me thirty-five dollars and then told me "You have to stay out of the dust for a while." Now I'm a farmer. How am I going to stay away from the dust?

As the group process developed, the expression of emotion intensified. When asked what might be done to improve the relationship between physicians and emergency medical services staff, one respondent evoked cheers from his fellows by suggesting we "nail the doctors' feet to the floor and burn the building!" One man, tilting his chair back against the cinder block garage wall with his baseball cap pulled low over his eyes, broke his evening-long silence with a simple request that seemed to summarize the group's position: "Look, just tell 'em that we're plain tired of being shit on." We did share these feelings with physicians, some of whom in turn were hurt and offended. But they were also sensitized to being more supportive of other players in the emergency medical system as well as to county needs. One outcome of this sensitization process was collaborative work around health fairs and the 911 project described below.

Quantitative Data

Group interview data was compiled alongside epidemiological statistics on mortality and morbidity and demographic and economic data provided by federal and state agencies. For example, the county death rate in 1986 was 9.04 per 1,000 compared to a state rate of 8.62. Heart disease was the leading cause of death and had a rate of 317 per 100,000; the state rate was 306 (North Carolina State Center for Health Statistics 1987; North Carolina Department of Environment, Health, and Natural Resources 1989). An important finding in the epidemiological data was that Madison County is not atypical statistically; its overall health is no better or worse than other American counties. However, an elevated diabetes mortality rate indicated a need for more attention to medical care and glucose monitoring, and diet. An elevated pneumonia/influenza rate (51.84/100,000 compared to a national 29/100,000) suggested greater attention be paid to respiratory illness and preventive measures such as influenza and pneumococcal vaccinations. Data on dental caries (27 percent to 63 percent of K–8 grade students in the county's eight schools), indicated the need for dental sealants and other preventive oral health care.

Decision Making for Community Action

Interview scores were totaled and ranked and, along with morbidity and mortality data, provided to the Madison Community Health Project Community Advisory Board, which provided the community-based leadership for action.

The CAB began as a small group of residents and county agency representatives who discussed the possibility of applying for the W. K. Kellogg Foundation funding in the summer of 1988. They hosted a foundation team site visit several months later and, when the grant was awarded, they were called together again and asked if they wanted to accept it. Leadership during this initial phase was provided by Suzanne Landis, the COPC-trained physician with the Mountain Area Health Education Center who later became the project director; the chair of the local community-based medical centers; and Tom Plaut, a sociologist teaching at a college within the county who later was given responsibility for the community assessment process. Landis, Plaut, and June Trevor, a county resident with a decade of experience working with the developmentally disabled in the county, became the project staff. In the fall of 1989, the project staff guided the CAB through an orientation to the COPC process and a community assessment. Data gathered in the assessment were presented to the CAB in the winter of 1990. A nominal group process (Abramson 1984) was employed to break down the CAB into small groups to discuss and prioritize needs and actions, which were then voted on by the plenary group. It was at this point that the staff began to transfer project leadership to the CAB, which initiated the following interventions over the next six years:

Flu and pneumonia vaccinations for people over sixty-five

Health fairs for seniors that continue to reach some five hundred people annually

Support for parents of newborn children in a pilot school district by specially trained lay volunteer women recruited by its Parent Teacher Association

Forums for high school seniors on AIDS, stress, and stress management

Cosponsored forums on national health care reform and infant mortality

A newspaper column on health issues, written on a rotating basis by CAB members

Walking trails and programs

An oral health program for school children, including the placing of dental sealants

Publishing resource guides for parents and senior citizens

Cooperatively writing grant proposals, two of which have funded the installation of a 911 emergency response system, while a third funded the development of a diabetes education and nutrition program (in response to a need demonstrated in the community assessment data)

From Community Advisory Board to Community Health Coalition

The experience of evaluating communitywide data and designing and implementing community projects over a four-year period gave CAB members a shared history of achievement and a new collective identity. A long-term planning committee was established in 1992 and an area resident with skills in meeting management was brought on as a consultant. This meeting manager later trained CAB members to facilitate meetings, so that by 1995 coalition meeting facilitation was rotated among the membership.

An evaluation survey of CAB members' results reported that "93 percent of the members responded that they are 'almost always' or 'often' enthusiastic about being a part of the CAB . . . over 85 percent . . . signified that the COPC project had helped them make use of community resources . . . 63.3 percent rated the CAB as 'very productive.'" The state of CAB morale was indicated in comments such as "meetings are informal and members feel free to express their opinions" and "[members have] freedom to share ideas" (Shaler 1992a:48).

By the spring of 1992, the CAB had grown beyond the Kellogg COPC project it advised. It renamed itself the Madison Community Health Consortium (MCHC), "a partnership that seeks to improve the overall health of Madison County citizens by networking community agencies and groups in the on-going process of needs assessment and project development, implementation and evaluation."

The consortium scored a major success in September 1992 when it received a $220,000 grant from the U.S. Department of Health and Human Services for a 911 emergency telephone system (to replace a maze of thirteen different emergency numbers) while offering emergency and injury prevention programs for county residents. The grant not only provided important and needed services, but affirmed the validity of years of collaborative efforts culminating in the winning of a competitive national grant (there were 260 applications for twenty-seven awards).

It is important to remember, given the anger and resentment found among volunteer firemen and emergency medical personnel toward physicians in the focus groups, that representatives of each group worked together on the 911 grant application. When the receipt of grant funds was threatened by county politicians, they were able to mobilize their neighbors to let the commissioners know that the loss of federal funds would not be tolerated. The 911 system went online in November 1993. A year later, the consortium won a second federal grant totaling more than $300,000 to help pay for the mapping and addressing required for a computerized , enhanced 911 system, in which the location of an emergency call automatically appears on a computer monitor screen together with a description of the site and directions for getting there. (Enhanced 911 is especially important in rural areas because it saves lives by reducing ambulance response times.) For a second time, the MCHC had demonstrated its ability to pull together agencies and individuals in collaborative efforts to compete successfully at the national level.

In July of 1995, the consortium grants team won another $175,000 to enable a local medical practice to develop a diabetes education, counseling, and nutrition program.

In October 1996, some 470 senior citizens received free physical examinations, medical consultations, and flu and pneumonia immunizations at the Senior Health Fair. In November, the health fair idea was expanded to the schools, and some twenty-five hundred students attended fairs in each of the county's schools. Both school and senior health fairs have been institutionalized as annual events.

The Consortium's Task Force on Physical Fitness organized coaches and parents to improve access to schools and other public facilities for community team sports. In response to the task force's advocacy, the county commissioners have appointed a parks and recreation director to coordinate community teams and facilities usage and, in the long run, create a county Department of Parks and Recreation.

A Task Force for Volunteers has been organized to better match high school and college students and other citizens with community needs.

In January 1996, the MCHC task force on substance abuse, collaborating with a another community coalition in a neighboring county, received a

$900,000 grant award for an Appalachian Substance Abuse Prevention Project, designed to better network community organizations and agencies for prevention efforts while also developing culturally appropriate educational materials for rural audiences.

As of July 1997, four years after the end of Kellogg Foundation funding, the consortium continued to mature as a force capable of articulating and advocating for the needs of the community-at-large. Looking back to 1989, the consortium's collaborative creativity was initially discovered, unleashed, and focused by a community-based research process in which social, epidemiological, and lay community researchers helped a county record its residents' definitions of "community," "health," and "community health needs." The researchers helped the project advisory board (which later became the consortium) create an understandable and workable summary of findings and the facilitation skills required for collective decision making and action. In a way, the consortium has become the community, organized, empowered, and actively working to improve its health and quality of life.

Lessons Learned from the Project

The health department director told an interviewer, "This is the best thing that ever happened to Madison County." What did happen? All the discussion and deliberation, consequent interventions and "wins," such as the funding of the 911 and the diabetes program, at bottom created a sense of trust and empowerment that is essential to genuine community. Visitors to health consortium meetings today are impressed by a group of people going about their business, people who have set goals and are confidently setting out to achieve them. A decade ago, many of these people did not know each other, and many of those who were acquainted did not trust each other. How was this change facilitated and what were the theoretical assumptions behind it? George Shaler, a graduate student at the University of North Carolina at Chapel Hill's School of Public Health, used the Madison project as a case study in his master's thesis on community-oriented primary care. He had been troubled by a recent trend in which physicians had become the dominant controlling players in COPC, defining community needs from the clinic perspective with little or no resident involvement. Entitling his paper "Putting the Community Back in COPC," Shaler made the following conclusion:

> Since its inception in the United States, the COPC framework has assisted countless communities to better facilitate the delivery of health care services to the community. COPC has come to mean many different things for differ-

ent communities. For some (medical) practitioners, COPC is a change in their practice's organization and service delivery, while some communities such as Madison County are slowly transforming the way health care is provided in their community. There then is a continuum of what constitutes COPC, ranging from the clinic-driven projects to more community-oriented projects. The more community oriented COPC projects attempt to engage residents in a process of determining the type of health services which meet their need. While being more time intensive for the practitioner, the outcomes of community-driven projects can be very positive. The Madison Community Health Project provides an example of an emerging community-driven project. The development of the CAB (consortium) and other successful community interventions justify this community-driven approach.

Renewed emphasis should be focused on the community in COPC. . . . There are many communities, Madison County among them, which have demonstrated their ability to include the community. As this discussion has attempted to show, community participation should not be relegated to a secondary status in COPC. (Shaler 1992b:56)

We have learned that community-oriented primary care must be based on community resident understanding and definitions of strengths and needs. W. I. Thomas's oft-repeated axiom, "as people define situations as real, they are real in their consequences," is a critical insight for coalition building. People will join in community action only if they understand the need for it in terms of their own language, definitions of the situation, and worldviews. The care taken in the Madison health project to ascertain residents' definitions of community, strengths, and needs was the key to releasing the store of knowledge and energy available for collective action.

We rediscovered the fact that many laypeople do not share the language and culture of professionals. Kark's comments on culture and the social context of Polela reflect his sensitivity to the cultural gap between the lay community and the medical center: "The whole process of the health centre's development was one which reflected an increased understanding of the individual in terms of his family situation, of the family in its life situation within the local community and finally the way of life of the community itself in relation to the social structure of South Africa" (Trostle 1986b:61).

David Liden, director of the Murphy Medical Center Foundation in Cherokee County, North Carolina, has mirrored the Karks' sensitivity in reflecting the foreign nature of his 50-bed hospital and 120-bed nursing home in a rural Appalachian community:

In many ways, a modern hospital is an alien institution for a rural community. We should have realized from the very beginning that our hospital has taken over a number of tasks that were formerly done in a family context. Birth, healing, death, [and] caring for the elderly traditionally took place at home. All of us working in the rural setting need to remember that we have replaced natural communities and families in many health care matters. This is symbolized every time a helicopter takes off with the most sick people of all, taking people away from the community to Asheville or Atlanta, Chattanooga or Knoxville. The helicopter represents in a very visible way the replacement of traditional community systems by "foreign" medical culture and technology. . . . The administrative staff members were outsiders, the technical staff members were outsiders, and the physicians, excepting one, were outsiders. The equipment, technology and language that go with hospital work are very different and unfamiliar to local people. (Landis et al. 1995:36–37)

Liden initially tried to reverse this foreign trend by making the hospital available for community meetings and encouraging staff involvement in local events. He studied the Madison COPC project and adopted its approach, holding public meetings and conducting focus groups to begin the process of local input and buy-in into the reshaping of health care delivery by public health departments, mental health centers, skilled care facilities, hospitals, and individual medical providers in a three-county area (Liden, personal communication).

The staff from the 1989–93 Kellogg grant has joined with other community-based researchers at the Mountain Area Health Education Center in Asheville as the Western North Carolina Community Health Research Services to provide support to people like Liden and other area health coalitions. We believe the COPC approach used in the Madison Community Health Project is replicable not only in western North Carolina, but also throughout Appalachia and, in fact, wherever viable human communities exist.

We also believe that COPC enhances the new collegiality between layperson and professional, discussed earlier in this chapter. The vertical relationship of expert to layperson can be replaced by a horizontal relationship of customer to craftsperson. (When asked to design an evaluation for a child care agency, one of the authors introduced himself to community staff members as "something like a plumber. You call a plumber to work on your pipes. I'm the 'data man.'") This "reframing" of the relationship between specialist and client suggested that they, not he, were in control of the research process. Of course, some reject such leveling in collaborative research: one physician responded to our suggestion that focus groups enhance the creation of community consensus and action with the statement, "Why should I listen to the opinion of someone who can't afford my services?" We think laypeople should define what is real and what is to be done in their communities. By leveling relationships, the potential for collaboration between residents and professionals is increased. The result is information that is accurate, accessible, and understandable for everybody involved and appropriate for preventive community-based health initiatives.

References

Abramson, J. H. 1984. *Survey Methods in Community Medicine: An Introduction to Epidemiological and Evaluative Studies.* 3rd ed. New York: Churchill Livingstone.

Banks, Alan, Dwight Billings, and Karen Tice. 1993. "Appalachian Studies, Resistance and Postmodernism." In *Fighting Back in Appalachia,* Stephen L. Fisher (Ed.). Philadelphia: Temple Univ. Press. Pp. 283–301.

Fisher, Stephen L. 1993. *Fighting Back in Appalachia: Traditions of Resistance and Change.* Philadelphia: Temple Univ. Press.

Gaventa, John. 1988. "Participatory Research in North America." *Convergence* 21:19–29.

Hinsdale, Mary Ann, Helen M. Lewis and Maxine Waller. 1995. *It Comes from the People: Community Development and Local Theology.* New York: Temple Univ. Press.

Landis, Suzanne, Thomas Plaut, June Trevor, and Judy Futch. 1995. *Building a Healthier Tomorrow: A Manual for Rural Coalition Building.* Dubuque: Kendall/Hunt.

Lewis, Helen, Sue Kobak, and Linda Johnson. 1978. "Family, Religion and Colonialism in Central Appalachia." In *Colonialism in Modern America: The Appalachian Case,* Helen Matthews Lewis, Linda Johnson, and Donald Askins (Eds.). Boone: Appalachian Consortium Press. Pp. 113–39.

Looff, David H. 1971. *Appalachia's Children: The Challenge of Mental Health.* Lexington: Univ. of Kentucky Press.

North Carolina Dept. of Environment, Health and Natural Resources. 1989. *Community Diagnosis: County Data Book—Madison County.* Raleigh: Dept. of Environment, Health and Natural Resources.

North Carolina State Center for Health Statistics. 1987. *Leading Causes of Mortality: North Carolina Vital Statistics, 1986.* Vol. 2. Raleigh: North Carolina Dept. of Human Resources, Division of Health Services.

———. 1989. LINK computer data base of 1987 U.S. Census of Agriculture, Advance State Report for North Carolina. Report number AC87-A-37(A). Washington, DC: U.S. Government Printing Office.

Plaut, Thomas, Suzanne Landis, and June Trevor. 1992. "Enhancing Participatory Research with the Community Oriented Primary Care Model." *American Sociologist* 23(4):55–70.

Shaler, George. 1992a. "An Assessment of the Madison Community Health Project's Community Advisory Board." Paper written for the Health Behavior and Health Education Dept., Univ. of North Carolina, Chapel Hill, January 13.

———. 1992b. "Putting the Community Back in COPC: The Madison Community Health Project." Master's thesis, Univ. of North Carolina, Chapel Hill.

Trostle, James. 1986a. "Early Work in Anthropology and Epidemiology: From Social Medicine to Germ Theory, 1840–1920." In *Anthropology and Epidemiology in the Twentieth Century: A Selective History of the Collaborative Projects and Theoretical Affinities,* Craig R. Janes et al. (Eds.). Boston: D. Reidel. Pp. 35–57.

———. 1986b. "Anthropology and Epidemiology in the Twentieth Century: A Selective History of Collaborative Projects and Theoretical Affinities, 1920 to 1970." In *Anthropology and Epidemiology in the Twentieth Century: A Selective History of the Collaborative Projects and Theoretical Affinities,* Craig R. Janes et al. (Eds.). Boston: D. Reidel. Pp. 59–94.

Waller, Maxine. 1991. "Local Organizing: Ivanhoe, Virginia." *Social Policy* 21(Winter): 62–67.

Waller, Maxine, Helen M. Lewis, Clare McBrien, and Carol L. Wessinger. 1990. "It Has to Come from the People." In *Communities in Economic Crisis: Appalachia and the South,* John Gaventa, Barbara E. Smith, and Alex Willingham (Eds.). Philadelphia: Temple Univ. Press. Pp. 19–28.

Weller, Jack. 1965. *Yesterday's People.* Lexington: Univ. Press of Kentucky.

Whisnant, David E. 1980. *Modernizing the Mountaineer.* Boone: Appalachian Consortium Press.

Contributors

LESLEY BARTLETT is assistant professor at Teachers College, Columbia University. Her teaching and research interests include the intersection between political and cultural change, the anthropology of education, and schooling in the United States, Latin America, and the Caribbean. She is coauthor of *Local Democracy Under Siege* (New York University Press, 2007).

KATHRYN M. BORMAN is professor of anthropology and affiliated with the Alliance for Applied Research in Education and Anthropology at the University of South Florida. She has extensive experience in educational reform and policy as well as evaluation studies. She recently completed (with the American Institutes of Research) the OERI-funded National Longitudinal Evaluation of Comprehensive School Reform directing the focus study of forty schools in five districts. She has investigated policy issues related to the training of skilled technical workers. Borman also participated in the Evaluation of Cincinnati Youth Collaborative (1992), assessing ongoing school-based support activities for youth. She served as editor of the *Review of Educational Research* and teaches a variety of courses, including anthropology and education and methods in qualitative analysis.

JEFFERSON C. BOYER is professor of anthropology and former director of the Sustainable Development Program at Appalachian State University. His ethnological work is on the political economy of highland peasants in Honduras. As a board member of the Highlander Research and Education Center, he continues to work to support the sustainable communities' movement in Watauga County and elsewhere in the Appalachian region.

SAMUEL R. COOK is associate professor in the Department of Interdisciplinary Studies at Virginia Tech, where he teaches Appalachian Studies and serves as director of American Indian studies. His research focuses on the politics of place and identity in relationship to local political economies, with a particular emphasis on explicating and participating in projects in which grassroots communities seek to empower themselves. He is the author of *Monacans and Miners: Native American and Coal Mining Communities in Appalachia* (University of Nebraska Press, 2000). Cook also serves as director of the Kentland Historic Revitalization Project on Virginia Tech's premier research farm, where he is working to establish a program in agri/eco tourism in association with the College of Agriculture and Life Sciences.

RHODA H. HALPERIN is professor emeritus of anthropology at the University of Cincinnati and professor of anthropology at Montclair State University. She is the author of *The Livelihood of Kin: Making Ends Meet the Kentucky Way* (University of Texas Press, 1990). Most recently, she worked in an urban Appalachian community in Cincinnati and chronicled this work in *Practicing Community: Class, Culture and Power in an Urban Neighborhood* (University of Texas Press, 1998) and *Whose School Is It? Women, Children, Memory and Practice in the City* (University of Texas Press, 2006). Her work on economic anthropology and archaeology, class, globalization, children, and urban studies can be found in articles and book chapters.

ELVIN HATCH is professor emeritus in the Department of Anthropology and the Department of Law and Society at the University of California, Santa Barbara. His research interests include both the history of anthropology and the study of small communities in industrialized nations, and he has conducted field research in rural California, New Zealand, and western North Carolina. He is the author of several books, including *Biography of a Small Town* (Columbia University, 1979) and *Respectable Lives: Social Standing in Rural New Zealand* (University of California Press, 1992). He is now completing a book on his research in a small county in the Blue Ridge Mountains.

SUSAN E. KEEFE is professor of anthropology at Appalachian State University. She has taught applied anthropology and placed more than three hundred student interns in community development agencies over the past three decades. As chair of the anthropology department, she fostered the Sustainable Development Program at Appalachian State and currently holds a faculty affiliation with the program. She is coauthor of *Chicano Ethnicity* (University of New Mexico Press, 1987) and editor of two volumes, *Appalachian Mental Health* (University of Kentucky Press, 1988) and *Appalachian Cultural Competency* (University of Tennessee Press, 2005).

MARY B. LALONE is professor of anthropology in the Department of Sociology and Anthropology at Radford University, where she specializes in economic/environmental, historical, and applied anthropology and in experiential teaching. Since 1992 she has organized and directed numerous projects focused on oral history documentation, heritage tourism, and park/museum planning with Appalachian Virginia communities. She has edited two volumes as part of these projects: *Appalachian Coal Mining Memories* (Pocahontas Press, 1997) and *Coal Mining Lives* (Radford University, 1998). Descriptions of her projects are available on her Web site at http://mlalone.asp.radford.edu/.

SUZANNE LANDIS is a practicing physician and teacher of young physicians at the Mountain Area Health Education Center in Asheville, North Carolina. She is a tenured professor in the Departments of Family Medicine and Internal Medicine at the University of North Carolina School of Medicine in Chapel Hill. She was the primary author of the proposal that led to the W. K. Kellogg Foundation funding the Madison Community Health Project and was project director from 1989 to 1995.

HELEN MATTHEWS LEWIS is a sociologist and community educator. She is fomer professor of sociology and anthropology and staff member at Highlander Research and Education Center. She is the author of numerous books and articles on Appalachian issues and community development, including *It Comes from the People: Community Development and Local Theology* (Temple University Press, 1995). She is currently semi-retired and lives in North Georgia, where she writes and continues to teach and consult part time.

Phillip J. Obermiller has helped found three nonprofit organizations and has served on the boards of each, as well as on the steering committees of two professional organizations. As a sociologist, he is interested in Appalachian migration and demographics and has edited or coauthored nine books about the region. Recent volumes include the fifth edition of *Appalachia: Social Context Past and Present,* coedited with Michael E. Maloney (Kendall/Hunt, 2002), and *African American Miners and Migrants,* coauthored with Thomas E. Wagner (University of Illinois Press, 2004).

Thomas Plaut is professor emeritus of sociology at Mars Hill College and worked with Community Health Research Services in Asheville, North Carolina. His research has focused on cultural barriers in professional-client relations, especially in health care. Beginning with the Madison Community Health Project in 1989, he has helped organize rural community health coalitions in North Carolina mountain counties. He currently assists health partnerships in needs assessment and program evaluation.

Jennifer Jervis Tighe lived in Over-the-Rhine and worked in nonprofit administration in this inner-city neighborhood of Cincinnati before beginning graduate studies at Miami University in Oxford, Ohio. She now teaches in the Xavier University Communication Arts Department, where she has developed curriculum focusing on philanthropy for nonprofit agencies. She has also produced a DVD on the intersection of Appalachian and African American studies. Tighe was the first executive director of SmartMoney Community Services.

Patricia Z. Timm is a public policy mediator and organizational consultant working in the Cincinnati, Ohio, area. Recently, she has directed the Hamilton County Environmental Priorities Project, the Metropolitan Growth Alliance, and the founding and development of the Ohio River Way, a regional cultural, water, and bike trail. She is currently the president of the Board of Friends of Women's Studies at the University of Cincinnati.

June Palmour Trevor directs a child care resource and referral program for the Madison County Partnership for Children and Families. From 1996 to 2000 she coordinated Western North Carolina Community Health Resource Services, a consulting team that provided training, technical assistance, and consultation in community health planning to county health partnerships across the region. Prior to 1996, she spent six years coordinating the Madison Community Health Project, a community-oriented primary care project funded by the W. K. Kellogg Foundation in Madison County, North Carolina, where she first worked with Landis and Plaut.

Melinda Bollar Wagner is professor of anthropology at Radford University, associate chair of the Appalachian Studies Program, and faculty advisor to the Appalachian Events Committee. She was president of the Appalachian Studies Association in 2004–5, and she has received awards in recognition of innovative undergraduate teaching. Since the mid-1990s, she and her students have turned their attention to efforts at cultural conservation by undertaking ethnographic study of cultural attachment to land in five counties. Her work on religion in America has included the ethnographies *Metaphysics in Midwestern America* (Ohio State University Press, 1980) and *God's Schools: Choice and Compromise in American Society* (Rutgers University Press, 1990).

Index

Plaut, Thomas, 13, 239
Plecker, Walter A., 94, 109n3
Polela Health Center, 234
political engagement, 81, 124
politics, local, 45, 47, 57, 123–24, 130–33, 212
postmodern critique, 7, 10
poverty, 6–7, 27, 158–60, 165; in Appalachia, 5–6
power, 9–11, 25–27, 198
powersharing, 216–17, 219–20, 242–44
progress, 2–3, 7–8, 14
progressives and conservatives, 45, 59–61
Putnam, Robert, 28–29, 68, 70

Quetelet, Adolphe, 233

race, 162, 166–67, 170n3
racism, 165–66, 170n3
Radford University, 142, 218, 220–24
rapport building, 201–2, 206–8, 217, 219, 225
reflexivity, 14, 19–20, 83, 93, 97
reciprocity, 23, 27, 29–30, 135, 146, 148, 173, 184, 201, 213–15
Rhoades, Ginger, 164–66, 169
Romberg, Raquel, 35n1
Rountree, Helen C., 100
Rutherford, Frankie, 24–25

Salamon, Sonya, 22–23, 33
Salstrom, Paul, 58
Sarnoff, Susan, 5
school dropout rates, 157–161, 179–80
schools, 165, 173–75, 180–85
scientific positivism, 2, 7–11
Selznick, Philip, 18
settlement schools, 5, 14–15
Shapiro, Henry, 14
Shield, Diane Johns, 91–92
slavery, 94
Smart, Alan, 30
Smith, Denise, 152
Smith, J. David, 109n4
Smith, Captain John, 93
Snow, John, 233
social capital, 8–9, 18, 25–34, 34–35n1, 45, 48, 50, 54, 62, 68, 70–71, 73, 76, 78, 85–86, 135, 137n3, 141, 145–46, 150–54, 154n1, 169, 173, 193, 196, 201, 213; bonding, 28–29, 32–33, 133, 146, 157, 161; bridging, 28, 33, 91, 124, 146; linking, 148–51, 153
social justice, 7
social networks, 22–23, 27–29, 115–17, 130, 133, 162, 173, 184, 213
Stack, Carol, 26
Stephenson, John, 63n6
stereotypes; of blacks, 166; of mountain people, 4–5, 15–16, 18, 24, 32, 56–58, 115–16, 130, 176–77
subsistence agriculture, 4, 31–32, 47, 58
Sustainable Communities Movement, 128, 132
sustainability, 9, 11, 14, 17, 67, 73, 86, 116–17, 120, 132–33, 137n2
Szreter, Simon, 32

Tennessee Valley Authority, 5
Third World, 3–4
Toennies, Ferdinand, 20–21
Torgersen, Paul, 103
tourism, 6, 46, 81, 117–18, 118, 120, 143, 202–203, 205, 212–215, 225
traditionalism, 2–3
Trevor, June, 239
Truman, Harry S., 3
trust, 9, 22–23, 30–32, 173, 184, 187, 197, 206, 208, 213, 232, 242

United Nations' Local Agenda 21, 133–34, 137n2
United States Forest Service, 151
Urban Appalachian Council, 164, 179
urban development planning, 178–79

Virchow, Rudolf, 233
Virginia Indian Nations Summit on Higher Education, 105–7
Virginia Indian Tribal Alliance for Life, 100, 102, 105
Virginia Racial Integrity Law, 94
Virginia Tech, 89, 103–7, 109

Wagner, Melinda Bollar, 152
Waller, Altina, 63n4

Participatory Development in Appalachia was designed and typeset on a Macintosh computer system using InDesign software. The body text is set in 10/13 Minion Pro and display type is set in Formal. This book was designed and typeset by Kelly Gray.